THE MECHANICS OF MONEY

By the same author

Editions Mazarine, Paris
Expansion Economique (1962)
Développement urbain: recherche d'un principe (1965)

Editions de l'épargne, Paris
Libéralisme et financement (1965)

Editions de la RPP, Paris
La vraie nature de la monnaie (1973)
Une monnaie pour l'Europe: l'Eurostable (1975)

THE MECHANICS OF MONEY

Jacques Riboud

Translated by
Stephen Harrison

Foreword by
Fritz Machlup

St Martin's Press New York

Stephen Harrison's English translation © Jacques Riboud 1980
First published as *Mécanique des monnaies, d'aujourd'hui et de demain*
© Editions de la RPP 1978

ISBN 0–312–52455–2

Library of Congress Cataloging in Publication Data

Riboud, Jacques.
    The Mechanics of money.

    Translation of Mécanique des monnaies, d'aujourd'hui
et de demain.
    Includes index.
    1. Money   I. Title.
HG221.R4913   332.4   80–22
ISBN 0–312–52455–2

'En science économique ou sociale la mythologie est au coeur même de nos pensées. Nous nous construisons un domaine bien abrité contre les vents, bien fortifié, même contre les maléfices qui sont les faits. Bien au chaud dans notre intérieur, nous fermons vite les fenêtres dès qu'arrive un courant d'air . . . .'

Alfred Sauvy, Histoire économique
de la France entre les deux guerres.

('In economics and the social sciences the very core of our thinking is all too often a tissue of mythology. We build ourselves a snug little home for our ideas, well protected against the icy blasts, fortified against everything, even those arch-nuisances, facts. Warm and comfortable indoors, we hasten to shut the windows as soon as we feel a draught . . . .')

Translator's Note

The term 'reduction', which is one of the key concepts of this book, is, I believe, new to the vocabulary of monetary theory. The word used in the original, *prélèvement*, has no exact English equivalent in this context. Its general connotations are those of 'withdrawal' or 'removal', whilst in financial usage it usually approximates to the English word 'tax'. Thus, the French expression *prélèvement sur la fortune* would best be rendered in English by 'wealth tax'. But 'tax' in English has the very specific connotation of an official impost levied by the government, whereas Mr Riboud's *prélèvement,* which he sees as the inevitable result of the introduction into circulation of any quantity of new money created *ex nihilo*, is something quite unofficial and, as he says himself, generally hidden from, or at any rate not obvious to, those who are affected by it. For this reason I have preferred to talk about the 'reduction in resources' that results from the creation of a new unit of money and to abbreviate this to 'reduction' in all cases where the context did not appear to require the use of the full form of the expression.

S. H.

Acknowledgements

I should like to take this opportunity of thanking Mrs J. Thuillier and Miss A. Bottega for most patiently typing what must have seemed at times a never-ending series of drafts of this English translation of Jacques Riboud's *Mécanique des monnaies*. Special thanks are also due to Miss Angela Milburn for reading the early drafts and making many valuable suggestions regarding style and the general presentation of the book.

S.H.

The author and publishers wish to thank Joseph Aschheim and Y. S. Park for permission to quote extracts from 'Artificial Currency Units: The Formation of Functional Currency Areas', *Essays in International Finance*, No. 11, April 1976. Copyright © 1976. Reprinted by permission of the International Finance Section of Princeton University.

Summary of Contents

Introduction

The creation, the life and the eventual destruction of a unit of money, its effects on the constituent elements of the economy and its relations with economic activity and prices, can all be described in terms of a kind of 'mechanics'. There is a mechanics of money just as there is a soil mechanics and a fluid mechanics, the expression being understood in the sense of a coherent theoretical structure derived from experience and intended to define in time and space the states, positions and effects of certain phenomena in terms of their mutual relations as well as of external factors.

PART ONE

THREE KEYS TO MONETARY ANALYSIS

1 What is money?

A unit of money is nothing more than a transferable claim on an institution, created arbitrarily and artificially and having a maturity and exchange value which are generally indefinite. There is no *natural* or *inevitable* connection between a commodity represented by this unit of money (or its backing) and its value in terms of exchange.

Thinking on these matters will continue to be confused, as will the monetary mechanisms themselves, as long as the old ideas of money as representative of a commodity, defined by the backing which constitutes its guarantee, have not been refuted and replaced.

2 How money works

'Lotto-money' is a game intended to show the arbitrary nature of the creation of payment instruments and reveal the uncertainties of present-day knowledge regarding those mechanisms that govern money, its creation and its circulation.

The game is played with small machines—kinds of printing presses— which are worked by handles and which produce counters representing consumption units or investment units. Another press prints monetary units, or MUs, simple pieces of paper which represent money and on which the leader has written 'I promise to pay the bearer x MUs.

3 Three keys to monetary analysis

If we want to study the mechanics of money we must begin by looking closely at how and where money is created, using three keys.

First, *payment*, or change of hands: the passage of a unit of money from agent X to agent Y in exchange for goods or services transferred from Y to X.

Next, *clearing*, the process which makes it possible for banks to superimpose new payment instruments, in the form of claims on themselves, on top of those that are issued by the central bank.

Finally, *reduction* of the liquid wealth of the holders of money, the inevitable corollary of the creation of a new unit of money.

4 The first key – Payment

The main lines of the analysis go beyond the economic agent's pocket or the bank's till and take us to the heart of the matter, the fundamental operation of payment (or transaction).

Some units of money have the transaction function, others do not; the two should not be confused. Demand deposits in a bank do have the transaction function, whereas time deposits in the same bank or deposits in a savings bank do not; in order to circulate and exercise their transaction function such units of money need to be exchanged first and replaced by other units (whether transferred from somewhere else or expressly created for the purpose) which do have the transaction function.

We should not rely on criteria such as the degree of liquidity or ease of withdrawal, nor should we take the notice necessary before a deposit can be withdrawn as the decisive factor in order to decide whether or not a particular unit of money has or does not have the transaction function. Nor should we stop too soon in the search for this function. Instead, we should go right to the end of the analysis and look for the final operation of exchange of a unit of money for a supply of goods.

5 *The second key – Clearing*

Clearing is generally neglected by monetary analysts. Nevertheless, it constitutes the basis of the power of monetary creation of a modern banking system.

It is thanks to the clearing mechanism that claims on banks which did not originally constitute money come to act as payment instruments. It is by looking to see whether or not clearing takes place that we can tell whether or not there is any creation of bank money over and above what the bank of issue has created. The mechanism of the clearing house can also be used to solve the perennial problem of whether or not Eurodollar banks are capable of creating money.

'Lotto-clearing' is a game specifically invented to demonstrate the mechanism of the clearing house and its role in the creation of money by the banking system. The game faithfully reproduces the clearing mechanism and the players represent the member banks of the clearing house. Tickets given to each player stand for the amount of cheques drawn on the other banks and deposited with each bank. The leader adds up on a clearing chart for each participant the amounts 'owed to' and 'owed by'. Comparison of total movements and total balances which each player has to settle in central bank money demonstrates the mechanism by means of which money is added by clearing banks to the total of money created by the bank of issue.

6 *The third key – Reduction*

The mechanics of money can only be properly revealed by using the concept of *reduction*, which is an aspect, an illustration and even a measure of what economists call seigniorage.

Once it has been created, a new unit of money has the power of procuring for the person who puts it into circulation for the first time a certain quantity of goods and services which have not been 'earned' and which in consequence constitute a reduction of the total wealth available to the holders of money. The effects of monetary creation such as inflation and savings and the problems of monetary regulation all become easier to understand when they are looked at from this point of view, that is, from the point of view of a reduction of the assets of those economic agents who hold money.

The mechanism of reduction—and its opposite, restoration—can be studied by analysing the disturbance which results in a stable system of exchanges by the addition or subtraction of a new unit of money. Analysis

further shows how a new unit of money, as it spreads through the money
supply as exchanges proceed, causes a series of partial reductions, the total
of which is equivalent to the value of the goods and services which the first
holder of the new unit of money consumed when he first put it into
circulation.

7 Use of the three keys, first example—Banks and Non-Banks

In monetary analysis, it is essential to distinguish between monetary and
non-monetary intermediaries.

A non-monetary intermediary is capable of multiplying credit but not
of increasing the supply of M1 payment money, whereas a monetary
intermediary can. The essence of creation of new money is not credit. The
formula 'loans make deposits' is true but misleading, since it makes no
distinction between a loan made by a non-monetary intermediary and one
made by a monetary intermediary.

It is only by referring to the mechanism of the clearing house that we
can hope to sort out the problems raised by the gradual assimilation of
savings accounts, whether demand or time accounts, and current accounts,
and thus assess the significance of the use of cheques and transfer orders
by depositors in savings banks from the point of view of the creation of
money.

8 Use of the three keys, second example—Eurodollars and Eurodollar banks

It is a common belief, especially in France, that when a bank operates in
the Euromarkets in currencies other than its own national currency it has
the same powers of creation of new money as it has in the national
currency of the country in which it is domiciled. To attempt to discover
whether or not this belief is justified involves comparing the points of view
of the two writers who have set out most clearly the two opposite
viewpoints: Michel Lelart, on the one hand, in his book *Le dollar,
monnaie internationale* and Jane S. Little, on the other, in a book
sponsored by the Federal Reserve Bank of Boston, entitled *Eurodollars –
the money market gypsies.*

9 Use of the three keys, third example—Investment on the basis of monetary creation

The very notion of reduction leads to the conviction that the use which new money is put to and the purposes to which it is allocated ought to be decided in terms of the general interest, which should in turn be determined according to appropriate rules.

PART TWO

Monetary regulation and the monetary indicators

1 Nature abhors a vacuum

There is no reason to believe that the fascination that gold has exercised on man's imagination for six thousand years will quickly disappear and that it will cease to be an investment hedge that is earnestly and justifiably sought after. But gold as a money is quite another question and the gold standard system even more so.

The gold standard is based on a wager and a probability. The wager is that the holders of notes will not all wish to exchange them for precious metal at the same time. The probability is that they will not. The wager was a reasonable one for over two centuries; today it would be one that bankers would certainly lose, because the probability is against them.

The real cause of the paralysis of those in power when faced with the present monetary disorders is a general refusal to accept the evidence and an obstinate preference for disciplines that now belong irrevocably to the past, rather than for innovation.

But societies and monetary systems abhor a vacuum, just as much as nature. This is the reason why, now that it is admitted that this vacuum exists, governments are turning towards new systems and new disciplines, such as the control and the regulation of those forms of money that actually or potentially constitute means of payment.

2 Monetarists and monetarians

The rise of the monetarist doctrine followed the disappearance of the old disciplines. The state cannot let the money supply get out of hand, devoid of control, propulsion and brake, in other words without any regulation. 'Monetarism', as it will be understood in this book, is the search for reliable indicators, intervention instruments, guides and rules according to which to apply them.

3 The uncertainties of monetary regulation

Whilst on the one hand the inevitability of monetary regulation and the
government's responsibility for it are no longer in question, on the other
hand the poverty of the means at governments' disposal, the inaccuracy of
the indicators and the defects of the existing instruments are all very much
in evidence. All these factors together constitute proof of the uncertainty
of knowledge which can only be dissipated by a rigorous analysis of the
mechanics of money. Some examples of this uncertainty and its consequences on the monetary policies of France, England, the United States,
Germany and Switzerland are given.

4 A flaw in monetary thinking

There is a basic flaw in monetary thinking which vitiates interpretation
of the indicators, causes wrong decisions to be taken, disrupts the
mechanisms and paralyses the regulatory machinery.

  This flaw is the confusion of those instruments that are money with
those that are not, the attribution of the same nature and the same role to
claims whose roles and natures are different, the unjustified confusion of
those kinds of money that are used for exchanges with those that do not,
those that have the payment function with those that do not, a failure to
distinguish between what may *become* money or cause the creation of
money and what *is* money.

5 The search for a new monetary indicator

The point of attempting to devise a new indicator is not so much to
provide better information for those whose responsibility it is to decide
monetary policy as to penetrate further into the nature of the mechanics
of money using a parameter which is rarely taken into consideration,
namely the nature of the transaction in which a given unit of money is
involved. To this end we shall use the fundamental data of National
Accounts relating to production, consumption and added value.

  The corrective factor to be added to M1, which is the ultimate aim of
these researches, is an aggregate derived from the following formula:

$$\frac{1.5}{V} \; \Sigma \; MR$$

in which V is the average transaction velocity, M the quantity of a given category of loan or savings deposit (whether bank or non-bank) and R the annual rate of turnover of each category.

The proof of this formula illustrates the monetary effect of a payment unit and confirms the special nature of M1, which distinguishes it from all the other indicators. At the same time, it gives some measure of the mistakes people make when they fail to distinguish, within the same money supply definition, between items that are money and those that are not, even if they are often called 'near-money' or 'quasi-money'.

6 Monetary creation and inflation

(1) Credit cards

The formula can help us to work out a corrective factor to be added to M1 in order to take due account of the increase in transaction volume brought about by the use of credit cards.

(2) International money

Looked at from the narrow point of view of creation of money as it takes place within the confines of a state, purely extranational currencies cannot be called inflationary, in spite of the fact that they undoubtedly constitute an artificial form of liquidity. It would be possible to define such a currency so that it retained its purchasing power and thus constituted the unchanging standard of value which every system of measurement requires.

7 The taboo of inconvertibility

The arguments of the previous chapters justify a definitive rejection of the notion of backing, which has dominated monetary thinking for so long and influenced the definition of money as representative of a commodity. In this connection, the example of John Law and his monetary system is discussed and the confusions which it gave rise to, and still gives rise to, are discussed.

PART THREE

Composite currency units, their future and their shortcomings: the Eurostable

1 The implications of present-day monetary disorders

If we look beyond the various unsuccessful attempts to create a new monetary system we can see an underlying tendency and a growing need— the need for a new international payment unit which is stateless, stable in terms of purchasing power, independent of foreign exchange market gyrations and price levels, and which is not the privileged instrument of the domestic policies of any national government.

2 The International Monetary Fund and its Special Drawing Right

The IMF is one of the most original institutions to have emerged during the post-war period. It was set up in order to prevent a recurrence in the field of monetary and economic relations between states of those mistakes that led the world into the Great Depression of the thirties. It has a dual role.

First, it is supposed to provide liquidity for international financial transfers and exchanges by lending to countries whose payments are in deficit the foreign currency they are short of, using funds provided by member states ('quotas').

Its second function—the one that concerns monetary theory most directly—is to devise a monetary system to replace the now defunct Bretton Woods system, which was characterised by gold definition of the par values of currencies, fixed exchange rates, the pre-eminence of the US dollar and its full convertibility into gold.

A new system is now being developed. It involves the creation of a new unit of value in the form of a composite unit, or basket of currencies, intended to replace gold as the yardstick by which the value of other currencies is measured. The IMF is thus venturing into promising but uncharted territory. The unit (known as the 'SDR'), such as it is defined at present, is in fact seriously affected by certain deficiencies that are likely to compromise its future. The most serious is its instability of value, which makes it unsuitable for use as a monetary standard. But this drawback can be obviated provided due note is taken of the exceptional quality that a purely extranational composite unit reserved exclusively for trade between states could have, namely constant purchasing power.

3 An American view of composite currency units

Professor Machlup recommends the creation of an extraterritorial currency unit, the value of which would be stabilised and the creation of which would be spontaneous.

Yoon Shik Park and Joseph Aschheim look at previous experiences in the field of composite currency units and analyse the reasons why they failed to work. Their conclusion is to call for innovation in this important field.

4 An extranational payment unit with constant purchasing power: the Eurostable

Governments are, by their very nature, ill equipped to invent, to experiment and correct on the basis of experience. Most innovations in monetary and financial techniques have been the work of the private sector. The Eurostable experiment, which would be carried out by a group of Eurobanks in a Eurostable Consortium, ought to help to overcome the obstacles arising from a project which differs so radically from traditional ideas.

Such an experiment would provide governments with useful information which they could use in order to develop the generalised use, within a given monetary zone, of a payment unit which would be peculiar to that zone and which would have the following advantages: it would be an unvarying standard of measure and would supplement the dollar and Deutschemark in their exclusive roles in the field of international finance; it would re-launch the grand design of European Union and give the monetary authorities better control of the Euromarket; it would stabilise international capital by 'fixing' floating masses of capital and constitute a stateless reserve and intervention instrument for central banks.

5 Thirty questions on the Eurostable

This chapter lists the questions most usually asked about the Eurostable. These questions concern: the price indices; the currencies that make up the Eurostable basket; the conversion formula into third currencies; the rules by which the system would function and the planned Articles of Association of the Eurostable Consortium; the problem of possible inflationary effects; the likelihood of the existence of a two-way market of depositors and borrowers; possible risks which the member banks of the consortium might run; the problem of lender of last resort; the position of the monetary authorities with regard to the idea and the adaptation of the experience gained from such an experiment to other international institutions.

Epilogue

Glossary

Foreword

The preface to the French edition of this book was written by an eminent economist and member of the *Institut de France*, namely Henri Guitton. I was honoured by the invitation to take his place for the English edition. If I approach my task in a way that is quite different from his, this is easily explained by the fact that our research backgrounds are different. On the other hand, we do share common philosophical and semantic interests and it is with pleasure that I take up some of the points raised by Professor Guitton, especially the questions whether we know what is money and whether money really exists.

These, I think, are questions that can be raised in connection with *all* concepts in the social sciences, all institutions, all artifacts, all things used by human beings. Since most things in society and in human action are defined by their actual or potential uses, and since different people, groups, or communities have different uses for similar things and use different things for similar uses, the relationship between things and uses exists only in the mind—mine, yours or somebody else's. Does a conception, a mental construction, 'exist' in a real sense? Or is it only an abstraction for which perhaps some 'referent', 'counterpart', or 'proxy' exists in the domain of observation? I am inclined to answer Professor Guitton's question about the real existence of money with 'no' if I think of money as a variable in a theoretical model, but with 'yes' if I refer to arbitrarily defined pieces of metal in my pocket, pieces of paper in my wallet or signs in printer's ink on my bank statement. But the definitions that make these things money are very arbitrary.

In his preface Professor Guitton expressed some qualms about the title of this book: may one, he asks, legitimately talk about the 'mechanics' of money and money transactions? Is there not a wide gulf between the physical world, with its constant, determinate and 'mechanical' relationships, and the social world, in which relationships are never mechanical, but always human, personal, mental and affected by the exercise of free will? Professor Guitton is quite right to emphasise this difference; but there is such a thing as a metaphor or figure of speech, something not to be taken literally. A great philosopher and economist,

William Stanley Jevons, one of the pioneers of methodological subjectivism, testified in support of Mr. Riboud's use of 'mechanics' by publishing a book called *Money and the Mechanism of Exchange* in 1875.[1]

For hundreds of years economists have listed the various functions of money and the better economists have understood that not all these functions are always fulfilled by what they agreed to call money. A typical list includes the following: general medium of exchange (to avoid direct barter); means of payment (to settle contracted debts); liquid reserve (for ready use for purchases and payments); store of value (over longer periods); standard (or measure) of value (for comparisons in decision-making); unit of account (for additions and subtractions in record-keeping). To these six functions some economists have added a seventh, namely as standard of deferred payments, but this could be seen as a combination of unit of account (for contracting a debt) and means of payment (for settling it). Most writers have preferred to select three functions as the essential ones.

The number Three has always fascinated classifiers, or at least those who were not addicted to the number Two, for binary division. In selecting the most eligible components of the triad, economists have had different tastes. Sir John Hicks proposed to distinguish two triads, a 'conventional' and a 'Keynesian'. The conventional triad consists of means of payment, store of value, and unit of account; the Keynesian triad consists of three reasons for holding money, the transaction motive, the precautionary motive, and the speculative motive.[2] Two triads give us six components, but these are not the six previously listed. The Keynesian triad represents an altogether different methodological position, in that it looks at the individual money holder's decisions and actions regarding the money balance he is willing to keep. These decisions presuppose that money may be used for purchasing goods and services, paying debts, and perhaps also for storing wealth. The functions of counting and comparing are of a quite different nature and have little to do with decisions to hold media of exchange or means of payment in a readily available reserve.

These remarks indicate that the enumeration of functions is sometimes less than logical. As a matter of fact, there have been times when the supposed functions of money were carried out by different things. For many people during the hyperinflation in Germany cigarettes were the most widely accepted medium of exchange; bank notes were the means of payment (in settling debts); foreign currency was the preferred liquid reserve; precious metals and diamonds were stores of value; some historically important commodity was the standard of value; and the hypothetical gold mark was the unit of account. Bank-notes, the means of payment, were held only for the shortest possible periods of time (a few hours, not days) and in the smallest possible amounts, as inevitable transaction balances between receipt and expenditure, and not at all for precautionary or speculative purposes. In these circumstances, one may well ask whether money 'exists' in any operational, empirical sense. Which of the things were money—cigarettes, bank-notes, American dollars, precious metals, bushels of grain or non-existent gold marks?

To be sure, times of hyperinflation are not exactly the best source of observational data, inductive generalisations, or theoretical models. If we want to obtain generalisations or theories applicable in more normal times, we had better base our models on more normal relationships, and this is what Mr. Riboud attempts to do in his *Mechanics of Money*. But even for the most normal relationships, definitions will always be arbitrary to a very large extent. If Mr. Riboud opts for the definition of money as the means of payment (usually payment for current purchases, rather than old debts), this is perfectly unobjectionable, provided that the effects of changes in the quantities of other assets which are endowed with considerable 'moneyness' (liquidity)—assets which he does not recognise as money—are not disregarded.

It is important, I believe, that students and general readers should understand that such differences in definitions of terms and concepts do *not* constitute differences in economic theory. Laymen often confuse linguistic preferences with substantive disagreements and this is apt to give a very wrong idea of the present state of economic science. Let me illustrate this by adding a few more terminological differences among some of the most respected authorities. The Swedish economist Knut Wicksell, writing in the first decade of this century, when all European countries were on the gold standard, decided that only the function of medium of exchange was an *essential* characteristic of money and that he would, for the sake of simplicity, treat only *metallic money* as money and deal with bank-notes and bank deposits as the chief determinants of the velocity of circulation of money.[3] It ought to be clear that for total annual expenditure, made with gold coins, metallic token currency, paper currency, and cheque deposits, expressed in M x V, or money times velocity, it makes no difference to the result what you consider to be included in M and what in V. Thus, for Wicksell, gold coins were M and all the rest were money substitutes, affecting V.

Almost a hundred years before Wicksell, David Ricardo had made a different terminological decision. He treated both gold and bank-notes as money, but bank deposits only as substitutes affecting velocity or, as he called it, 'the degree of economy practised in the use of money.' Perhaps some readers would like to savour the original formulation by Ricardo:

> The value of money and the amount of payments remaining the same, the quantity of money required must depend on the degree of economy practised in the use of it. If no payments were made by cheques on bankers, by means of which money is merely written off one account and added to another, and that to the amount of millions daily, with few or no bank notes or coins passing, it is obvious that considerably more currency would be required, or, which is the same in its effects, the same money would pass at a greatly increased value, and would therefore be adequate to the additional amount of payments.[4]

In view of monetary developments since the times of Ricardo and Wicksell and, in particular, the enormous increase in payments by cheque, it is hardly surprising that virtually all specialists on monetary affairs have expanded the definition of money to include various kinds of bank deposit. Because of the large variety of these deposits it has become customary to accept several alternative concepts of money, usually distinguished by subscripts or postscripts to the letter M, such as M1, M2, and so on. Mr. Riboud is quite determined not to allow such promiscuous tastes: he is wedded to the one and only M that appears to him legitimate, namely, M1, which admits demand deposits with commercial banks subject to transfer by cheque. His reason is that these are the only deposits that can be used for payments, whereas all other deposit balances have to be transferred to a current account (or withdrawn in bank notes) before payments can be made. Again, Mr. Riboud's decision is unobjectionable, provided that he does not disregard the effects of changes in other kinds of bank deposit.

When statisticians and economists take the trouble of collecting, compiling, and combining figures for different classes of assets, they do so because they believe that these aggregates or their changes have some influence on other things which they consider important. In those cases where monetary aggregates are put together in different arrangements, the experts are uncertain about which arrangements deserve to be considered as the most relevant 'money stock measures' affecting total economic activity, gross national product, employment, wage rates, commodity prices, foreign-exchange rates, and so on. They have good reasons for being uncertain; their uncertainty is not ignorance of things that could easily be found out, it is not inability or unwillingness to think logically and it is not sheer prejudice or superstition. One of the theoretical reasons is that the total of effective demand and the total of actual purchases are not the same as the total of money payments and large orders for later delivery may affect prices and production long before payments are made. This, of course, means that liquidity, or the expectation of being *able* to pay for what is now being bought, may include holding assets other than means of payment and may even include the existence of borrowing facilities not yet utilised. Hence, many monetary experts think that some measures of domestic liquidity, of the prospective ability to liquidate easily negotiable assets, may be more important in determining economic activity than the total of means of payment currently held. Another reason for the experts' uncertainty and vacillation is that institutions change over time and that classes of assets that were not means of payment a few years ago have become so now.

An example of such a promotion of what Mr. Riboud would call a non-money to the rank of money is the case of thrift deposits in banks in New England. These deposits, previously not subject to transfer by cheque, have become transferable by what in every respect looks like a cheque but is officially called a Negotiable Order of Withdrawal (NOW). These NOW accounts are savings accounts, but differ from demand deposits at commercial banks only in that they pay interest to the depositors. (I do not live in New England but as soon as this service was offered I opened a NOW account in which my salary is deposited and on which I draw my cheques with a New England bank. Thus I have less money in my demand account in New Jersey, but more money in the NOW account in Massachusetts.) The law may be wise or silly, but in either case the economist must adjust his operational definition to the new situation. This is the origin of Item 5 in the table on page 159 and this is why it is included in M1 +. Mr. Riboud will have to recognise it as a means of payment and therefore as money.

Another example of an institutional change requiring an adjustment in operational definitions occurred when banks in New York and New Jersey, noticing that their customers had shifted their accounts to competing banks in New England, tried to offer similar advantages to depositors. Barred by law from making savings accounts subject to transfer by cheque, they offered 'automatic transfer services' (ATS) in New York and telephone transfer services in New Jersey for balances in savings accounts. Thus, cheques drawn on demand accounts would be covered by an automatic or telephone transfer of the needed balance from the customer's savings account. (Needless to say, I immediately took advantage of the new service and carry almost my entire transaction balance on the interest-earning savings account; the balance on my demand deposit is now only large enough to cover the cheques I draw.) In this case, the balance on the savings account has not become a means of payment and hence is not money under Mr. Riboud's definition. However, the reduction (or reduced growth) of the amounts held on demand deposit would deceive the observer, and perhaps mislead even the policy maker, if the shift of balances from demand to savings account were not explicitly taken into account.

A third example of institutional change bearing on our problem of monetary aggregates is illuminating. The jumble of banking regulations, including in particular the ceilings on interest rates which various kinds of banks and other financial intermediaries may offer their depositors on balances of various size in different types of accounts—designed by benighted legislators to restrict competition—presents a constant temptation for financial entrepreneurs to look for loopholes and escape-hatches. In the last few years a novel device has been developed by means of which liquid funds, so-called 'money-market funds', could be managed without the encumbrance of being subject to the monetary authorities' regulations. Their regulations and interest ceilings apply to deposits in banks and thrift institutions but not to dividends and shares. Thus, instead of depositing your money in a bank, you buy shares in a mutual fund that invests only in liquid money-market instruments and distributes its earnings, calculated day by day, to its 'shareholders' in the form of cash dividends or share dividends. (Having opted for share dividends, I receive my regular statements indicating that I hold such-and-such a number of shares plus fractions of shares, at a constant value of one dollar, or ten dollars, per share.) A telephone call suffices to get any part of these share holdings, or rather its constant money value, back into the owner's current account with a commercial bank. Since the dividends represent almost twice the maximum interest that may legally be paid on savings deposits, while the transfer of funds from the money-market mutual fund takes not an hour longer than the transfer from a savings account, it is understandable that informed asset holders now hold large portions of their liquid balances in the form of shares in money-market mutual funds.

Nobody knows, or can possibly know, what portions of these holdings are held to satisfy the holders' requirements for transaction balances or their demand for precautionary and speculative balances, or their wish to obtain a relatively high yield on their investment. These shares in liquid mutual funds may therefore be accumulated at the expense of balances on demand deposits, savings deposits, or time deposits with commercial banks, of demand or savings deposits with savings banks or other thrift

institutions, of government bonds of all kinds—or even of the ordinary
shares of all sorts of companies. Experts are racking their brains trying to
find some formula and measure that would tell the story of what has
happened or is happening in the money markets since these convenient
money substitutes, in the form of perfectly liquid shares, have developed.

A fourth and last example of an institutional development that plays
havoc with the operational counterparts of the theoretical conception of
money may be described here. Demand deposits with commercial banks have
been subject to government regulations burdening the banks as well as
the depositors. The banks have to meet reserve requirements on their
deposit liabilities and the depositors get no interest on their deposit
balances. Non-deposit liabilities of banks are free from these regulations.
Consequently both parties gain if demand-deposit liabilities can be
transformed into equally liquid non-deposit liabilities of the bank. This
is done by the bank selling the depositor securities with a repurchase
agreement at an agreed price. Assuming the depositor knows that he will
have to make a payment in two or three days, he can buy securities from
his bank and return them on the day he needs the funds for the payment.
He receives interest in the form of the difference between the repurchase
price and the selling price of the securities. Thus the transaction balance
otherwise required for the payment disappears from the books of the
bank for the intervening period. The bank avoids holding the required
reserve and the customer earns interest. This substitute for balances on
demand deposit or time deposit is commonly called the RP (repurchase).
The device makes the statistics of the money stock unrepresentative of
what most of us understand by 'money'.

Mr. Riboud's solution has the advantage of giving an unambiguous
figure for the narrowly defined money stock. This is of little help,
however, because the ambiguities, uncertainties and information gaps
are merely shifted from the supply side to the demand side. If money
substitutes are expelled from the money supply, their existence and
particularly their variability over time will make the demand for money
more problematic. But I am not opposed to the Riboud conception: it
gives a cleaner and clearer picture of the supply and shoves all the mess
under the rug that covers the demand side.

I have mentioned the fascination with triads. Mr. Riboud, having
rejected the triad of functions of money, substitutes for it a triad of
'keys' to monetary analysis: payment, clearing, and what I prefer to
call 'encroachment', though it is called 'reduction' in this book. This is an
original way of organising monetary analysis. That so much emphasis is
placed on the working of the clearing mechanism is very helpful, though I

believe that the connection between clearing and the banks' power of
money creation is not quite as Mr. Riboud sees it. A strict Ricardian,
however, may be satisfied with the analysis, because the reduction in the
need for money transactions as a result of balancing out credit and debit
entries and the extension of bank credit resulting in redepositing and a net
increase in the banks' deposit liabilities are two important factors in the
'economy in the use of money'.

The important place which Mr. Riboud gives to the processes of
encroachment and its opposite, relinquishment (restoration, as it is called
in this book) is another welcome feature of his book. Not that the ideas
are new, but many treatises and texts fail to explain satisfactorily the
transfers of real resources that are inherent in the spending of new money
freshly injected into the money stream and, on the other hand, in the
non-spending of income by recipients who either add to their holdings of
idle balances or repay their bank debts and thereby reduce the stock of
money. In recent decades there has been little net relinquishment of
command over goods and services but a great deal of net encroachment,
by first and early spenders of new money, upon the purchasing power of
those whose incomes have increased too late, too little, or not at all.

I want to close this preface with a few comments on Mr. Riboud's plan
for the *Eurostable*, a new European international monetary unit with
constant purchasing power. Mr. Riboud first advanced this plan in an
earlier book, *Une monnaie pour l'Europe: l'Eurostable* (published in
1975). The main feature of the project is that it is based neither on
intergovernmental agreements nor on the decisions and actions of an
international organisation such as the European Monetary System. The
new monetary unit is to be created by a consortium of private banks,
swapping credits among themselves, granting loans to nonbank borrowers
and accepting deposits, all denominated in the new unit. The unit is a
composite of several currencies, a basket of national currencies, similar
to the ECU now planned by EMS and to the SDR issued by the IMF, but
with the difference that the number of units of national currencies in the
basket is regularly adjusted in accordance with the price indices for the
particular countries. Thus, if the price index in France rises by ten per
cent, the amount of French francs in the currency basket, and hence in
the Eurostable, is increased by ten per cent. In this fashion each
component of the Eurostable could buy a commodity basket of
unchanged contents in the country in question and, in consequence, the
Eurostable could be regarded as a monetary unit with constant purchasing
power.

It is particularly important to note that the Eurostable is not designed merely to serve as a unit of account or as a standard of value but is to serve as a means of payment in international transactions. One may ask why it might not also be used in domestic transactions; the answer is that legal obstacles would probably prevent such use. The banks creating, lending, and borrowing Eurostable would be the same that now deal in Eurocurrencies, banks that are largely serving a clientele not resident in the country where the banks operate, banks not subject to the same tight rules and regulations that are imposed on domestic banks or on domestic operations.

How would the Eurostable be converted? 'The conversion rate of the Eurostable into a third currency is calculated each day by means of a formula that incorporates two sets of parameters: the median cross exchange rates, as they are determined by the market, and the consumer price indices in the countries of the reference currencies, as calculated by the national statistical services' (Part 3, Chapter 4). The choice of the consumer price indices may be questioned, since the Eurostable is designed chiefly for transactions arising from international trade and capital movements. One may argue that export-price indices would be more appropriate for the purpose, even if there is a strong connection between the prices of traded goods and the exchange rates of currencies of the trading countries.

Mr. Riboud does not discuss all the technicalities involved in his scheme. Readers interested in different techniques of value maintenance of a composite currency may like to refer to a recent book exclusively dedicated to an analysis of the inherent problems: *Composite Reserve Assets in the International Monetary System* by Jacob S. Dreyer.[5] While it discusses chiefly the Standard Basket and various forms of Adjustable Baskets, adjustable, that is, for changes in par values or transaction values, it contains a section on stabilisation of the purchasing power of the composite monetary unit. Previously, a number of staff memoranda of the Research Department of the International Monetary Fund had dealt with these problems. One of the lessons learned in the course of the studies carried out at the IMF was that it would be extremely difficult and perhaps impossible to obtain the agreement of the Executive Directors and Governors of this international organisation, that is, in effect an agreement of many governments which probably cannot muster the expertise required to comprehend the provisions of the inevitably complex scheme and the arguments behind them. This difficulty of getting an international agreement on a novel monetary experiment is the main reason for Mr. Riboud's proposal to make it nongovernmental—a voluntary consortium of some far-sighted and enterprising banks with 'offshore' branches.

Even on the mere banking aspects many problems beyond those solved by Mr. Riboud remain to be tackled. I doubt that the scheme could be started just by mutual swap arrangements among a few banks; it would take a central agency created by the consortium, a private clearing house which could issue Eurostable reserves to the members of the consortium. But I may be wrong on this point; and even if I am right, it would not be much more difficult to establish the clearing house than to set up a swap arrangement. The idea is worth some experimentation on a trial basis. If bankers and multinational firms are really as concerned about exchange-rate risks and inflation risks as they say they are they ought to be prepared to engage in a pilot scheme with a self-made international means of payment with constant purchasing power.

FRITZ MACHLUP

Princeton and New York,
June 1979

NOTES

[1] William Stanley Jevons, *Money and the Mechanism of Exchange* (London: H. S. King and Company, 1875).
[2] Sir John Hicks, *Critical Essays in Monetary Theory* (Oxford: Clarendon Press, 1967), p. 1.
[3] Knut Wicksell, *Lectures on Political Economy*, vol. 2, *Money* (London: Routledge & Kegan Paul, 1935, translated from the second Swedish edition, 1911), pp. 3 and 27.
[4] David Ricardo, *Proposals for an Economical and Secure Currency* (London: John Murray, 1816), p. 12. Reprinted in *The Works and Correspondence of David Ricardo* (ed. by Piero Sraffa), vol. IV (Cambridge: University Press, 1951), p. 58.
[5] Greenwich, Connecticut: JAI Press, 1977.

Author's Preface

As he turns over the pages of this book, the reader will come across certain mathematical formulae. Let no one be dismayed by this; these formulae are only there in order to illustrate certain technical points, such as the question of converting SDRs into currency. Those who wish to ignore them can do so without fear of missing anything important.

The main ideas discussed in this book are, or ought to be, accessible to everyone. Essentially, the reader will find analyses and, more particularly, criticisms of traditional monetary doctrines.

These doctrines are those that are supposed even now to guide public policy in a wide range of everyday matters; to this extent they are the concern not only of professionals but of the educated public as well. Nowadays, stimulated by the frequency with which they see monetary matters reported in the newspapers, people are coming to ask more and more fundamental questions about money. This book attempts to provide some of the answers.

In order to make the book approachable, certain ideas, as well as certain quotations, have been put into supplementary notes, which are placed at the end of each section. These supplementary notes take the form of a series of articles which can be read without referring to the main text.

Finally, the book also offers three 'games'—Lotto-money, Lotto-clearing and Lotto-Eurostable. The purpose of these games, which are similar to the well known parlour game 'Monopoly', is to demonstrate with greater clarity certain basic concepts that may appear too complex in words alone and at the same time reveal defects and merits that may not be immediately obvious.

It is the author's hope that by giving his readers entertainment as well as argument he may the more firmly convince them of the truth of his conclusions.

One final point: the reader who has not time enough to read the whole book may obtain a good idea of the import of the work by reading the final section, entitled 'Epilogue'.

J.R.

Introduction

In the modern world, money has long since ceased to be expressed in terms of coins made of a precious metal having its own intrinsic value. Everywhere money is nothing other than a claim on an institution, whether central bank or commercial bank, and takes the form of banknotes payable to the bearer or credits to a current account.

Money is created, it starts to circulate, and is divided into smaller units or added to others. It stays for a certain period of time in someone's pocket and then moves on somewhere else; as it passes from one person to another it fulfils its primary function, which is to act as the vehicle of exchanges of goods and services and to promote the conversion of production into consumption or investment. After it has taken part in a certain number of transactions, thereby oiling the wheels of the economy, it dies, or, in monetary terms, it is destroyed. This death is imaginary rather than real when the note enters a bank's till (it is no longer counted as part of the total money in circulation); but it actually is destroyed when a current account deposit disappears in consequence of a repayment of a loan or a transfer to a deposit or savings account.

The way a unit of money is created, used and then destroyed, the effects upon it of the various constituent elements of the economy, and its relations with economic activity and prices, are all factors that obey the laws of a certain mechanics. There is a mechanics of money just as there is a soil mechanics and a mechanics of fluids, this term being understood in the sense of a coherent theoretical structure, based on experience and intended to define in time the states, characteristics and effects of certain phenomena in terms of their mutual relations and in terms of external factors.

It is not my aim here to address myself to such matters as inflation, unemployment, income distribution, the equilibrium of the balance of payments, exchange rates, the 'snake in the tunnel' etc. These matters have already been more than adequately dealt with elsewhere and do not constitute the subject of this book. What is studied here is the process by which a unit of money is created and put into circulation and by which it is then destroyed when its natural life is at an end. Human beings produce, consume, build, procreate, make and unmake societies, but this is not what biology—another form of mechanics — studies. This science does not concern itself with society, but only with the process by which living cells are formed, combine and are then animated by the mysterious power of life and the ability to procreate. In 'monetary biology' this same process can also be studied. The uncertainty which surrounds it is the prime cause of monetary disorders, their persistence and our impotence to correct them.

But we shall not succeed in properly managing national economies and regulating trade within states and between states as long as we have no precise knowledge of the natural or artificial mechanisms, whether spontaneous or planned, which control the movements of units of money (or which are controlled by them) and as long as the differences of opinion which separate so many well-meaning people have not been eliminated. These differences of opinion concern what is money and what is not; the definitions and the interpretation of the indicators, whether or not certain institutions have the power of creating means of payment, the objectives, the means and even the principles of monetary regulation, the meaning and the role of composite currencies, the ability (or not) of the Eurocurrency system to create money and many other aspects and problems of monetary economics.

It is not very often that in books dealing with money, without excepting the most distinguished, one finds explanations of these things. Even when the word 'money' is on the cover or included in the title, one generally finds that the problems that are dealt with are exclusively economic in nature. People cannot help referring to money because money is the inevitable vehicle of any economy, but they do not explain the process by which money is created and distributed. In the same way, books dealing with war refer to fire-arms because without fire-arms there can be no war; nevertheless they do not go into the details of how guns and missiles work. This is the reason why the banker's clearing house, a vital institution by means of which a banking system creates means of payment, is only mentioned *en passant* in the *General Theory* of Keynes. In fact, the author only gives it a few lines. For the management of affairs in the fields of politics, social studies and economics to be efficient, reliable interpretations of events, accurate analyses and precise forecasts of the effects of decisions are required. Unfortunately, there is no such certainty in monetary affairs. The progress that has been made so far is rather in the recognition, now more or less general, that things are uncertain, that something, somewhere has gone wrong. Fortunately, this new awareness has now replaced the self-assurance and the intellectual arrogance of the high priests of finance, the guardians of orthodoxy, who, forty years ago, dictated the dogmas of the moment.

It would be wrong to say that the Great Depression was caused solely by erroneous monetary doctrines, but it was ignorance of the monetary mechanisms that transformed what ought only to have been a passing crisis into a deep and lasting malaise, which in turn plunged the world into recession and then into war. These dangerous beliefs have not all been abandoned; some still persist. But whereas in the fields of demography, industry, agriculture and military and social matters these mistakes have been denounced and the opinions of our forefathers abjured, in France, at least, no one has dared to have the public hangman solemnly burn the sacred books. Instead, people have simply been content to cease to apply the teachings and have preferred to adopt, and to modify according to circumstances, a purely pragmatic approach. In many respects this is preferable but it is not without its risks.

We cannot continue living on pragmatism for very long. Once we have finished denouncing and destroying we shall have to start to put forward some more positive suggestions and begin the work of reconstruction. The time will come when we shall have to put financial relations between states on a more solid basis, create a payment unit that will not be a national currency and equip the monetary system with a stable standard of value, independent of exchange rates and prices.

Sooner or later we shall have to discipline floating masses of 'hot money' and reinforce the role of the International Monetary Fund, thus putting at the disposal of those responsible for monetary regulation within states undisputed indicators, efficient intervention instruments, properly defined principles and a coherent doctrine. When this moment comes, an exact knowledge of monetary mechanisms will be an essential prerequisite of success. The study of monetary mechanisms requires an approach midway between that of the world of business, which keeps the members of the banking profession decidedly earthbound, and the lofty intellectual abstractions on which university researchers spend their time. The former need to gain altitude, whilst the latter need to come down out of the clouds a little. Only in this way shall we be able to correct the errors and confusions which characterise contemporary thinking on monetary matters and which constitute the greatest obstacles to progress.

Part One

Three keys to monetary analysis

1 What is money?

All aspects of money, the question of its circulation, the problems of supply and demand, its uses, its abuses, and other desirable and undesirable effects, are subjects of considerable controversy at present and give rise to contradictions which aggravate the uncertainty and the doubt that assail those whose task it is to make choices and take decisions.

The fundamental cause of this is the persistence of the old notion of money as 'representative of a commodity, defined in terms of the backing that guarantees its value'. Instead of accepting a unit of money for what it is, namely a simple acknowledgement of debt (more usually known as a claim on an institution) created *ex nihilo*, many people prefer to look at it as something that 'represents' a commodity, or, failing a commodity, some substitute for a commodity in the shape of another claim, this time on the person to whom the monetary unit is lent, i.e. a borrower.

Money is nothing other than a *transferable acknowledgement of debt, a promise to pay, arbitrarily created and usually with an indeterminate maturity and exchange value*. Any such acknowledgement of debt which is put into circulation and used directly as a means of payment for goods and services is *money*. There is no natural link between the commodity which this unit of money represents, the backing in terms of which payment is guaranteed and its actual value. The backing is only a form of protection, which may be useful but which is not a necessary precondition for the actual creation of the money.

This belief in the nature of money[1] as representative of a commodity has given rise to a complex mythology in which 'genuine claims' are contrasted with 'false claims', 'artificial' money with 'real' money, an astonishing system of verbal sophistry which explains the creation of money by the banking system as the result of the 'monetisation of a non-monetary asset'. If the consequences of such ideas were confined to the arena of academic debate it would not matter very much. But unfortunately they have gone far beyond that. In the eyes of many people these are still the ideas that ought to govern public policy on money and credit.

The rules governing the creation of money based on the idea of a commodity backing have become dangerous because they preserve the appearance of security whilst the substance of it has disappeared. This traditional definition should be expunged from the monetary canon. Apropos of the central bank reserves on which money is supposed to be 'founded', the Bank of France writes: 'Such a conception goes back to the time when bank notes and, indirectly, bank deposits, were officially convertible into precious metals. It is now obsolete'.[2]

In fact, it is only by going back to the beginning and submitting the traditional ideas on the nature of money to critical analysis that a doctrine can be developed which will be appropriate for the monetary mechanisms such as they really are in the modern world.[3] No progress can be made until the fundamental ideas have been revised and this traditional doctrine of money as a claim which stands in place of a commodity has been definitively refuted. This is what one contemporary writer, M. Michel Lelart, says on this subject:[4]

> Nowadays money is exclusively fiduciary. . . . Such a complete transformation in the nature of money has made it impossible to continue to assimilate it to a commodity.
>
> Consequently, it has become necessary to develop a theory which will account for the peculiar qualities of money and which will, in particular, explain the mechanism by which it is created. . . In fact, however, in spite of this radical transformation which the nature of money has undergone, the temptation of comparing money to a commodity is one that few economists have been able to resist. On the contrary, it has been reaffirmed, defended and, as far as possible, justified. Although he considered money to be a form of claim rather than another commodity, Keynes' responsibility in this respect is very great. He did not emancipate himself from the well entrenched habit of defining money not in terms of its nature but in terms of its function.
>
> The nature (of money) has fundamentally changed. . . Treating money as just one more commodity, the liquid commodity *par excellence*, has naturally led people to ignore the problem of how it is created. . . .

The concept of money as 'representative of a commodity' results from the transformation into a revealed truth of a mechanism which in its day had great merits, namely the mechanism of the gold standard. Before they stood for quantities of gold, units of money had stood for other things, such as shares, as in the system of John Law. Then they stood for property confiscated from *émigrés* during the French Revolution, as in the case of the *assignats*, and finally they came to stand for goods and then claims on borrowers or on the whole economy.

A new unit of money certainly represents something, but that something is not what most people think. It represents a *drawing* on or a reduction of the resources of the community; more precisely, a drawing on the holders of currency. The effect of this 'drawing' or 'reduction' continues until the new unit of money is destroyed. To try to base this new unit of money, created by an institution and credited to a borrower, on the claim on the borrower that the issuer thereby acquires, is as illogical as the harlequinades of circus clowns. There is no doubt that such a claim is necessary as a guarantee for the lender, but that does not justify the theory. The creation and the functioning of an instrument is something that should not be mixed up with a device intended merely to reduce a lender's risks.

A motor car is not defined by the insurance policy which covers the risks entailed in car ownership any more than pictures or jewels are defined by the alarm systems and locks that protect them. It is a fundamental fault of reasoning to take as the basis of a process something which is nothing more than a guarantee for the lender or, at most, a more or less automatic mechanism which helps to oil the wheels. This kind of muddled thinking and the muddle it leads people into when they try to regulate monetary mechanisms will continue as long as these old ideas have not been refuted and replaced.

NOTES

[1] The nature of money is a fundamental theme of the author's previous writings. *La vraie nature de la monnaie* is the title he gave to a book published in 1973 by the 'Editions de la RRP'. For further discussion of this topic, see page 106.

[2] *La Banque de France et la monnaie* (Bank of France).

[3] 'The notion of wealth leads to an impasse. This impasse derives from an unjustified comparison of money to a simple asset or item of liquidity . . . What gives money its economic importance, however, is its payment function.'
Michelle de Mourgues, *Economie monétaire* (published by Daloz).

[4] *Le dollar, monnaie internationale* (published by Editions de l'Albatros).

2 How money works

'Lotto Money' is a game designed to demonstrate the arbitrary way in which payment instruments are created and to show how little we really understand about money and the way it passes into circulation. I recommend it to everyone who has to deal with money and more especially to those whose job is to talk about it.

The players, who number twenty in all, are divided into two groups of ten (called group A and group B) and each group has a leader. Each player has a little machine, a kind of die-stamping press, which is worked by a handle and which makes counters or 'units of production', UPs for short. The counters are of two sorts. Some are edible, black in colour and made of liquorice. These are called 'consumption UPs'. The others are hard and inedible; they are made of red plastic and can be used as accessories to the machines that produce the UPs, in order to improve productivity. These counters are 'investment UPs'. Each of the two group leaders has a printing press on which he prints monetary units, or MUs, simple pieces of paper bearing the words 'I promise to pay the bearer 1 MU_a' (in the case of group A) and 1 MU_b in the case of group B. The MU press is worked manually and requires no special effort, even at great speed. It can also be controlled by a kind of automatic pilot which is connected to the player's machine and eliminates any deliberate intervention by the group leader. This is called the 'discount window'.

The game is divided into sessions, each one consisting of several rounds. At the end of each round the players exchange UPs they have made for MUs, which have been made by the group leaders. At the end of the following round, each player uses the MUs he has 'earned' in order to buy UPs. He consumes or saves the black UPs (the consumption UPs) and uses the red ones in order to improve the productivity of his UP machine, his aim being either to produce more UPs in the same time or to produce the same quantity for less effort.

Each group is awarded points calculated by means of a formula incorporating two parameters. The first parameter is the number of UPs produced during one session and is called the GNP. The second parameter is the number of UPs that can be obtained on average during this session in exchange for 1 MU. This is the purchasing power of the MU. The

winner is the group that obtains the greatest number of points; the
number of points awarded to a group rises in proportion as its GNP and
the purchasing power of its MUs rise.

The game is about to begin. Each group leader must first of all supply
his players with enough MUs to enable them to obtain the maximum
number of points. To this end he must print and distribute a certain
quantity of MUs, but how many and to whom? Each group leader can
only find out by trial and error, according to his own temperament. The
first, *A*, putting his faith in the purchasing power parameter, distributes
his MUs parsimoniously; the leader of group *B* distributes three times as
many MUs.

The group leader distributes the MUs by lending them to his players,
which means that he becomes a creditor instead of a debtor, as the words
'I promise to pay·the bearer 1 MU' imply. But the maturity date is
omitted from the MUs, as are also the repayment terms, whereas the
promise to pay that the leader of the group receives from the player to
whom he lends MUs has a precise maturity, as well as an interest rate.

The game begins, the players start to turn their handles and after a few
rounds the first group starts to run out of MUs. At each halt in the game
there is a shortage of cash; a certain number of sellers find no buyers for
their UPs and in consequence reduce production. In addition to this
shortage, which derives, as it were, from purely mechanical reasons,
there is also the psychological element of speculation. The value of the
MUs starts to rise. The holders prefer to keep them in their pockets, rather
than spend them. The conversion of production into consumption or
investment, the process on which the whole system is based, is slowed
down.

In the second group, on the other hand, this process of conversion is
working and even expanding because the participants are using some of
the red counters they produce in order to make their machines more
efficient. But if the GNP parameter is progressing well and causing the
total of points to increase, the second parameter, purchasing power, is
tending to work in the opposite direction. The players themselves, by
speeding up their exchanges, shorten the gaps between rounds. The total
quantity of MUs has not increased but they circulate faster. The time-lags,
and therefore the production that takes place between each exchange, are
reduced.

The group leaders are starting to get worried, the first because his total
of points is too small, which he attributes to the fact that his MUs are
circulating too slowly, the second because the velocity of circulation of his
MUs is too great, which causes him to worry about the purchasing power.

They consult the experts. Some suggest linking the MU to gold, whilst others mention a lot of so-called 'monetary indicators', called M1, M2, and M3 but without explaining how to use them. The two group leaders are perplexed.

The leader of group *B* has acquired a taste for liquorice and is no longer content with just making credits; instead he now uses the MUs he prints in order to purchase UPs, which he consumes cheaply. The leader of group *A*, who is more prudent, continues to print MUs and lends them to players whom he chooses on the basis of their ability to invest wisely and work hard. Soon his team catches up with the other and then overtakes it.

The harmony that has reigned so far in each group is gradually replaced by differences of opinion, something economists call 'sectoral tendencies'. They assume different forms in each group. In group *A*, one of the players decides to increase the price of his UPs. The reasons for his decision are not clear. Perhaps he thinks that his liquorice is better than the liquorice the other players produce. But more probably recent events have given him cause to expect a rise in prices, so why not anticipate it? The embarrassed replies which he gives to his group leader suggest that he is motivated less by calculations of profit than by pure impulse. What was at first only a sectoral tendency becomes more general. One by one the players, noticing that the price they are paying is higher than the price at which they sell, whilst their number of hours worked remains the same, also raise their prices. The team leader is worried because his total number of points is likely to be affected. Up to this moment he has tried to keep the production of MUs equal to a growth rate in line with the production of UPs by his players, i.e. about 5 per cent per session, but the players have been affected by the price rise, which is higher than the agreed 5 per cent.

At the end of the seventh round, several players find they can no longer afford to buy what is offered with the MUs they have available. Those players who have not been able to sell what they have produced slow down. At the end of the next round they too can no longer buy the goods on offer, even at the old prices.

Production is strangled: it is the beginning of a process of asphyxiation. The same thing is happening in group *B*, though the causes are different. One of the players, growing tired of turning his handle and considering that he is being discriminated against, starts to raise his prices faster. Others start to imitate him, but the leader of the group decides to stop regulating things manually, switches on the automatic pilot and connects it to the MU machine.

As the rise in prices, which at first was purely sectoral, spreads through the system, the automatic pilot takes over. The MUs are produced faster and faster by the machine and pass into circulation. Whether the machine is badly regulated or whether it is operating on false premises, too many MUs are being produced. Prices start to rise faster and faster.

In group A, weary players cause more and more new MUs to be produced and as long as they do so they are able to consume without producing. The team leaders consult their textbooks: 'The Compleat Monetarist' and 'Keynesianism in Five Lessons — Results Guaranteed'. The two books are in flat contradiction with each other. All they have in common is the peremptory nature of their assertions and the contempt they have for any attempt at contradiction. The group leaders are no better off for having consulted them. The leader of group A, in order to check the price rise and get production going again, decides to curb demand, brake the MU printing machine and increase interest rates so as to attract some of the MUs that have begun to trickle through from the other team. Finally, he imposes taxes on the players in order to absorb some of the liquidity he has so generously created himself in the form of loans.

The hoped for result is not achieved. Demand is effectively curbed, but so is production. The majority of the players have contracted debts because they wished to make their machines more efficient. They accepted high rates of interest only because they were counting on both an increase in production and a continual fall in the purchasing power of money, which would reduce their repayment costs proportionately. In fact the reverse has happened. The negative effects have been magnified by pessimistic expectations and the collapse of confidence on the part of the most enterprising players, who were also the most frequent users of red counters (investment UPs).

In group B, the leader, instead of curbing demand, attempts to increase it, believing that by spreading his fixed costs over greater production he will be able to limit price rises. He lowers interest rates and even considers creating more MUs in order to give them as presents to the players, rather as President Carter intended when he planned to give $50 to every American man, woman, and child. Once again, unfortunately, the results are not those that were expected; various things happen.

The first is a shortage of raw liquorice; the second is a loss of control over the machine that produces the MUs. Having relieved the players of the task of turning the handle, the machine has gone wrong and has increased, rightly or wrongly, the demands made on it. In the formula used for working out the total points, the GNP parameter looks fine, but the MU parameter looks less favourable.

Let us leave the players there. At the end of this fourth session neither of the teams has succeeded in working out the rules of the game that will enable them to win the contest. The conclusion they come to — which is also mine — is that it is preferable to analyse the mechanisms in question, to take them apart and to try to understand the way they work, rather than continue to cling to beliefs of doubtful value and to continue to subscribe to doctrines that lack any foundation. Only in this way can one hope to learn how to make good use of the instruments one has available.

3 Three keys to monetary analysis

No attempt to control and direct monetary phenomena can succeed if it is not based on a proper understanding and a correct interpretation of the mechanisms by which money is created and by which it circulates. This means that we must take these mechanisms apart, separate the components from each other and try to discover how they interact, using exactly the same method an engineer would adopt if he wanted to understand how a piece of machinery worked. We are not concerned here with the economic theories of money: our aim is rather to try to understand the phenomenon of money itself and the way it works.

The usual method of economics is to study the way money is distributed and its effects on production and on prices, just as the manufacture of lorries is studied by drawing up statistics, making comparisons, looking into the transport of goods, trade and the distribution of commodities. In other words, economics takes units of money, just as it takes lorries, as they come out of the factory, and remains outside.[1] This is useful but it is not always enough. The purpose of this study is to go *inside* the factory and study in detail the process of manufacture by using one basic premiss and three keys.

The basic premiss, as we saw in Chapter 1, is that a unit of money is nothing more than a claim on an institution arbitrarily created without any natural link with a commodity which it is supposed to represent, a backing which guarantees its value or any tangible counterpart remitted to the issuer in exchange for it.

The three keys are the following.

Payment, the fundamental activity by which money carries out its function. It is nothing more than the transfer from one economic agent, X, to another, Y, of a unit of money in return for a transfer of goods or services between Y and X,

The clearing process, which makes it possible for banks to create their own means of payment and superimpose them on those deriving from the bank of issue.

The drawing on the total wealth of the holders of money which is the inevitable result of the creation of a unit of money. The analysis of this phenomenon of *reduction* (and its opposite, restoration) demonstrates, on the one hand, the relations between money, its velocity, its quantity and the uses it is put to, and, on the other, economic activity and prices. It also causes the artificial divisions between the various sources of money to disappear and provides a basis on which credit may be distributed selectively.

With the help of these three keys one can successfully analyse monetary mechanisms, about which little is really known or, which is worse, which people *think* they know, though the blunders they make prove that the opposite is the case. This happens, for example, in the case of the Eurocurrencies. Many experts — and in France most of them — attribute powers of monetary creation to the Euromarket; some, such as the late Jacques Rueff, consider that it is partly responsible for world inflation.

In fact, to the observer who has not looked closely enough into the subject, it may indeed seem that there is no difference between a payment order to a London Bank in pounds sterling and one given to the same bank in dollars, hence the conclusion that London banks have the same powers of monetary creation in dollars as in sterling, though when they operate in dollars they are not obliged to abide by any discipline, whether British or American. But the truth is that the Eurobanks act as *non-monetary* intermediaries in currencies other than those of the countries they are domiciled in and thus do not create any new money. This can be seen if one analyses what happens using the two keys, payment and clearing.[2]

Another example is provided by the choice and definition of monetary indicators; economic analysis looks for and registers the flows, the quantity and the velocity of money, which presupposes that the indicators that reflect these factors are clearly defined and correctly interpreted. In fact, this is not the case. Of course, it is possible to call into question the very idea of controlling the money supply but certain established facts cannot be called into question: for example, firstly, the fact that in every country the money supply has become an essential indicator; secondly, the fact that qualified experts question the interpretation of these indicators and, consequently, the measures of monetary control based on them.

These three keys help to make the interpretation of monetary

statistics more accurate and to distinguish what is really money from
what is not. They also lead to a corrected indicator which reflects more
faithfully than M1 the volume and effects of money transactions. At a time
when the old concepts and disciplines that governed our thinking are
coming to appear more and more discredited it is important that the
mechanism by which money is created, put into circulation and finally
destroyed should be understood. This is the purpose for which these
three keys are proposed.

NOTES

[1] In his book *L'Impôt sur le capital et la réforme monétaire* (published by
Editions Hermann), Maurice Allais writes: 'The application in France of
senseless monetary policies has merely been the result of an incredible
intellectual backwardness with regard to the nature of money and credit.'

[2] In a well-documented book on Eurodollars with a preface by Henri
Bourguinat, entitled *Mécanisme de change et marché des eurodollars*
(published by Ed. Economica), Pierre-François Champion and Jacques
Trauman write, apropos of the multiplier in the Eurodollar system:
'This is a difficult and very controversial question to which many
economists have tried to give a reply, without any success'. This is true:
it *is* a difficult and controversial question. Nevertheless, the need to
draw some solidly founded conclusions, on which theoreticians and
practical men can agree, still exists. How else can one hope to
discipline, let alone regulate, international capital flows, which are
essential for the health of the world economy? But there is little hope
of rationally analysing the Euromarket as long as the first key to proper
understanding of these matters, namely the concept of payment, is
neglected and the second, which is the clearing mechanism, continues
to be ignored.

As far as 90 per cent of their activities are concerned, the Eurobanks
are non-monetary intermediaries, just like savings banks. It is only the
assets that the Eurobank has in banks domiciled in the United States
which possess the 'payment function'. The deposit at a Eurobank does
not have the payment function which a deposit at a bank in national
currency has, i.e. the currency of the country where it is domiciled.
The fact that Eurobanks do not function as monetary intermediaries is
due to the absence of a clearing mechanism. It is this lacuna in the
system that explains why a Eurobank does not settle its debts by means
of a claim on itself but by means of a claim on a third party (its asset in
a bank domiciled in the United States) which consequently means that
it does not create any new money.

4 The first key – Payment

Payment, or the exchange of a unit of money – i.e. a claim on an institution – for a delivery of goods or services is a fascinating process, both in its nature and in its effects. Take a simple piece of paper such as a bank-note or a note confirming that a current account has been credited, or the document that often takes its place, namely a cheque. In each case, the document in question is an acknowledgement of debt (also called *a claim on an institution*) which is completely artificial in its nature since the debtor who acknowledged the debt, a cashier at the central bank or at a clearing bank, i.e. the person who has signed the piece of paper 'promising' to pay twenty pounds, has in most cases not received anything at all, except perhaps another piece of paper – a receipt – signed this time by a borrower. This piece of paper has the even more miraculous power of transforming the issuer, whether it is the Bank of England or a commercial bank, from debtor into lender.

This claim on an institution – a bank-note or a cheque – changes hands many times and as it does so the whole economic apparatus is set in motion. Raw materials are extracted, refined and gradually converted into finished goods; to use the language of econometrics, 'value is added'. Eventually the process comes to its logical conclusion: the goods are used, that is, they are consumed or invested. This cycle is almost biological in nature: it is comparable to the phenomenon of life and this is the origin of the old image of money as the life-blood of society. The different forms money takes on are as various as life itself, but behind them all one still comes back to the same two complementary flows: on the one hand goods and services are supplied and on the other they are consumed or invested.

Let us take some examples. A bank gives a customer an overdraft. It credits his account and enters on the asset side of its balance sheet a claim for the same amount. The borrower, who now becomes a depositor, draws a cheque and, hey presto, £1 000 starts to circulate, passing from one person to another, causing added value to accumulate in the process of production until it is finally used up, that is until there is a conversion into non-productive consumption on the part of consumers or the government or until it is invested.

A manufacturer delivers a machine which he has just produced. His customer accepts the bill of exchange drawn by his supplier and the latter discounts it at his bank. His bank in turn discounts it at the central bank. Here we have another acknowledgement of debt (a bank-note or central bank asset) which takes the place of the first and becomes a means of exchange, passing from hand to hand. An exporter receives a payment in dollars, i.e. claims on an American bank. He converts them into pounds at the Bank of England and thus he acquires another claim, on the Bank of England this time, which replaces the one he had on the Federal Reserve System and which starts to circulate. The Bank of England buys some gold from a hoarder. This act produces a claim on the bank which passes into circulation and goes from one person to the other, in turn promoting a parallel flow of business.

All these examples show that the fundamental guide-line to follow in monetary analysis leads beyond the bank counter and goes right to this basic operation, the transfer of a unit of money (claim on an institution) from one economic agent, X, to another, Y, in exchange for a supply of goods or services from Y to X. Certain claims have the *payment function*, i.e. the property of being directly exchangeable for goods or services, others do not; the two sorts should not be confused. Current account deposits in a bank have this power because they can be used directly in exchanges, which does not mean that every time a payment unit changes hands there is inevitably a corresponding delivery of goods and services, but simply that such a unit has the property peculiar to it of being used to effect such exchanges. Other claims, such as deposits in savings accounts in banks and savings banks have no payment function because they cannot be used directly for payments; they must first be exchanged for claims that do have the payment function, i.e. that can be exchanged directly for a supply of goods and services.

If the deposits at a savings bank could be used as direct means of payment they would have to be included in the money supply: this is the case, for example, for a limited number of Loan and Saving Associations in the United States, and it is true of the municipal *Sparkassen* in Germany. It is not whether the deposits are demand or time deposits that is important, nor whether they are interest-bearing or not. There are some demand deposits that in practice are subject to greater advance notice than is the case with a time deposit on which a banker agrees to permit drawing before the maturity date. The real difference is of another sort; it lies in the direct transfer of money in exchange for a corresponding transfer of goods and services.

Looked at from this point of view, a bill of exchange endorsed over to another payee or a Treasury Bill handed directly to a creditor must be considered items of payment money. On the other hand, a very large denomination bank-note may well have no payment function because in practice it is never used directly in a transaction but is always changed into notes of smaller denomination first. In practice, however, bank-notes and current account deposits constitute by far the greater part of the means of payment in circulation. The amount of other claims used for this purpose is negligible. It is therefore justifiable for the purpose of statistics to limit the stock of payment money to the constituents of M1, i.e. notes and current account deposits. It is a constant source of mistakes to talk of 'near money' as if it were payment money and to include the two things in the same category. What is important is the mass of claims that actually have the payment function, which implies that in order to analyse the process of monetary creation and the meaning of monetary indicators', the role of financial intermediaries and the power of monetary creation of the Eurobanks, one must first of all find out where the *final* exchange of money for the supply of goods or services takes place.[1]

Here some more examples. X has bought a car from Y. In order to pay for it he borrows £2000 from A. A asks his solicitor to transfer the sum to X. The solicitor, N, gives £2000 in notes to his clerk, C. Since C prefers to make the payment by cheque rather than in cash, he deposits the notes he has received at his bank B_1 and draws a cheque on it, which he gives to the purchaser of the car, X. X endorses the cheque and sends it to Y, who deposits it at his bank, B_2.

Out of all these operations, which is the actual act of payment? The transfer order given by A to his solicitor? The bank-notes given by the solicitor to his clerk? In fact it is neither the one nor the other. Instead we must look for the final transfer: the precise moment at which the supplier, or his representative, receives in exchange for the goods or services that have passed out of his hands the monetary unit or claim on an institution which takes their place.[1] It is the *replacement of one possession* (in this case the car) by another (claim on the Bank of England or on another bank) which must be emphasised. In our example, the element which effects the payment is the cheque drawn by C on his bank, B_1. In fact, if we wish to take the analysis a step further we should consider the following.

This cheque, or claim on B_1, is given by Y to his bank B_2. B_2 then becomes creditor of B_1, but the process does not stop there. Thanks to the mechanism of the clearing house, which causes mutual claims to cancel each other out, the final payment between B_1 and B_2 is made by means of, say £1 500 in cleared money, i.e. mutually self-cancelling claims, and £500 in central bank money credited to the account of B_2 with the central bank. It is reasonable, therefore, to conclude that the final payment of the £2000 owed by X to Y was made to the extent of £1500 of the original sum by the claim of the seller, Y, on B_1 passed on by him to his bank B_2, and as regards £500 of the total by a claim on the central bank. The total, £1500 + £500 = £2000, represents the full price of the vehicle delivered by Y to X. In England, M1 includes current account deposits but not the assets of the banks at the central bank. Nevertheless, the fact remains that part of the payments that are counted in M1 were ultimately effected in central bank money. The total of the movements constituted M1 and nothing but M1. Later on, in Part 2, we shall come to a theoretical justification of this search for the final transfer of a unit of money as the counterpart of a payment. The reason for this will become more apparent to the reader once he has gone through the various stages of the analysis contained in Parts 1 and 2. The fundamental feature of modern economies is the way money claims pass from hand to hand as the counterparts to exchanges of goods. The whole vast edifice of production, investment, salaries etc. is based on it. If we wish to get to the heart of this process, we must look for the unit that balances the supply of goods and services. This is why so much emphasis is laid here on going right to the end of the line to find the ultimate claim that effects the payment.

It follows from this that we must distinguish the deposits a bank accepts – when it is a monetary intermediary – all of which constitute liabilities for it, from those balance sheet entries which, on the contrary, constitute assets, such as reserves and loans. Amongst the bank's various liabilities, the only ones that have the payment function are current account deposits because only they can be exchanged *directly* for goods and services. The other deposits, such as savings deposits, do not have this power; they have lost their vital principle. When a unit equipped with the payment function is deposited in a bank account and converted into a savings account deposit, this same unit is destroyed and withdrawn from M1.

The mobilisation of a savings account causes the creation of a 'living' unit of money because it becomes transferable and is therefore equipped with the payment function. As such, it is added to M1. In the case of a deposit with a non-monetary intermediary, such as a savings bank, the unit of money is either put in reserve or transferred to a borrower who makes use of the right to goods and services represented by that unit of money in place of the depositor. If we want to take the comparison farther we can say that a unit of money is 'asleep' whilst it is in someone's account, because it preserves the vital payment function

without putting it to use. This payment function only takes effect
when the unit of money 'wakes up', that is, when it passes from the
holder's account to someone else's.

A unit of savings money, on the other hand, is not asleep: it is dead.
It is not freely transferable and therefore has no payment function. This
function has passed to another unit — the one the bank effectively
transfers if it is a savings bank or the one the bank creates on the basis
of the extra liquidity it has gained in the case of a monetary intermediary.
The mobilisation of a unit of savings money thus requires the transfer of a
pre-existing unit, in the case of a savings bank, and the creation of a brand
new unit, in the case of a monetary intermediary such as a commercial bank.
The traditional expression 'mobilisation', if taken literally, may give rise
to misunderstanding since it gives the special character of 'resuscitation'
to a process which, in fact, is the same whether the payment unit is
created in exchange for foreign currency or notes, gold, a discounted bill
or a simple advance.

If we wish to explain the creation of a new unit of money, it is better
to speak of *paternity* rather than resuscitation. This paternity can be
just as easily attributed to the mobilisation of a unit of savings money as
to conversion of foreign currency or discounting of a bill. In this case
there is creation of offspring, not resuscitation. These figures of speech
may be questioned; their virtue, however, is to bring out the fundamental
role of the payment function and thus help to elucidate the Mechanics
of Money.[2]

Of the three keys proposed here, the payment function is perhaps the
one which, more than any other, is, or ought to be, systematically used in
the process of monetary analysis. Since the time of Aristotle, the role of
money as medium of exchange has been recognised and taught in the
schools and universities. It is therefore all the more surprising that this
payment function should be so rarely singled out and recognised and
that it should be so frequently confused with other functions. It can, on
the contrary, help our analysis, providing we do not rely upon criteria
such as withdrawal notice in order to decide whether a claim has or has
not the payment function. Nor must we hesitate to take the analysis to
its logical conclusion, till the ultimate exchange of a unit of money against
supply of goods is found. Only in this way can we hope to make progress
in the analysis of the nature of money.

NOTES

[1] In the interests of correct analysis, one cannot insist too much on the importance of looking for the final stage of the process and the claim that ultimately effects the payment when a transaction takes place. Appearances are often deceptive, and superficial observation easily leads to error. Some additional examples will be found on page 108.

[2] Is there any need to point out that these figures of speech are only chosen for the purpose of illustration? The analysis must be taken further. A note is deposited at a bank and thus withdrawn from circulation. It is no longer counted in the money supply, in the narrow sense of the M1 money supply. The note has effectively been destroyed, and if it hadn't it would be duplicated by the credit to the current account of the depositor, which has the same payment function as the note.

But this note constitutes for the bank in question an asset at the central bank which may perhaps be used by it in order to pay a depositor who withdraws part of his deposit or in order to carry out a final transaction, such as the payment of a negative balance at the Clearing House. Because of this, though it is not counted in the total money in circulation, this asset makes it possible for the bank to create claims on itself which constitute new money, which is why it is included in the monetary 'base', or 'high powered' money, which, added to the notes in circulation, constitutes M0.

In order to complete our series of monetary metaphors, we could say that the bank's assets at the central bank are the 'soul' of the note which has just been destroyed. This soul is in heaven (central bank) and intercedes with God (monetary authorities) on behalf of those beings left behind on earth (the bankers).

The ratio of reserves which the banks have at the Bank of France is less than 7 per cent of the total payment money in circulation.

5 The second key – Clearing

The clearing mechanism is generally neglected by monetary analysts; nevertheless, it is the basis on which the power of creation of payment instruments by a national banking system rests. It is thanks to this process that claims, or acknowledgements of debt, which originally had no monetary function, come to act as means of payment. It is also thanks to the clearing mechanism that money can be increased in quantity. By looking to see whether clearing takes place one can discover whether new bank money really is created independently of the central bank over and above the supply of primary money. By analysing the mechanism of the clearing one can also solve the problem, which has been at the origin of so much controversy, of the powers of self-multiplication of Eurodollars.

The essence of the clearing mechanism is the settlement by bank A of its debts towards bank B by means of its claim on bank E, which is also creditor of bank B. Let us take an example. John has drawn a cheque on bank A and has used it to pay his supplier, Peter, who in turn has deposited the cheque at bank B. John's claim on bank A has been replaced by Peter's claim on B, whilst B is the holder of a claim on A. But at the same time another transaction has taken place. Robert, for example, has deposited at A a cheque drawn on B. The consequence of this is that whereas B is creditor of A, A is also creditor of B. Only the balance when the mutual claims have cancelled each other out is actually transferred in central bank money to A or B, whichever is the final creditor.

Current account deposits constitute the biggest part of the total of payment money. A deposit in a current account is created by a financial intermediary which is called 'monetary' (or 'bank') precisely because it has the power to create payment money as a consequence of the fact that the claim on itself, or acknowledgement of debt, that it gives its customer, whether he is a depositor or borrower, can be exchanged *directly* for goods or services. It is thanks to this operation, that claims on private banks (current account deposits) can come to constitute a mass of means of payment which are added to the claims on the central bank (notes) to make up the total of M1.

If the clearing process were only carried out within individual banks or on a bilateral basis by two banks at a time it would not have much impact.

It is precisely because it takes place between a large number of banks which together make up the banking system that it succeeds in multiplying the mass of bank money. An example will make this clear:

> *A* owes £1000 to *B*,
> *B* owes £1000 to *C*,
> *C* owes £1000 to *D*,
> *D* owes £1000 to *A*.

If the clearing mechanism did not exist, *A*, *B*, *C* and *D* would each have to transfer £1000 to its creditor. Each bank would therefore have to have this amount available in central bank money. The effect of the clearing is to make this necessity disappear: *A*, *B*, *C* and *D* do not need to move any funds at all.

What's more, the clearing mechanism makes it possible for banks to lend by using claims on themselves, instead of lending with freely available central bank funds. In order to grant a credit, all a bank needs to do is to enter on the asset side of its balance sheet its claim on the borrower and put his claim on it on its liability side, thereby creating new money which becomes part of M1. The amount lent, once it has been used by the borrower in order to make a payment, is deposited at another bank which becomes the creditor of the bank that granted the credit. The latter knows that, thanks to the clearing system, it will not actually have to pay in central bank money more than a fraction of its obligations, the balance, in fact, that remains after the day's clearing.

So as to be able to deal with withdrawals in notes or settle any clearing house balances in central bank money, a bank keeps a certain quantity of liquid or semi-liquid assets which it can quickly turn into legal tender money (also called primary money, central bank money or, as Milton Friedman recommends, 'high-powered money'). The total quantity of these assets is in direct relation to the bank's liabilities, according to the legal ratio of compulsory reserves to deposits. In England banks keep a cash reserve of 7–8 per cent of their total assets and an amount of easily mobilisable reserves at the central bank equal to 30 per cent.

A deposit in a savings account or in a deposit account is governed by the same accounting procedures as a current account deposit, whether created by a deposit or by a loan. On the liability side, there is the debt owing to the depositor; on the asset side there is the sum paid over (claim on another bank or savings bank). These time deposits, or near-money, do not have the payment function and therefore do not enter into M1, but they do act indirectly as the base for lending operations through their effect on bank liquidity (central bank money) and, through the ratio of loans to deposits, on the total of current account deposits that the bank can create by lending.

In practice, the clearing process works by means of a third party, the Clearing House, which receives and pays out in central bank money the balances that result from each day's transactions. For each debt there is a corresponding claim, so that the balance of accounts with the clearing house is always nil. It is easy to imagine that instead of using the Clearing House each participant could settle his obligations himself, using his claims: for example, A could transfer to his creditor B his claim on F; B in turn would use his claim on F in order to pay his debts to C, etc. But as soon as the participants exceed a certain number the operation would become long and complicated, whereas it needs to be completed within the space of one business day.[1] In any case, for the clearing mechanism to have its proper effect, the whole process of transfers of claims would have to lead to a 'binomial' of two banks with mutual claims and liabilities; the mutal obligations of A and F would be cancelled out because the claim of B on A, for example, has gone as far as F, who is also A's debtor via E, D and C.

A break or gap in this chain prevents the final binomial position from being reached. A creditor who has no obligations with regard to the other participants in the system, or the absence of a clearing house, paralyses the whole mechanism and causes the clearing to be replaced by actual payments in primary money (central bank money in the case of a national banking system, dollars in the case of the Eurodollar system). The Eurocurrency system is full of such gaps, and moreover it has no clearing mechanism. The result is that Eurodollar banks are obliged to settle their reciprocal debts directly in dollars. The following analysis aims to cast further light on the role of the clearing mechanism in the creation of payment instruments by a banking system and on the negative effects that the following factors would have:

> absence of clearing house
> wide geographical spread of participants
> absence of mutual claims
> leaks or breaks in the system, withdrawals in cash (in a national banking system) or return to the US banking system (in the case of a Eurodollar).

Let us imagine that the clearing session, which takes place daily at the

Clearing House, has just started. The participating banks have been reduced, for the convenience of the exercise, to four: *A*, *B*, *C* and *D*. Each one has brought with it the cheques deposited with it and the transfer orders it has received and has added them up and classified them according to drawee or payee. What each bank owes to each other bank and what is owed to it by the other banks is thus worked out. The difference for each one between what it owes and what is owed to it is the *clearing balance*. It is this balance that is paid at the end of the session in central bank money by crediting or debiting the bank's account at the central bank.[2]

For the sake of the clarity of this demonstration, the various operations are entered into double-entry charts. For example, 9 in column *B* and line *A* means that the total of cheques drawn on *A* and deposited at *B*, to which are added the payment orders in favour of *B* received by *A*, equals 9. The section outlined in bold at the bottom right-hand corner of the chart shows the total movements, i.e. the total payments carried out by the banks −63− and the fraction of the total payments which has been carried out in Central Bank money, in this case 15. The difference, i.e. 63 − 15 = 48, corresponds to the total of mutually clearing claims on the banks, 12 for *A*, 13 for *B*, 12 for *C* and 11 for *D* (= 48).

The overall mass of payments, i.e. 63, has therefore ultimately been carried out (that is in the banking system) by 48 in claims on the banks and 15 in central bank money, although the statistics[3] have registered 63 in claims on the banks (current account deposits). The reason for this is that the usual statistical practice in calculating M1 is to count only current account credit balances and disregard the banks' central bank assets. In practice, the clearing operation is very simple. Each bank adds up its claims and its liabilities and the balances are paid over in central bank money. *A* is therefore debited 7, *D* is debited 8 and *B* and *C* are credited with 5 and 10 respectively.

The *mechanism* implied by this, however, is very complex: the balances are the results of imaginary intermediate operations which have been analysed stage by stage in Tables II, III and IV. In table II the process is binomial: in III the process becomes trinomial and in IV it becomes quadrinomial, with the result that only the central bank transfers are left (15, 15, 15 and 15). The internal breakdown of each stage of the process may be compared with Table I. Here the reader will observe how the simple fact of comparing claims and obligations and the calculation of the balances by subtraction is in fact equivalent to a whole series of instantaneous transfers between the participants (I, II, III and IV).

The clearing process makes it possible to compare very quickly how much each member bank of a banking system owes to every other member bank and how much each of the other member banks owes to it. The balances (figures outlined in heavy type in the bottom right-hand corner of each table) must be paid in central bank money. In this case the amount in question is 15.

The difference between the total amount paid over and the balance, that is 63 - 15 = 48, represents the proportion of the payments that has been carried out in claims on the banks.

On the four tables, successive clearings are carried out by the banks, first two by two, then three by three and so on. After four operations they arrive at the same final balance to be paid in central bank money, i.e. 15, as in the first table. It can thus be seen that if there were no such overall system of clearing the number of operations to be carried out singly by individual banks would be very much greater and would increase in proportion as the number of participating banks increased.

CLEARING CHART SHOWING TRANSACTIONS BETWEEN FOUR BANKS

First example

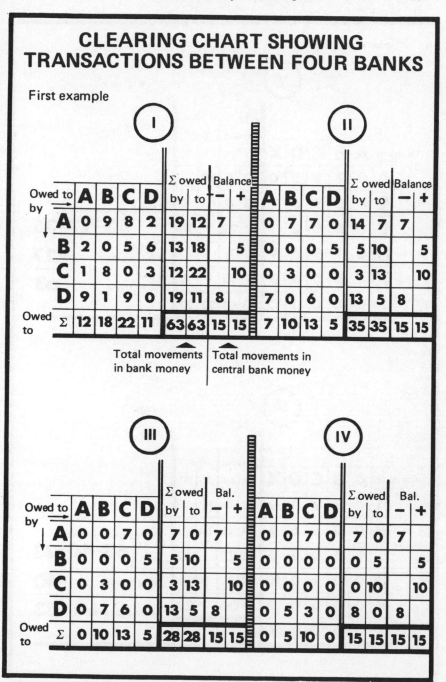

	A	B	C	D	Σ owed by	Σ owed to	Balance −	Balance +
A	0	9	8	2	19	12	7	
B	2	0	5	6	13	18		5
C	1	8	0	3	12	22		10
D	9	1	9	0	19	11	8	
Σ	12	18	22	11	63	63	15	15

I — Owed to (by →); Owed by (↓); Owed to (Σ)

	A	B	C	D	Σ owed by	Σ owed to	Balance −	Balance +
A	0	7	7	0	14	7	7	
B	0	0	0	5	5	10		5
C	0	3	0	0	3	13		10
D	7	0	6	0	13	5	8	
Σ	7	10	13	5	35	35	15	15

II

Total movements in bank money | Total movements in central bank money

	A	B	C	D	Σ owed by	Σ owed to	Bal. −	Bal. +
A	0	0	7	0	7	0	7	
B	0	0	0	5	5	10		5
C	0	3	0	0	3	13		10
D	0	7	6	0	13	5	8	
Σ	0	10	13	5	28	28	15	15

III

	A	B	C	D	Σ owed by	Σ owed to	Bal. −	Bal. +
A	0	0	7	0	7	0	7	
B	0	0	0	0	0	5		5
C	0	0	0	0	0	10		10
D	0	5	3	0	8	0	8	
Σ	0	5	10	0	15	15	15	15

IV

Second example

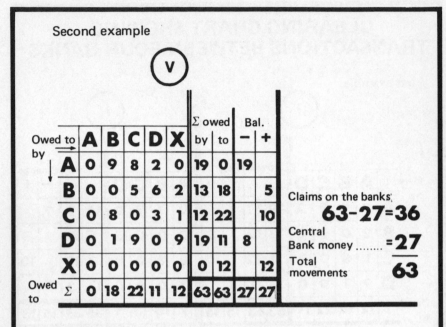

V

Owed to by ↓	A	B	C	D	X	Σ owed by	to	Bal. −	+
A	0	9	8	2	0	19	0	19	
B	0	0	5	6	2	13	18		5
C	0	8	0	3	1	12	22		10
D	0	1	9	0	9	19	11	8	
X	0	0	0	0	0	0	12		12
Owed to Σ	0	18	22	11	12	63	63	27	27

Claims on the banks,
63-27=36
Central
Bank money .... **=27**
Total
movements **63**

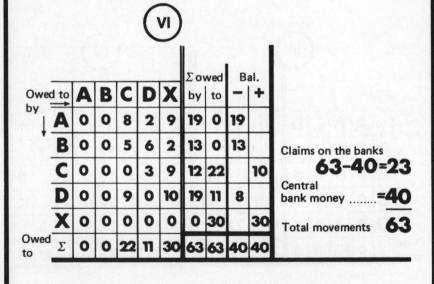

VI

Owed to by ↓	A	B	C	D	X	Σ owed by	to	Bal. −	+
A	0	0	8	2	9	19	0	19	
B	0	0	5	6	2	13	0	13	
C	0	0	0	3	9	12	22		10
D	0	0	9	0	10	19	11	8	
X	0	0	0	0	0	0	30		30
Owed to Σ	0	0	22	11	30	63	63	40	40

Claims on the banks
63-40=23
Central
bank money .... **=40**
Total movements **63**

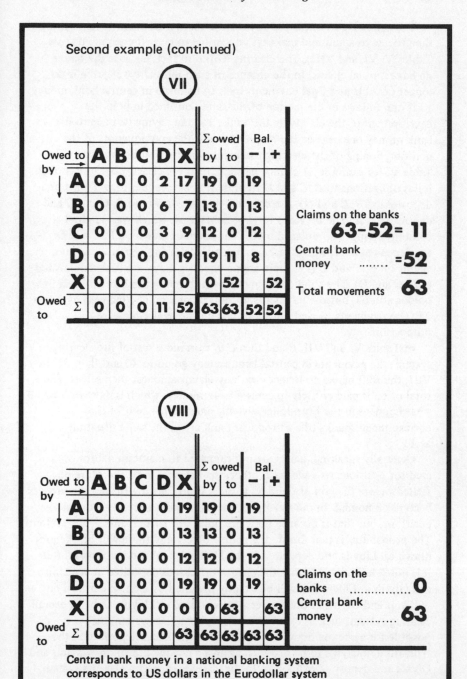

Second example (continued)

VII

Owed to by → ↓	A	B	C	D	X	Σ owed by	Σ owed to	Bal. −	Bal. +
A	0	0	0	2	17	19	0	19	
B	0	0	0	6	7	13	0	13	
C	0	0	0	3	9	12	0	12	
D	0	0	0	0	19	19	11	8	
X	0	0	0	0	0	0	52		52
Owed to Σ	0	0	0	11	52	63	63	52	52

Claims on the banks

63-52= 11

Central bank money .... **=52**

Total movements **63**

VIII

Owed to by → ↓	A	B	C	D	X	Σ owed by	Σ owed to	Bal. −	Bal. +
A	0	0	0	0	19	19	0	19	
B	0	0	0	0	13	13	0	13	
C	0	0	0	0	12	12	0	12	
D	0	0	0	0	19	19	0	19	
X	0	0	0	0	0	0	63		63
Owed to Σ	0	0	0	0	63	63	63	63	63

Claims on the banks **0**

Central bank money **63**

Central bank money in a national banking system corresponds to US dollars in the Eurodollar system

The following example shows how the absence of mutual claims brings the process to a halt and makes it impossible to clear the payments (see Tables V, VI, and VIII). The clearing works, in fact, because the banks do have mutual claims. In the absence of such mutuality, clearing is no longer possible and final payments have to be made in central bank money.

If one follows in the section of the tables outlined in bold the development of the claims on the banks and the payments in central bank money one can see the reasons for and the consequences of the non-functioning of the clearing mechanism in the Eurodollar system. In Table V, for example, A cannot participate in the clearing because though it has obligations to B, C and D (represented by cheques drawn on A and deposited at B, C and D), there are no cheques drawn on B, C and D and deposited at A. The previous total of debts to A, which was 12 (first column) disappears, replaced by 0. The cheques drawn on B, C and D are deposited at X, who is either outside the clearing system or has no claims on B, C and D (i.e. there are no cheques drawn on X and deposited at B, C and D). The total of the movements given in the box outlined in bold is still 63, but the payments in central bank money increase by 12 to 27. The payments carried out by claims on the banks decrease proportionately.

In Tables VI and VII, B and then C in turn move out of the clearing system; the payments in central bank money go up to 40 and then 52. In VIII, the four banks no longer clear any claims amongst themselves. The total of 63 is paid entirely in central bank money, which is more or less what happens in the Eurodollar system, since 90 per cent of the correspondent banks of a Eurodollar bank are in the same situation as X.

Generally speaking, banks are not prepared to maintain debtor or creditor positions *vis-à-vis* each other; the balances must therefore be settled before the end of the day. If there is no Clearing House, the process becomes binomial. In our examples, there are quite a lot of binomial positions, but that is because there are only four participants in the system. The probability is that during the course of any day there will be cheques drawn on Lloyds and deposited at the Midland Bank, and *vice versa*. But it is much less probable that the cheque on Lloyds deposited at Williams and Glyn's at Chichester will be exactly matched by a cheque drawn on Williams and Glyn's at Chichester and deposited at Lloyds. Only an overall clearing system, such as exists in a national banking system, makes it possible for a cheque drawn on the Midland Bank and deposited at the Williams and Glyn's to be matched against a cheque drawn on Williams and Glyn's and deposited at Lloyds. In the absence of such a clearing system,

Lloyds, the Midland, and Williams and Glyn's would each have to pay the amounts corresponding to the cheques in central bank money. The final result would of course be the same, and so would the final balance in central bank money but the banks' needs in central bank money would be so much greater.

Given that a bank can only pay what it really has available in its reserves and that it must never be overdrawn at the central bank, the transfer orders that would be needed to replace the clearing system would call for extremely high levels of reserves. If it could not use its reserves, a bank would have to wait to be credited before it could make a payment. For example, A, before it could pay 9 to B, would have to wait till it had received 9 from D, but D, before it could pay 9 to A, would have to wait till it had received 6 from B and 3 from C. B would in turn need the money owed it by A before it could pay D. . . .

It is nevertheless true that the acceleration and the centralisation of banking transactions and the replacement of cheques by payment orders or giro transfers would make clearing less necessary or, more exactly, would diminish its advantages. As the banks acquire new ways of making effective transfers of payment money the payments will be made in central bank money instead of through claims on the banks. The role of bank money as a payment instrument will diminish in favour of central bank money, the velocity of circulation of which will increase proportionately.

The preceding remarks underline two aspects of the creation and circulation of money. The first is the unreliability and the often illusory nature of attempts to regulate the money supply by means of reserve requirements. Apart from notes held by the public, the mass of central bank money held by the banks does not change; however, it may be distributed amongst the individual banks. What one lacks, another one has available, ready to be lent overnight or longer through a purchase of money-market instruments. These transactions are included in the payment orders cleared in the Clearing House along with the cheques.

The second is the role of the velocity of money transfer techniques. The latter, by increasing the velocity of money, undermine the theories of the monetarists concerning the supposed constancy of velocity which they use as a convenient excuse for taking the stock of money as sole monetary indicator and means of intervention.

'Leaks' occur in a national banking system every time the holder of a current account withdraws cash. The bank is obliged to pay out in notes, which constitutes a drawing on its reserves. In the Eurodollar system, the equivalent of a 'leak' is a payment order in favour of a bank in the US to an account held by a US resident, whether the resident is an individual or another bank.

The fact that monetary analysis generally ignores the clearing system is a constant cause of confusion between the balancing of mutual debits and credits by banks and the cancelling out of receipts and payments in the accounts of any economic agent. Let us take the example used on page 49 and expand it to include six banks: A, B, C, D, E and F.

> A owes £100 to B
> B owes £100 to C, etc.

At 9 o'clock, A pays B in central bank money. B had nothing in his till at 9 o'clock, but at 10, having received £100 from A, he is able to pay C. At 11 o'clock, C, who previously had an empty till, can now use his payment from B to pay D, etc. . . . . In the end, all the banks settle their obligations by means of a clearing of debits and credits in their own books. All economic agents are capable of doing this, and frequently do; this does not give them a power of monetary creation. All they are doing is increasing the velocity of money. A contented group treasurer is one who has nothing in his current account at the beginning of the day and nothing in the evening and who, in the meantime, has used his 'incomings' to settle his 'outgoings'. But this does not mean that he has created any money.

There are generally several different levels of clearing, distributed along territorial lines. Not all the banks in a given banking system are participants in the clearing system. The minor ones (correspondent banks) are affiliated to member banks to whom they delegate their debts and claims. A member bank will therefore clear the mutual debts existing between itself and its correspondents. Only transactions which the correspondent's banks have entered into with third parties are settled in the Clearing House along with the member bank's own transactions.

Enough has perhaps been said by now to show the vital importance of the clearing process in the creation of bank money. Those who wish to study this mechanism further cannot do better than play the game of 'Lotto-clearing', which is played as follows.

Ten players are seated round a table. They represent ten banks: $A, B, C, D, E, F, G, H, I$ and J. On a blackboard there is a clearing chart, which shows the sums owed to the banks in the horizontal rows and the sums owed by them in the vertical columns. In all, there are ten rows and ten columns. Further columns outside the table indicate the balances between what the banks owe and what is due to them.

Each player receives ten tickets, each of which represents the total of the cheques deposited with him and drawn on him or other banks. Thus, one ticket will represent (in the case of bank *A*) all *B*'s claims on him, another all of *C*'s claims etc. First of all, he adds up the total of the cheques deposited with him. In the case of bank *A*, let us suppose that the total of the ten tickets is 100, of which 8 have been drawn on *A* himself and deposited with *A*. The other banks *B*, *C*, *D*, *E* etc, therefore owe *A* $100 - 8 = 92$.

Next, each player distributes to each of the other players the tickets that represent the total of the cheques deposited with him and drawn on them. For example, *A* may have a ticket indicating a total of 15 drawn on *B* and deposited with *A*. This ticket for 15 is then handed by *A* to *B*. The total of the tickets deposited during this second stage represents what each player owes to the other players. On the clearing chart, the columns and rows are added up and checked to see that they balance. At the bottom of the chart, on the right, the overall movements are represented, including the total claims on the banks (liabilities) and the compensatory movements in central bank or primary money. The difference between these two totals is the amount of bank money which has been added to the central bank money to complete the transactions. The next stage of the game is designed to show how the presence of a participant who does not take part in the clearing process, or an absence of reciprocal claims, increases proportionately the total of central bank money which must be paid over or received by each participant.

The ten original players are joined by two new ones, *X* and *Y*. Each of the ten players cuts *one* of the tickets he received at the beginning of the game, representing a claim on another player, in two.

Example: *A* has a ticket representing 12 owed by *D* to *A*. He divides this ticket in two thus:

owed by *D* to *A*:7,
owed by *D* to *X*:5.

The ten new tickets, representing debts to *X*, are collected and handed to this eleventh player, *X*. The latter now has claims on the ten other players and no debts with regard to them. This is what happens when there is an absence of reciprocal claims or when cash is withdrawn from a bank. The totals are established as before. The overall movements do not change but the balances in central bank money increase.

Now *Y*, the twelfth player, enters the game. During the next round each player chooses once again one of the tickets he has received and cuts it in two.

Owed to → by ↓	A	B	C	D	E	F	G	H	I	J	X	Y	Totals owed by	Totals owed to	Balances −	Balances +
A												O				
B												O				
C												O				
D												O				
E												O				
F												O				
G												O				
H												O				
I												O				
J												O				
X	O	O	O	O	O	O	O	O	O	O						
Y																

Total payments ◄

Payments in central bank money ◄

This game shows how, thanks to the mechanism of the Clearing House, banks are able to superimpose claims on themselves with the payment function on the stock of money issued by the central bank (primary or central bank money). It further serves to show that it is only by looking for the *final* transfer of claims that the monetary analyst can discover which claim *really* effected the payment.

As the boxes on the table are filled in and the 'owing to's' and the 'owed by's' are added up and the balances worked out, the reader can see how the wide geographical dispersal of banks (as in the Eurodollar system) and the absence of mutual claims (as in the cases of banks X and Y) limit the role of the claims on the banks and increase proportionately the amount of payments that must be made in central bank money.

If counters are substituted for the negative clearing balances, which must be paid in central bank money, the extent to which the clearing process reduces banks' needs in reserves of central bank money can be clearly seen. The game also gives some idea of the effects of the various instruments of monetary regulation such as compulsory reserves, open-market dealings and refinancing costs.

Example: owed by *A* to *C*:8;
this becomes:

> owed by *A* to *C*:5,
> owed by *Y* to *C*:3.

The new totals are added up and communicated to *Y*: they represent
a debt on the part of *Y* towards the other players. He however has no
corresponding claim on them. Once again, the overall movements are the
same, but the transfers in central bank money have increased.

The next stage of the game is to show how a clearing operation replaces
the series of bilateral dealings which would be necessary if every
participant used his claims on third parties to settle his debts towards the
others. The clearing process, such as it was simulated at the beginning of
the game, produced positive and negative balances, which represented the
total of central bank payments. These totals are now distributed to the
players, whose balances are negative in the form of counters. For example,
if *A* has to pay over to the clearing house 10 in central bank money he
receives ten counters. Those players whose balances are positive receive
nothing because they they do not have to pay anything. The game is then
divided into a series of rounds. During round *N*, each player pays his
debts by using the counters which he has at hand, i.e. those he received
during the preceding round, *N* − 1, but without using those which he may
receive during round *N*. During round *N* + 1 he carries on paying his debts,
this time using the counters he received during round *N*, and so on till the
end of the game.

Once everyone's debts have been cleared, the total number of payments
is found to have been made with the same amount of central bank money
as during the clearing session. The difference is that the end result had to
be achieved by means of a large number of rounds, whereas the clearing
process only required the simple addition of two totals on the part of each
player.

In the final part of the game the players are separated and put in
different rooms; at the same time, the intervals between the rounds are
extended (this is what happens in the Euromarket). Consequently the time
necessary to clear the accounts becomes proportionately longer. Soon the
players find that they are obliged to ask for more counters and then
eventually they are forced to replace the cheques by payment orders
carried out entirely in central bank money without any clearing. There is
then no longer any bank money over and above the central bank money;
all the payments are made in central bank money.

The game shows how the clearing process makes it possible for the banking system to superimpose claims on the banks on the claims on the central bank, the total of the two being M1, the narrowly defined money supply. It illustrates the reserve constraints to which banks are subject and the use the monetary authorities make of these restraints to regulate the money supply. It also shows how and why Eurobanks do not add any additional claims to those represented by American payment dollars, which constitute for them their central bank money. Finally, the game also shows how the replacement of cheques by payment orders with a centralised system would speed up transfers of central bank money and would make it possible to reduce proportionately the creation of money by the banks, whilst the velocity of this same central bank money would also be accelerated.

NOTES

[1] The clearing balances have to be settled each day. This requirement is the consequence of a system which makes it possible for a member or corresponding bank to indebt itself to another bank for as much as it likes without any specific previous agreement on the part of the latter. This is effectively what happens when a cheque drawn by a client of bank A is deposited at bank B and this is the effect it has on the credit which this bank has granted to the drawer (by means of a credit to his current account) and consequently on the money which the bank has created.

This debt on the part of A towards B only lasts for a few hours. If the cheque is sent to be cleared at mid-day, the debt is settled that same evening. The debt of A towards B has become part of the clearing balance paid in central bank money.

[2] For the sake of simplicity, movements within the same bank have not been included, e.g. a cheque drawn by the customer of a bank and paid to someone else, who deposits it at the same bank. A more complete estimation of the total movements would be obtained by adding these internal movements to the external ones (63 in the case of Table 2).

[3] Banks' assets at the central bank are not counted by statistics in the active money in circulation (M1), which consequently only includes a fraction of central bank money — the most important fraction, namely that which is held by the public and by non-monetary financial intermediaries.

M1 includes, amongst other things, the money created by banks, i.e. all their deposits which have the transaction function (current account deposits). If central bank assets held by the banks were included in M1 they would distort the interpretation because of the double counting this would involve — the central bank money used for clearing and the fraction of the same money used for payments to the public would be counted as separate.

An analysis on a clearing chart shows the total transactions at the bottom of the table in the box outlined in heavy type and the total of the movements in central bank money are represented on the right in another box (transfer of balances in central bank money): 15. To include central bank money in M1 would be equivalent to adding together the two totals in the two boxes and would give an excessive overall transaction volume. The excess would be an amount equal to the total of central bank movements carried out at the end of the clearing session (in the table, 63 + 15, i.e. 78 instead of 63).

If one wishes to represent the situation more accurately, one is still obliged to take account of the total of central bank money, including, consequently, the assets of the banks at the central bank. This may also be the 'intermediate target' used in monetary regulation by, for example, the Bundesbank.

6 The third key – Reduction

The monetary mechanisms are revealed in all their variety if one looks at them in the light of 'reduction', which is an aspect, an illustration and even a measure of what economists call 'seigniorage'.

Reduction and its opposite, restoration, have the merit, from the point of view of monetary analysis, of being easily perceptible phenomena, which means that they are less subject than other factors to subjective and therefore controversial interpretations.[1] Starting from one basic fact which everyone can observe and upon which everyone should be in agreement, certain relationships between money, its quantity, its velocity, the uses to which it is put and other features of the economy, such as activity and prices, can be demonstrated. Furthermore, the role of the time factor and the *gradual* effect of an addition of a new unit of money to the total of money in circulation may be observed.

This basic fact is that when a new unit of money is introduced into circulation it gives the holder the right to consume a certain quantity of the total production of society without first having had to make an equivalent contribution in the form of goods and services. In other words, he has a claim on the wealth of society, and if he exercises it, the total wealth of society will be proportionately diminished or 'reduced'.[2] The various effects deriving from monetary creation, such as inflation, in the sense in which it is usually understood, i.e. as a diminution of the purchasing power of money, the contrast between loans made by a non-monetary intermediary and those made by a monetary intermediary, etc., can all be better understood if one looks at them from the point of view of this reduction, which is a kind of tax on the holders of money.

The idea of reduction is at the same time a consequence and a justification of the basic concept already discussed, namely that a unit of money is a claim on an institution, created arbitrarily, without any link to a commodity. Once it has been created, a new unit of money has a quite miraculous power – the power of procuring for the person who puts it into circulation for the first time a certain amount of goods or services which, unlike the unit of money, have not been created *ex nihilo* but which have been taken from the total wealth of society, and which are, in other words, 'unearned'.

A bank creates *ex nihilo* £2000 and lends them to a borrower. It enters in its books its claim on him as an asset and his claim on it as a liability. The borrower uses the money to buy a new car. A certain quantity of goods and services which have at some time been produced have thus been consumed. The borrower enjoys the fruit of the efforts of others without having contributed anything himself. Who was the real originator of the goods and services consumed? It is not the garage owner who sold the car, because with the sum which he receives he buys another; nor is it the motor car manufacturer, who pays the sum received from the garage owner into his bank account and draws on it to pay his employees and his suppliers; nor is it the employees or the suppliers, since they use the money they earn to buy the wherewithal to live and work. The real originators of the item of wealth consumed here in the purchase of a new car must be the active members of society as a whole: in the last analysis the claim is exercised on them. This fact is the basis of the following argument: nothing comes of nothing; if goods are consumed without having been earned, somewhere there must be someone who has provided the goods and who has suffered a reduction in his resources.

The creation of a new unit of money always has the result of momentarily reducing in this way the total available wealth of the holders of money; the destruction of a unit of money has the opposite effect and constitutes a restoration of a certain quantity of goods and services to the stock of freely available resources. This remains true whether or not there is any tangible counterpart to the new unit of money in the form of gold, a claim on someone else, a quantity of raw materials or a finished product. This can easily be proved by comparing what happens when a quantity of gold is bought or when a bill is discounted or when a bank overdraft is created: in each case there is the same equilibrium in terms of production and consumption, whether the unit of money used for the purpose was earned (i.e. through an addition to total production) or whether, on the contrary, it was created specifically for this purpose, *ex nihilo*, and added to the mass of M1 without any parallel addition to total production by the person who benefits from the creation of the new money.

The extreme case is that of the issue of paper money against a purchase of gold, the archetype in traditional monetary lore of a commodity-backed money, symbol of 'genuine' as opposed to 'false' claims. Let us compare the addition of goods and services and the consumption that results in the two following cases. In the first case, an economic agent buys a kilogram of gold and pays for it with money that he has earned, deducted, for example, from his salary. This money corresponds to a certain number of hours of work that he has done. In the second case, the same kilogram of gold is bought by the central bank, which pays for it by printing bank-notes. In this second case there is a creation of purchasing power over and above what there was in the first case, a supplementary purchasing power which has *not* been earned, expressed in the form of the new bank-notes which, once they have been put into circulation, cause an appropriate diminution of the total stock of available wealth for everyone except the first user.

The same thing happens, and the same conclusions are valid, in the case of any creation of money, e.g. in the case of a discounted bill. Suppose a craftsman sells an article he has made. The purchaser could pay him with pre-existing units of money which he had earned; alternatively, he could pay with a bill of exchange which is accepted and discounted by the craftsman. The latter receives units of money that have been created *ex nihilo*, and the corresponding unearned purchasing power is added to that which existed in the first example.

A bank grants a credit by overdraft. It enters a claim on the asset side of its balance sheet and a liability on the other side, in the form of a current account deposit which is added to M1. The bank's customer draws a cheque and this cheque is accepted in payment. The money used for the payment was created *ex nihilo*. If there is not at the same time, somewhere else, a corresponding destruction of a unit of money to balance the money created, there is a reduction in the total quantity of freely available wealth.

The customer of a commercial bank wishes to withdraw money from his savings account. The money in his savings account has no payment function. It is a claim on the bank that cannot be used directly in a trans-action, that is, it cannot be directly exchanged for goods and services. In order to mobilise the money in this account, the bank has to put into circulation a unit of money equipped with the payment function, which the depositer then uses in order to purchase something. This purchase constitutes a withdrawal from the total wealth of society which balances out the *contribution* the bank's customer made when he first made his savings deposit.

On the other hand, when money is destroyed there is a corresponding restoration of the wealth withdrawn by the first user of the new unit when it was first created. An economic agent repays a loan from a bank. His current account is debited and the bank's assets and liabilities diminish proportionately. The total of current account deposits in the bank falls, thus causing M1 to contract. In order to repay the loan, the person in question had to earn the requisite sum. There was an addition to total production without equivalent consumption by him. Consequently,

there was a *restoration* to total production — the opposite of what
happened when the bank granted the loan. The customer who pays his
supplier by accepting a bill of exchange pays the bill at maturity with
earned money. The sum paid over is withdrawn from both the assets and
the liabilities of the bank and also from M1. This restoration balances the
reduction resulting from the discount. The supplier and his customer
are then in the same position as if there had been a cash payment without
the issue and subsequent discount of a bill, but with the difference that
there has been an interval of thirty to sixty days during which the bill
has continued to circulate and a credit has been guaranteed by means
of new units of money created by the bank and provided thanks to the
process of reduction.

A customer makes a transfer from his current account to his deposit
acccount and M1 is reduced proportionately. A right to consume a certain
quantity of goods and services is abandoned by the holder; as such, this
abandonment constitutes an active contribution to the total wealth of the
community, as opposed to the corresponding reduction in the opposite
case, i.e. if a savings account is mobilised, leading to an entry in a current
account and then a payment. In the case of a deposit in a savings account
with a non-monetary intermediary, such as a savings bank, the unit of
money which the customer deposits is not destroyed, as it is in the case of
a deposit with a monetary intermediary; it is simply transferred by the
bank to a borrower, who makes use of the right to goods and services
which it represents in the place of the original depositor.

Supposing the Bank of England sells gold or foreign currency. Its stock
of bank-notes or central bank money is augmented. At the same time, M1
diminishes proportionately. This amounts to a restoration to the wealth
of the community. The purchaser of the gold or the currency has earned
the bank-notes which he pays over to the central bank. This means that he
has made his own contribution to total production, in exchange for which
he receives (or 'consumes') a certain quantity of gold or a certain quantity
of currency. As far as the purchaser of the gold is concerned, there is an
equilibrium between production and consumption. But the same is not
true of the Bank of England. The notes which it has received are
withdrawn from circulation, which means that a certain quantity of
money has been destroyed. Thus the central bank abandons the claim on
goods and services that it acquired when it accepted the notes and in so
doing it restores to the total wealth of the community the amount by
which that total was reduced at the moment the new notes were brought
into circulation.

We can sum up by saying that whenever a new unit of money equipped with the payment or transaction function is put into circulation, there is a reduction in available resources in favour of the person who first makes use of the right to goods and services represented by that unit of money. Conversely, there is an addition to, or restoration of, available resources when a unit of money is destroyed or when the right to goods and services represented by that unit of money is abandoned by its final holder. Overall, the net reduction in available resources is the balance remaining after the total of money that has been destroyed has been subtracted from the total that has been created. In other words it corresponds to the increase in the stock of M1 and probably amounts by now, in France, to something in excess of 1,000,000 millions in constant francs.

How does this reduction take place? How is it distributed? In order to find out we shall make use of a method well known in the physical sciences. Starting from a well-defined, stable, exchange situation, we shall cause a single, equally well-defined, disturbance (e.g. the addition of a quantity ΔM of new money) whilst at the same time 'freezing' a certain number of components of the model so as to work out the relationship between the disturbance and those components that have been left free to change. This disturbance modifies the system of exchanges through a series of partial changes and then gradually settles down, so that at the end of the period in question a new stable exchange system has arisen. A comparison between the initial stable state and the new stable state that results from the changes makes it possible to schematise the way in which the disturbance has spread and thus demonstrate the effects it has had on those components of the model that were left free. If the algebraic sum of the partial changes that have taken place between the initial and final states is equal to the difference between these initial and final states, we have proof or, at least, strong presumptive grounds for believing, that the way in which the gradual diffusion of the disturbance throughout the model has been demonstrated is correct. The great advantage of this kind of analysis is that it rests on two easily observable states: the initial state and the final state. The result should therefore be fairly conclusive.

This seems to me to be true of the following demonstration. It shows how money, as it circulates, causes the model to change from its initial to its final state, thanks to the numerous partial contributions by holders of money, until the sum of these contributions is equal to the value of total production consumed by the user of the new money. Each one of these partial reductions is carried out between the moment the money enters someone's pocket and the moment it leaves. This 'partial reduction'

Two groups of economic agents, A and B, exchange their production (P_A and P_B) and pay for it with a quantity of money, M, (total money supply = $2M$) during the course of a series of movements. The consumption of A (or B) is equal to what B (or A) has produced during the previous movement.

The diagram represents the monetary exchanges during the course of the movements 1, $n + 1$ and q. During movement 1 a sum of money in addition to M, $\Delta M (= \Delta_A M + \Delta_B M)$, is put into circulation and procures a quantity of goods $\Delta P (= \Delta P_A + \Delta P_B)$ for its holders, who are outside the AB exchange system.

The diagram shows how, from movement to movement, $\Delta_A M$ and $\Delta_B M$ gradually spread through the money supply (e.g. payment by A at the end of movement n using $\Delta_A - \mathrm{d}_n^A M$) and how the result is a gradual reduction of δ_1 up to δ_n on the holders of money by means of the variation in the purchasing power of money.

The reduction ceases at movement q, when prices stabilise, production and consumption having remained unchanged, so that $\Delta_A M$ and $\Delta_B M$ are now operating at the same exchange rate as the two initial quantities of money, M.

It can be seen that the sum of partial reductions carried out during each movement from 1 to q, which take the form of a diminution of the consumption of A and B compared with what they have produced, is equal to ΔM, that is to say, in terms of production, ΔP.

DIAGRAM SHOWING PARTIAL REDUCTIONS ON A AND B FROM MOVEMENT I TO MOVEMENT Q

A	Movement	B
$\delta_1 M \begin{cases} + M \\ -(M + \Delta_A M - d_1^A M) \end{cases}$	(1)	$\delta_1' M \begin{cases} + M \\ -(M + \Delta_B M - d_1^B M) \end{cases}$
$\delta_2 M \begin{cases} + M + \Delta_B M - d_1^B M \\ -(M + \Delta_A M - d_2^A M) \end{cases}$	(2)	$\delta_2' M \begin{cases} + M + \Delta_A M - d_1^A M \\ -(M + \Delta_B M - d_2^B M) \end{cases}$
$\delta_{n+1} M \begin{cases} + M + \Delta_B M - d_n^B M \\ -(M + \Delta_A M - d_{n+1}^A M) \end{cases}$	(n+1)	$\delta_{n+1}' M \begin{cases} + M + \Delta_A M - d_n^A M \\ -(M + \Delta_B M - d_{n+1}^B M) \end{cases}$
$\delta_{q-1} M \begin{cases} + M + \Delta_B M - d_{q-2}^B M \\ -(M + \Delta_A M - \varepsilon_A) \end{cases}$	(q-1)	$\delta_{q-1}' M \begin{cases} + M + \Delta_A M - d_{q-2}^A M \\ -(M + \Delta_B M - \varepsilon_B) \end{cases}$
$\delta_q M \begin{cases} + M + \Delta_B M - \varepsilon_B \\ -(M + \Delta_A M) \end{cases}$	(q)	$\delta_q' M \begin{cases} + M + \Delta_A M - \varepsilon_A \\ -(M + \Delta_B M) \end{cases}$

is the difference between what the holder of the money had to provide in the form of goods and services in order to earn the money, and what he receives in goods or services when he spends it.

Let us take a finite monetary area and a stable exchange system. Let $2M$ be the quantity of money. This mass $2M$ changes hands in a certain period of time which we shall suppose constant and which we shall call a 'movement'. Let us now follow the exchanges that take place in one movement. The economic agents can be divided into two groups, A and B, each of which has a quantity M of money. Group A produces and sells to B a total P_A and receives M in return. B, for its part, produces and sells P_B, also in return for M. Total production during one movement is $P (= P_A + P_B)$.

The diagram shows, for each movement, the total received from the sales of the previous movement, illustrated by the sign + ; the total spent on a purchase is represented by the sign −. During the course of movement 1, new money from outside is introduced into the monetary area AB. This new money is $\Delta_A M$ in group A and $\Delta_B M$ in group B.

$$\Delta_A M + \Delta_B M = \Delta M.$$

ΔM therefore gives the first holders of the money

$$\Delta P_A + \Delta P_B = \Delta P.$$

ΔM was created and ΔP was consumed outside the monetary area AB, without having been 'earned'.

The exchange system, which was $M = P_A$ and $M = P_B$ during the first movement, is modified by the introduction of ΔM (movement 1); A now has a bigger stock of money, $M + \Delta_A M$ in all, but finds that B has a smaller total of production, diminished by ΔP_B, i.e. $P_B - \Delta_B P$. B, for its part, only has $P_A - \Delta_A P$ to consume with the funds it has at its disposal, i.e. $M + \Delta_B M$. Prices therefore start to rise, each party keeping a part, $d_1^A M$ and $d_1^B M$, of $\Delta_A M$ and $\Delta_B M$, without spending it, because of insufficient supply.

During movement 1, the transfer of money is

from A to B: $M + \Delta_A M - d_1^A M$,
from B to A: $M + \Delta_B M - d_1^B M$.

The overall consumption of A and B, which was originally P, will diminish and will be only $P - \Delta P$ because ΔP has 'left' the monetary area AB, to the advantage of the first holders of ΔM (external to AB).

During the second movement, production returns to normal and is matched by a money stock of $M + \Delta M$. But equilibrium is not re-established immediately. The prices paid by each group for P_A and P_B only rise progressively, whereas ΔM is already making its way into the exchanges.

Let $\delta_{n+1} M$ for A and $\delta'_{n+1} M$ for B be the differences between what each party has received during one movement, n, for the production that he has sold and what he has to spend during the following movement, $n+1$, in order to buy what is on sale. $\delta_{n+1} M$ and $\delta'_{n+1} M$ are negative because at each movement A or B has to spend more to buy P_B and P_A than he received, or, which comes to the same thing, the agents A and B, who can only pay out what they receive, have a negative production differential and, consequently, consume a negative consumption differential $\delta_{n+1} P$, the monetary value of which is equal to $\delta_{n+1} M + \delta'_{n+1} M$.

In order to have a chance of paying for and thus buying what is offered, each group has to put up a bigger and bigger part, at each movement, of the sum it received (ΔM), when ΔP was sold outside the system. The diagram indicates by movement (running from 1 to q) the monetary exchanges (+for payments in, – for payments out). As the movements proceed, the point of equilibrium at which the production of each party, P_A and P_B, is exchanged respectively for $M + \Delta_A M$ and $M + \Delta_B M$, is reached after q movements.

At the penultimate movement, $(q-1)$, before the point of equilibrium is reached, the gap is only ϵ_A and ϵ_B. The differentials δ tend towards 0. The sum of the differentials is equal to $-\Delta M$. In fact the sum of $\delta_M + \delta'_M$ $= 2M - (M + \Delta_A M) - (M + \Delta_B M) = -\Delta M$. The production of A and B amounted to $q.P$, but their consumption was only $q.P - \Delta P$, lower by ΔP than it would have been if ΔM had not been introduced into circulation. This is the overall reduction in resources, the sum of the partial reductions δP corresponding to the fractions δM, the total of which is ΔM. The two stable states, the initial and the final, are easily observable (first, exchange of $2M$ for P, then exchange of $2M + \Delta M$ for a quantity of production which has supposedly remained unchanged, namely P). If we add up the simple variations at each stage of the disturbance, we reach the final stage. It is clear that the sum of the variations is equal to the difference between the initial and final stages. Thus we have the proof that ΔM, once it has been introduced, is gradually distributed in a series of tiny fractions as the exchanges proceed, and thus effects the reduction in available production which balances the production consumed by the first holder of ΔM (1).

The process of *restoration* is the opposite of *reduction*.[3] It follows on a withdrawal of money from circulation. In the monetary area which is under consideration, two groups of agents, A and B, exchange a mass of money $2M$. A produces P_A and sells it to B for M. B produces P_B and sells it to A for M. During each movement, as in our first example, each group consumes what it has bought from the other group. ΔM is then deducted from the money stock, $2M$. This operation is parallel with and opposite in direction to the one examined in the previous example; in other words, it is a case of restoration. The reason for the withdrawal of ΔM may be the wish to repay a bank loan. In order to get ΔM, the economic agent in question has produced ΔP which he has sold to A and B. In return, he has received a sum ΔM_A from A and ΔM_B from B.

$$\Delta M_A + \Delta M_B = \Delta M$$

This sum ΔM is paid into the bank in cash or by means of a direct debit of a current account. The operation, taken in isolation and independently of any other additions to the account or withdrawals from it, causes ΔM to be deducted from the total money stock $2M$. At the same time, the bank's customer has made his own contribution to production, which for the monetary area AB constitutes a net profit, as he has consumed nothing with the ΔM he received in return for his production ΔP and subsequently remitted to the bank to be destroyed. How is this profit or restoration, which balances out a previous reduction, distributed throughout AB? The purchasers of ΔP are not the beneficiaries, because they themselves had to earn ΔM in order to be able to purchase ΔP. Nor, for the same reason, was it the people to whom the purchasers of ΔP subsequently sold it. The real beneficiaries of the quantity of production represented by ΔP are all the participants in AB, i.e. the holders of money. The vehicle by which ΔP is shared out amongst them is the money they use in their transactions.

The mechanism that comes into play is the mechanism of exchange of money in return for production, an exchange which is gradually modified as the subtraction of ΔM spreads. The withdrawal of ΔM causes prices to fall gradually as the movements proceed. Finally, when the point of equilibrium has been reached, A sells P_A to B for $M - \Delta_A M$ and B sells P_B to A for $M - \Delta_B M$. Total production, which previously had fallen for lack of money, has gradually returned to the previous situation (P at each movement).

Meanwhile, each holder of money in groups A and B has received, in the course of the movements, a slightly greater quantity of production than he contributed himself, because of the progressive rise in the purchasing power of money. During the course of each movement, with the money which he has just received he purchases from the other group more than he would have purchased if the withdrawal of ΔM had not taken place. The amount thus consumed over and above what is supplied by each person is equal to ΔP_A for A and ΔP_B for B.

$$\Delta P_A + \Delta P_B = \Delta P$$

During movement 0, before the withdrawal of ΔM, A produces P_A, sells it for M and consumes P_B, which he also pays for with M. The production—consumption balance sheet can be set out as follows. (Production bought and consumed = +, sold = −.)

for A : $+P_B - P_A$,
for B : $+P_A - P_B$.

It can thus be seen that at the beginning, the overall balance sheet of the monetary area AB is equal to exactly 0, in other words consumption equals production. In fact, $(P_A - P_B) + (P_B - P_A) = 0$.

The succeeding movements show that, thanks to the withdrawal of ΔM, this will no longer be the case, and an excess of consumption over production equal to ΔP will emerge at the same time as a fall in production. At the beginning of the first movement, A has P_B, which he bought during the previous movement, whilst B has P_A. ΔM is then withdrawn from circulation by a person external to the area, who brings a contribution to group A of ΔP_A and a contribution to group B of ΔP_B, which has been produced outside AB. A only has a quantity of money equal to $M - \Delta M_A$, whilst B only has $M - \Delta M_B$.

Under the previous price system, A could only sell B a total of $P_A - \Delta P_A$, whilst B could only sell A an amount which had been similarly reduced. But production pressures, given that the total stock of money is reduced, cause prices to start to fall. In consequence, A sells rather more than $P_A - \Delta P_A$: in fact he sells $P_A - \Delta P_A + d_1 P_A$. B does the same. Prices continue to fall during the following movement. The quantity of money which each group holds has not changed; it is still equal to $M - \Delta_A M$ and $M - \Delta_B M$; but the total quantity of goods that each quantity of money can purchase increases because of the fall in prices.

By the last movement the point of equilibrium is reached:

A consumes P_B, paid for with $M - \Delta_A M$,
B consumes P_A, paid for with $M - \Delta_B M$.

At each movement, each group benefits from a production—consumption differential of δP_n because of the difference between what it actually buys and what it would have received for the same sum if prices had not fallen (this is an example of partial restoration). The grand total of the differentials, δP, for the two groups is $+\Delta P$. The addition of ΔP to the two groups after the destruction of ΔM has thus been gradually distributed to the holders of money as exchanges have taken place. This total ΔP represents the surplus of A and B's consumption over production.

The privilege of consuming without having to produce is the benefit that results from the withdrawal of ΔM. But it has a price; the surplus of consumption over production has been obtained thanks to a significant reduction in overall production which itself is far superior even to ΔP. At the same time the deleterious effects of a deflation of the money supply can be clearly perceived. Whereas the addition of ΔM did not cause production to fall but simply caused a reduction and redistribution of available wealth, the subtraction of ΔM caused a fall in production which went on from movement to movement, because of the delay with which prices adapt to a new exchange system. There was certainly an excess of consumption over production, but at the same time there was an overall fall in production during the movements, so that total consumption, though it remained higher than production, nevertheless suffered a contraction. This is exactly what happened during the deflationary spiral of the thirties. It is also what happens when, after an inflationary upsurge, the authorities try to bring prices under control by severely restricting the growth of the money supply. (1) The destruction of ΔM (e.g. repayment of a loan) has the opposite effect to an addition of money. A form of restoration takes place and there is a corresponding rise in the purchasing power of money. The only thing that needs to be taken into consideration is the balance, or difference between additions and subtractions, represented by the variations in M1 as recorded by the monetary statistics.

The way in which, as we have seen, the reduction is distributed and gradually diffused throughout the system makes it possible to see certain traditional concepts such as, for example, the equivalence of the velocity of money and its total volume, in a new light. At the same time, we may recognise others that are less well known, such as the role of the time taken by new money to spread through the economy. A change in the rate of production or in the velocity of circulation has an effect on prices. An increase in the total quantity of money (ΔM) may be compensated for by an increase in production (ΔP) which may even completely mask the reduction suffered by the holders of money when it changes hands. So there may be an addition of ΔM, and a simultaneous increase, instead of a reduction, in purchasing power under the influence of factors acting against ΔM, such as a fall in the velocity of money, a rise in production, etc. But there is still a reduction in total resources in the sense that, if there hadn't been an addition of ΔM, the holders of money would have received more in goods and services at the moment they spent the money than they had previously acquired. The reduction in resources due to ΔM may be more than adequately compensated for, but it still exists in the form of a possible missed opportunity for profit by the holder is of money.

If prices rise by 1 per cent, 0.5 per cent may be caused by an increase in the velocity of money, 0.3 per cent may be caused by expectations of further inflation, psychological factors that act independently of any purely mechanical factors. Alternatively, -0.5 per cent may be due to an increase in production and 0.7 per cent due to a phenomenon of purely sectoral importance, such as a localised rise in one particular price, e.g. the oil price, which brings with it other increased costs, such as salary rises. These factors are either independent of each other or may act upon each other in varying ways, or may take each other's place. Official statistics only record the final prices, which are the result of all these factors. Rises and falls due to ΔM are hidden amongst these various factors, scarcely perceptible and certainly refractory to any statistical presentation. They all have similar effects, which add to or subtract from the overall result, but it is only the balance which appears at the end, the result of innumerable, hidden transactions which are impossible to identify individually but which are still very much there.

It would be surprising if the preceding description of the processes of resource reduction or restoration, which are necessary in order to balance an addition (or destruction) of money, was not accused of quantitativism. It is well known to what extent opinions are already hardened on this topic, the battle lines laid out and the clashes inevitable. But in this instance, I believe that to talk of quantitativism, as it is usually defined, is not justified. Whether or not one accepts the quantity theory of money, it seems to me that there are certain facts one cannot deny, such as that the first recipient of a new unit of money consumes a certain quantity of goods and services without having earned them; in other words, that he has the benefit of hours of work that have been accumulated by others. Somebody must have contributed to the common stock the goods and services that are thus consumed; these people, and the vehicle by which the contributions have been made, must be found.

The vehicle cannot be anything but money, and the anti-quantitativists must be prepared to admit as much. But they can also point out that the

variation in purchasing power by means of which the reduction on the
holders of money is effected is entangled with a number of other
variations which result from quite other factors than resource reduction.
It is a rule of scientific analysis that the final size of a variation is the sum
of the partial variations caused by each factor as it intervenes separately.
The mistake of the ultra-quantitativists is to ignore these other factors
and to concentrate on only one of them, namely the growth of the money
supply. The fact that this final factor may be different in nature from one
of the intervening components (the one that corresponds to the reduction)
by no means contradicts the role of this component; it simply means that
the other factors may be dominant.

The analysis given above of the phenomenon of reduction does not
take sides over how money, employment and prices are related, nor does
it even imply a specific choice in this distressing nexus. In fact one could
just as easily turn the whole mechanism round and make it operate in
reverse by precipitating the disturbance of the exchange system not
through an increase in the money supply but by varying the rate of
production, the velocity of money and the price level. The way in
which the disturbance is diffused through the model from the initial
stage to the final one would remain exactly as it was described, which
would provide convincing evidence of the neutrality of the mechanism.

The relationships between different economic factors, such as
production, the velocity of money and prices, and the reversibility of
causality appear when one introduces a disturbance other than ΔM into
the model, such as a price rise. Under the pressure of an exogenous factor
other than ΔM prices start to rise. The rise is not instantaneous. It is
gradually transmitted throughout the economy as trade develops. If A is
to buy the goods on offer, an addition of δM of new money must be
introduced into circulation during each movement. The sum of the factors
δM is equal to ΔM. The reduction in real resources corresponding to ΔM
is ΔP. If there was not a constant flow of new money to oil the process
of exchange, trade could only continue on condition that the velocity of
money increased. In the absence of this, production would be strangled. A
would be unable to purchase P_B and B would be unable to purchase P_A.
In fact, the velocity of money is rarely affected by a rise in costs. A price
rise deriving from exogenous causes and not accompanied by an increase
in the money supply thus brings about a slowing-down of production.

The reduction of resources resulting from a variation in purchasing
power affects not only holders of money but also economic agents with
mutual liabilities in nominal terms, namely lenders, borrowers and in
general all those who enter into fixed-rate contracts involving money

which has *not* been created *ex nihilo* but is in fact pre-existent, since the institutions involved are non-monetary intermediaries. What about the purchase of an issue of bonds, for example? If the bonds are not indexed, the bond subscriber, who is thereby a lender, is affected, just like all holders of money, by the fall in purchasing power which provides the reduction in resources. One may wonder whether the lender should not be included among the contributors to the reduction, the total of which balances out the ΔP consumed by the first user of ΔM. But this is in fact not the case because the beneficiary of the resource reduction is the borrower and not the first user of the new money. The contribution to the reduction by the lender is somehow 'intercepted' by the borrower, and has no part in the supply of goods and services balancing out those that are consumed by the first user of ΔM.

In cases where the monetary system is backed by a standard with constant purchasing power, into which the circulating units of money are freely convertible – this was more or less the case under the gold standard – there is, by definition, no fall in purchasing power of the monetary unit. The mechanism by which it effects a reduction of the net resources of the community, as we have described it in the preceding pages, no longer works. But this does no mean that there is no reason to find out how and by whom the goods and services consumed by the first user of the money are in fact provided. The issue of a new unit of money equipped with the special property of being directly exchangeable for goods or services – which we have called the 'payment function' – always results, as we have seen in the preceding chapters, in a drawing on or a reduction of the resources of the other holders of money, whatever the monetary system may be. The gold standard system is no exception to this rule. The reduction takes place, whether the new unit of money is backed by gold or not, whether it constitutes an advance to the state, whether it results from a discount or whatever the reason for its creation. It affects all the holders of money, whether their holdings are in paper or gold coins. The question is : how?

In such conditions, one of two things must happen: either the rate of production remains the same, or it changes (prices remaining *ex hypothesi* the same in both cases). If it does not change, the holders of money are prepared to hold money longer and wait before spending it. But if the rate of production increases enough, it becomes possible for the economic agent to receive, over the same period, a proportionately greater quantity of goods and services.

If we go back to the model described above and draw up a table of movements, we can see more clearly how the reduction is distributed in the special conditions of a system of immutable prices and production rates. A and B sell each other $P_A + P_B$ and pay for them with M. During movement one ΔM is introduced. ΔP is then consumed by the providers of ΔM, outside the space AB. A and B then hold $2M + \Delta M$. Prices and production rates remain, *ex hypothesi*, unchanged, and A and B both continue to spend only M in order to purchase each other's production. ΔM is then in some sense surplus, the average velocity of money having diminished proportionately. The series of exchanges from movement to movement simply causes ΔM to be divided amongst the economic agents $A + B$.

If we add up the exchanges from the first movement to the last we can see that A and B have consumed less than they produced. In value, this differential was ΔM and in production it was ΔP. This is the reduction. In practice it is probable that the pressure of ΔM will have an effect that will take the form of an increase in production and thus a rise in prices. If, as a result of convertibility into gold, prices remain at the same level, the final result of the introduction of ΔM will be a rise in production. Here we can see, incidentally, one of the great merits of the gold standard, and at the same time its vulnerability and the special conditions required for it to work properly. All that is needed for the mechanism to go wrong is for P not to follow an excessive increase in the money supply or for the quantity of gold not to rise fast enough.

The analysis demonstrates the time necessary for the monetary effects of an addition or a subtraction of ΔM to make themselves felt, now that 'pegging' to a fixed standard has been abolished. The point of equilibrium (a situation of stable purchasing power) is only reached after a certain number of movements of M. The factors involved include not only the time necessary to effect the exchanges but also the number of participants (holders of money). It is certain that a long time goes by before the point of equilibrium is reached. In such circumstances, it is easy to see that it is a waste of time to expect rapid results from an injection of new money, illusory to trust to purely quantitative calculations, and imprudent to put one's faith in weekly variations in M1, as many experts in the USA do. Precisely because of the diffusion time, the total effect at any one moment of a quantity of money is the sum of innumerable partial effects, the origins of which may go back months and even years.

Our analysis of resource reduction shows that the effect produced by an addition to the money supply of new means of payment, whatever their origin, is always identical. This is in contradiction with the fundamental principles which have dominated economic thinking for more than a century and which have governed techniques of financial and monetary management. An example is the discounting of bills of exchange with maturities of thirty, sixty and ninety days. The corresponding monetary creation is not considered to have any monetary effect since the new money is 'based on an already existing asset', namely the merchandise which gave rise to the discountable piece of paper. A five or seven year loan, on the other hand, has traditionally been considered inflationary because it is not based on anything that actually exists and its repayment is planned for a very remote time in the future. In fact it was only after the war and against the advice of financial orthodoxy that medium-term loans were introduced by the banks.

In actual fact, what counts is the overall increase in means of payment. The reduction in available resources that results is identical, whatever the origin of the addition made to the money supply, whether it is a ninety-day bill or a five-year loan. This very fact leads us on to pose the question of the use that is made of the resource reduction. Even if it is hidden, even if it is compensated for by an increase in production, there is a contribution by the holders of money, which implies a particularly judicious choice in the attribution of new money and also poses the problem, which we shall look at in Chapter 9, of selective distribution of monetary creation, whether the source of this creation is the central bank or the banking system.

NOTES

[1] In a chapter of his book (op. cit.), Maurice Allais writes:

Corresponding to the increase of the money supply there is a creation of purchasing power *ex nihilo*, for which no services were rendered, so false claims are created. . . The sums in question are very large. . . The false claims are added to the genuine claims, which take their effect outside the creation of these false claims and can only be used by causing a rise in prices, which works in favour of the holder of false claims and at the expense of the holders of genuine claims.

It should be noted here that Maurice Allais takes up the term 'false claims', the paternity of which may be attributed to Jacques Rueff, though Maurice Allais gives it a different meaning.

[2] The concept of reduction brings out the secret, unnoticed character— unnoticed, that is, by those on whom it is exercised—of the phenomenon of seigniorage, or that reduction of available goods and services resulting from the creation of a new unit of money.

Robert Mundell in the United States, and Alexander Swoboda in Europe, have both looked at the question of seigniorage, from the point of view of the profit margin of the 'seigneur', namely the difference between the interest he receives from borrowers and the interest he pays to depositers of money he has created.

Here the notion is looked at from the point of view of the use by the first holder of a new unit of money of a title to goods and services *which has not been earned*. The merit of this approach is that it defines more precisely the role of the units of M1, which have an active role because of their payment function, as opposed to the inactive role of that money which can be considered to have been destroyed (near-money, savings deposits).

Active units of money set off a reduction in available resources as soon as they are created; when they are destroyed they cause a corresponding increase in available resources. The notion of reduction of resources, and its corollary of an increase in resources, reinforces the difference and even the opposition between the nature of those units of money which have the payment function and those that do not have it or no longer have it.

[3] There is surely hardly any need to point out that the model which has just been described is deliberately and arbitrarily simplified. It nonetheless makes it possible to show — and indeed demonstrate — the effect of an addition of a new unit of money in a stable system of prices, production and exchanges. Starting with this theoretical model, one can, by modifying or completing certain parts of it, get a bit closer to reality. On page 73 some further examples are given.

See also the supplementary note on anti-inflation policy on page 110.

7 Use of the three keys, first example–Banks and Non-banks

There are fashions in monetary economics, just as there are in most of the social sciences and even in the exact sciences.[1] Sometimes these fashions are useful; sometimes they are pernicious, especially if they only serve to render concepts which are already vague and more or less refractory to any rational interpretation even more vague and confused. Such, it seems to me, is the case of one of the latest fashions, which claims that there is no difference between monetary and non-monetary financial intermediaries and which attributes to all institutions that take in savings from the public and make loans the power of creation of payment instruments.[2] (1) The development of savings accounts and passbook deposits in the banks, the provision to industry and to other sectors of the economy of long-term loans, the role of 'transformation' — 'borrowing short' and 'lending-long' — carried out by the banking system—all these factors help to explain this trend of modern thinking, especially in the absence of clear and properly based ideas on the way the monetary mechanisms work. The planned introduction of cheque-books and giro transfer orders in savings banks, which has recently been the subject of much discussion, only adds to the confusion.

that a claim on itself issued by a bank is accepted as a means of payment outside the banking system, is freely transferable, and has a *de facto* legal-tender force. Thanks to the mechanism of the clearing house, the banks can keep in circulation a mass of claims on themselves in bank money which is greater than their total liquid claims on the central bank. The mechanism that comes into play in the case of a non-monetary intermediary is quite different. Such an intermediary can multiply *credit* but cannot, unlike the monetary intermediary, increase the quantity of payment money, or M1. Let us look at some examples.

Paul has a thousand pounds which he deposits in savings bank A. This institution then proceeds to lend the thousand pounds it has just received to Peter, who uses the money to settle a debt with John. John decides to deposit the money in a savings account in the same bank, or at another bank, *B*. The whole operation starts all over again: the notes are lent to Robert and then go through another savings bank, *C*. The total of M1 has not changed but the volume of credit has increased by three thousand pounds. If Peter decides to withdraw his money or gives a transfer order in order to make a payment, savings bank *A* does not give him the money or effect a payment by means of a claim on itself. It hands over bank-notes or draws a cheque on a bank where it has an account, i.e. it pays by means of a claim on another institution than itself, whether bank of issue or commercial bank. In order to do this, it uses funds from another deposit or draws upon its reserves, or simply refinances itself by borrowing.

A bank receives a deposit, in bank-notes, of a thousand pounds. It credits the current account of the depositor and transfers the money to its account at the Bank of England. The thousand pounds in notes are replaced in circulation by a thousand pounds in bank money, credited to the depositor's account. The bank then proceeds to create, on the basis of the deposit it has at the central bank (£1000), two thousand pounds of credit, by simultaneously entering two thousand pounds on the liability side of its balance sheet as the borrower's claim on it and on its asset side as a claim on the borrower. Thus one thousand pounds in central bank money have been withdrawn from circulation, and therefore subtracted from M1, whilst three thousand pounds in bank money have been added. The initial deposit of one thousand pounds has, as it were, 'melted' into the bank's overall liquidity in terms of central bank money without having really been re-lent.[3] (1) The operations appear as follows in the bank's balance sheet:

Assets	*Liabilities*
£1000 (reserves)	£1000 (initial deposit)
£2000 (claim)	£2000 (borrower's current account)

M1 = £3000

In the case of a non-monetary intermediary, such as a savings bank, the initial deposit of £1000, allowing for a reserve of £100, can only be used for a loan of £900.

Assets	*Liabilities*
£100 (reserves)	£1000 (deposit)
£900 (claim on borrower)	

*M*1 = £1000

The units transferred through the loan or put into the bank's reserves in the case of a deposit, remain part of M1, whereas the depositor's claim of one thousand pounds, which has no payment function, ceases to be part of M1.

The essence of monetary creation is not credit. The formula 'loans make deposits'[4] is true but misleading, since it fails to distinguish between a credit or a loan granted by a *non-monetary* intermediary, such as a savings bank, and a loan made by a *monetary* intermediary, such as a commercial bank. Both produce deposits, but the savings bank does not create new money because the receipt which it hands over to its depositor in the form of an entry in his passbook account does not have the payment function, whereas the commercial bank receipt, in the form of a cheque, does. The final payment that results from the use of this claim to settle a debt is effected partly in claims on the bank and partly in central bank money as regards the balance remaining at the end of the clearing process. The savings bank, on the other hand, simply transfers to the borrower a pre-existing right to goods and services which has been temporarily abandoned by the depositor; it does not add to this any claims on itself.

In fact, the credit is only, as it were, the wind or the insect that transports the pollen to the flower: in this instance the bank counter. Conception only takes place behind this counter once the pollen has penetrated it, and only if circumstances are favourable, i.e. if the bank counter has the payment function. In this case, the result is the birth of a new unit of money which duplicates the unit that has been deposited, is added to it or replaces it. Any deposit made at a bank increases its liquidity: in the previous example this was in the form of £1000 in notes. When this same deposit is made by means of a cheque, the liquidity is communicated to the bank through the clearing in the form of a credit to its account at the central bank. The deposit is added to the bank's reserves in order to cover any requests for withdrawals or debits to accounts. The more stable this deposit is — i.e. the less likely it is to be withdrawn — the more suitable it is as a base upon which to create bank money.[5]

If we refer back to the clearing mechanisms discussed in Chapter 5, we can solve the problems raised by the gradual blurring of the distinctions between savings accounts, whether time deposits or not, and current accounts, and the use of cheques and payment orders by depositors at savings banks. Discussion of these matters has hitherto concentrated more than anything else on commercial considerations, each party concerned attempting to cling to its privileges and at the same time encroach on those of its competitors. In fact, the whole debate should be carried on on a higher plane. The really important thing is surely to calculate the repercussions that the measures envisaged would have on monetary creation and, more precisely, on the creation by the banks of payment instruments having the payment function.

As far as a bank, or monetary intermediary, is concerned, the parallel between the demand deposits and savings deposits which it receives is as follows. In order to be used, the savings deposit must first of all be mobilised, that is, it must give rise to the creation of a sight deposit or bank-notes; or, on the other hand, it may be directly transferred to effect a payment. In the first case, the savings deposit does not have any payment function; in the second, it has. In the case of a savings bank which issues cheque-books to its customers and accepts payment orders from them, the problem of monetary creation can only be solved by following the process of clearing at its different levels. Let us take first of all the case of clearing within the same institution. John pays his supplier, Peter, with a payment order which he sends to his savings bank. If Peter has an account at the same savings bank he is credited, and the payment order has effected the payment. If we take things a stage further, to the level of clearing on a local basis involving several savings banks, the clearing process would make it possible for the banks to settle their obligations with claims on themselves and therefore to operate, to a limited extent, as monetary intermediaries. At the highest level, finally, the savings banks might participate fully in the bankers' clearing house. In this case, there would no longer be any difference between a savings bank and a commercial bank: both would have the same power to create money in the form of claims on themselves.

These distinctions make it possible to answer a crucial question: will the introduction of the cheque and the payment order enable the savings bank to create money? In themselves, these things do not necessarily imply the ability to create bank money as long as the bank, when it pays the cheque, is only transferring assets it has at the central bank, or at another bank. In this case, there is no claim on the bank and therefore no creation of new money. Even if a process of clearing did take place, certain restrictions, such as the limiting of deposits to physical persons, loan ceilings etc., would considerably reduce its effects.

The thirty-second annual report of the *Conseil National du Crédit* (1977) says:

The permission to open current accounts and to distribute cheque-books which has been granted to savings banks marks an important milestone in the history of these establishments. . . During recent years, in fact, they have made great efforts to diversify their activities. . . So as to complete this development, whilst at the same time retaining the traditional character of savings instrument for the savings bank passbook, the *décret* of 12 January 1978, complemented by the *arrêté* of 23 January, prescribed that depositors may henceforth enjoy full current account services independently of their passbook . . . on condition that their accounts are never overdrawn.

No mention is made here of clearing. Strictly speaking, there is no reason why savings banks should be confined to lending — which is, after all, what they are in business for — to customers other than their depositors. It is not by rigorously prohibiting overdraft facilities that the risk of *ex nihilo* monetary creation, of which, incidentally, there is no mention in the annual report of the *Conseil National du Crédit*, will be eliminated. Let us suppose that a customer of the savings bank has a current account in credit and uses his cheque-book to pay a shopkeeper. If the cheque thus drawn on the savings bank enters into the clearing, there will be an *ex nihilo* creation of payment instruments. If it does not, the bank will have to transfer to the payee the whole of the amount represented by the cheque. In that case, there will be no creation of new money. It makes no difference whether the customer's account is in credit or overdrawn.

This example shows that if one wishes to work out the effects of a particular measure it is advisable to analyse the mechanisms in questions using our three monetary keys.

NOTES

[1] Traditional economic theory is extremely fond of the 'multiplier'. It makes use of it for a variety of purposes, some of which are contradictory. On page 111 a supplementary note will be found which quotes Professor Henri Guitton on the multiplier, and provides some further reflections on the contradictions to which this overworked concept can give rise.

[2] See page 113 for the opinion of André Delattre on this important question.

[3] 'A banker does not lend monetary assets deposited with him by individuals. He has the power to create all the money that he needs for credit operations. . . He offers, in a word, new money'. André Chaineau, *Mécanisme de la Politique monétaire* (PUF).

[4] The author of this expression, Hartley Withers, emphasised with some reason that he was talking about *bank* credit. By quoting the expression out of context, people have, if not perverted its sense, at least deprived it of any real significance.

[5] The analysis of the mechanism of monetary creation by the banking system which is still to be found in textbooks has scarcely changed for 250 years. See page 114 for another note on this, and a quotation from Richard Cantillon.

8 Use of the three keys, second example – Eurodollars and Eurodollar banks

It is a commonly held opinion, especially in France,[1] that when a bank operates in the Euromarket in currencies other than its own national money, it retains the same power of creation of new money as it has in its own national banking system. This is one of those mistaken beliefs that illustrate very well the uncertainty of present-day knowledge with regard to monetary mechanisms.

In order to keep the discussion within clearly defined limits, let us compare the two writers who have set out most clearly the two opposed theses. Firstly, we shall take Mr. Michel Lelart, who maintains, in a paper published under the auspices of the Centre National de Recherche Scientifique (the principal French scientific research body), the following:

> That the Eurobanks are monetary institutions capable of creating money and that they can and do create dollars outside the USA is no longer a matter of any controversy . . . The question of whether or not a Eurobank creates Eurodollars does no seem to me to justify the interminable controversy to which it has given rise. . . .[2]

Miss J. S. Little, says, for her part, in a book published under the auspices of the Federal Reserve Bank of Boston, that Eurodollar deposits in themselves are almost completely sterile and the Eurobanks, like all non-bank financial institutions, only have a very limited capacity to increase the total amount of credit: 'The Eurobanks are largely non-bank financial intermediaries which by themselves can do little more than raise the supply of dollar loans to final borrowers by a small amount'.[3]

This is also the opinion of the well-known monetary expert, Professor G. Haberler, who maintains that it is misleading to speak of a special money-creating function of the Eurodollar market.[4]

Far from considering, like Michel Lelart, that the debate is over, we ought to consider that it is in fact only just starting; and far from regretting this fact, we should be glad. The analysis of the Eurodollar system and the controversy it provokes is fruitful for two special reasons. Firstly, because of the importance of the Eurodollar market in terms of size: international financial flows are indispensable for the prosperity of the world, and there is no prospect of their being properly organised until people know with some measure of certainty how they work. The second, and more important, reason is that nowadays monetary regulation—the control of the quantity of money—governs economic life in all countries. But the very idea of regulation presupposes that these mechanisms should be properly understood and properly interpreted and that the interpretations should be based on a certain degree of consensus. In fact, however, this is not the case, which justifies devoting a certain amount of reflection to this matter. Let us look first of all at the conclusions Michel Lelart arrives at regarding the Eurobanks' power of creation of dollars.[5]

> In the Eurodollar system, as in any monetary system, the multiplier effect may be defined and measured starting with the distinction between:
> The central institution that creates and issues the primary or high-powered money that acts as the basis of the system. In the Eurodollar system the American economy acts as central bank. Its external obligations constitute the monetary base.
> The secondary institutions which multiply central bank money by creating their own money. This category consists of the Eurobanks which, starting with the dollars they hold, credit the current accounts of their clients in dollars.[5]

Nothing could be clearer or more precise than this statement, and Michel Lelart goes on to say:

> In the United States, the base money is the money created by the central bank. The Eurodollar system has no such institution. . . Once the central bank in question is no longer a bank whose liabilities consist only of bank-notes and deposits but an entire national economy, which includes other economic agents, whose liabilities may be Treasury Bills, shares and bonds, it is quite normal that liabilities of this sort should be a part of the central bank or base money. Eurodollars cannot be separated from US dollars. They cannot be excluded from the multiplier, which explains the growth of Eurodollars in terms of the growth of US dollars. The money stock we must bear in mind is not

just the total supply of Eurodollars; it is the supply of all dollars, whether created in the United States or in Europe. . . This is what we shall call the international supply of dollars.[6]

Here we have a statement that certainly ought to be taken seriously. If it is true, steps must be taken immediately, because the whole American monetary system, and with it all the monetary systems in the world, runs the risk of being swallowed up in a vast flood of dollars. If Michel Lelart is right, the mechanism by which the American monetary authorities attempt to control the money supply is nothing but a sham, and one can reasonably compare the American economy to a lorry racing down a hill with its driver completely oblivious of the fact. Sitting at the wheel, he looks at the instruments on the dashboard, which indicate the monetary aggregates, M1 (notes and current account deposits), M2, M3 etc., which no longer have any meaning, and he applies a brake which is no longer connected to the brake drums, since the Eurobanks' power of monetary creation is out of the authorities' control. What an amazing sight: the chairman of the governors of the Federal Reserve Banks, traditional epitome of financial orthodoxy, at the wheel of the American economy, happy and trusting in the instruments and statistics, whilst all the while his vehicle is plunging to its doom!

The chairman of the Fed. is not the only one who ought to be alarmed by Michel Lelart's conclusions: monetary authorities in all countries ought to be worried, not only because of the consequences for them that are bound to flow from disturbances in the USA, but also because of the deficiencies in their own systems of regulation which Michel Lelart points out to them.

Nowadays, in fact, whether one approves or disapproves, all countries try to 'regulate' the growth of their money supply, check the development of the monetary aggregates, establish objectives and impose, not without a certain amount of difficulty, new disciplines in place of those which used to follow automatically from the gold standard. Monetary regulation works through the base of primary money issued by the central bank, on which, as Michel Lelart reminds us, the banking system erects its own pyramid of money. It is by controlling the base and the multiplier that the monetary authorities attempt to control the creation of new money. If, as Michel Lelart argues, the Eurobanks can create as much money as they wish, independently of the monetary authorities and on the strength of a base which is itself multiplied independently of the authorities, then the techniques of regulation no longer have any meaning and the monetary systems are completely out of control.

Happily, this process of multiplication of dollars does not really take place in the way Michel Lelart claims. Why? Because, as Miss Little tells us, 'Eurobanks generally play the role of non-bank financial intermediaries and do not create money, in sharp contrast to the commercial banks that manufacture money by permitting both depositors and borrowers to have the use of checking accounts at the same time.'[7] Eurobanks act as pure intermediaries and simply transfer to borrowers funds which investors have decided not to make use of. A bank has the power to multiply and create new money in the case of its own national money but in the case of a foreign currency, in which it operates as a Eurobank, it has no such power of creation: it is a *non-bank*. This is the key word; this is the main cause of differences of opinion concerning the power of monetary creation of Eurobanks.

The second cause of error is to consider that all the deposits in a bank are 'money', in the sense of *payment* money. 'The statistics published by the BIS', says Michel Lelart 'help us to calculate accurately enough the total quantity of Eurodollars. We shall of course only count those liabilities of the Eurobanks which are incontestably money'.[8] But the deposits in a bank need not necessarily be money, even if they are classified as 'near-money' and even if they are included in the money stock by official statisticians. As we have seen, the confusion over what is money and what is not is so great that we ought to take advantage of the opportunity which Michel Lelart has given us of attempting to clarify the matter, and it is Michel Lelart himself who will help us, in his excellent book *Le dollar, monnaie internationale*[9] by directing our attention to the very fundamentals of the question, namely the theory and nature of money.

A deposit in a Eurobank, even if it is a demand or current account deposit, is not money, any more than a deposit in a savings bank is money, because it is not used directly in payment for goods and services. It must either be mobilised beforehand or give rise to a transfer of a claim on a third party, i.e. on an institution other than the bank itself. It is this claim on another bank which has the payment function (in the case of the Eurobank it is the dollar asset which the Eurobank has in a bank in the United States). A Eurobank is certainly a bank, but it does not have the same power of monetary creation when it operates as a Eurobank as when it operates as a member of its own national banking system. As Miss Little puts it:

Most Eurobanks are commerical banks and behave accordingly when they deal in domestic currencies. For this reason, some analysts have asked how anyone can argue that a group of banks which is granted money-creating abilities in the domestic market mysteriously loses these abilities when functioning in the foreign currency market. Nevertheless, banks operating in the Eurodollar system do have two hats, and they switch to the non-bank financial intermediary topper when dealing in Eurodollars.[10]

But why, then, do banks lose the power to create money when they become Eurobanks? For the simple reason that there is very little clearing of debts in the Eurodollar system, unlike the national banking systems, where reciprocity of transactions permits a great deal of clearing. It is this mechanism, as we have seen, which makes it possible for a bank operating in a national banking system to create new money. When a Eurobank domiciled in London, for example, receives a payment order in dollars from a customer, it does not carry it out by means of a claim on itself, as it would do in the case of its own national currency. Instead, it effectively transfers dollars by giving, in its turn, a transfer order for the appropriate sum to an American bank where it has an account. Here we have the proof that a Eurobank operates in a currency that is not its national currency as a non-monetary intermediary. This is the case because the wide dispersal of Eurobanks throughout the world and the consequent rarity of mutual claims amongst them precludes the use of a clearing house. It is, therefore, not surprising that the total of mutually cleared claims in the Euromarkets is estimated by the BIS at only 10 per cent of the total money flows involved.

Let us take the analysis further and consider what would happen if all the Eurobanks had their accounts in the same bank in New York. This fact would not modify in any way the mechanism described above and the consequences would still be the same. In other words, the Eurobanks would continue to function as non-monetary intermediaries. Let us suppose that an Arab oil producer has received $100m. from a customer in the United States, and has a credit to his account for this amount at Chase Manhattan in New York. He deposits this sum at Lloyds bank in London. Lloyds lends the money to an importer in Hamburg, who in turn pays his Brazilian supplier. The latter deposits the money at a bank in Rio. The bank in Rio lends the money to the Central Bank of Zaïre, which uses it to pay its French supplier, Renault. Renault deposits the dollars it receives at the BNP. For the sake of simplicity, we shall suppose that each one of the various banks involved has an account at Chase Mahattan in New York. The various movements in the Chase's books will then be as follows:

	Debit	Credit
(1)	US buyer	Arab oil producer
(2)	Arab oil producer	Lloyds
(3)	Lloyds	Bank in Hamburg
(4)	Bank in Hamburg	Bank in Rio
(5)	Bank in Rio	Central Bank of Zaïre
(6)	Central Bank of Zaïre	BNP

The final result is that the Arab oil producer has a deposit of $100m. at Lloyds; Lloyds has a claim of $100m. on the bank in Hamburg; the bank in Rio has a claim of $100m. on the Central Bank of Zaire and the BNP has a deposit at the Chase Manhattan bank. Altogether, that makes $400m., all held outside the USA, which means they must all be Eurodollars, i.e. a total of $400m. Eurodollars, where before there were only $100m. A multiplier of sorts has thus certainly been at work, but the result is only a multiplication of *deposits denominated in dollars* held outside the United States, not a multiplication of payment dollars. The only link in this chain which has the payment function is the deposit held by the BNP, which replaces the original deposit held by the Arab oil producer. But Lloyds' claim on the bank in Hamburg has no payment function, and neither does the claim by a depositor at Lloyds. Should our Arab oil producer wish to make use of the deposit he has at Lloyds in order to pay for a Cadillac he has just bought, he will give a transfer order to Lloyds requesting them to credit General Motors' account in New York. But Lloyds no longer has the dollars it received from the Arab oil producer because it has lent them to someone else. Consequently, it must refinance itself by borrowing or use deposits from other sources which it has received in the meantime. If the Arab oil producer wishes to buy a Rolls-Royce instead of a Cadillac, for which he must pay in sterling, Lloyds will not need to transfer the corresponding amount in primary money, i.e. in claims on the Bank of England; instead it will use a claim on itself. This makes all the difference.

It is not true, as Michel Lelart maintains, that no distinction should be made between dollars created in the United States and Eurodollars. It would be just as logical to claim that the deposits in a savings bank should be included in the domestic money supply, whereas in fact they are not even included in the stock of near-money. It would be much more accurate to speak, not of Eurodollars, but of 'deposits denominated in dollars outside the United States'.

In order to give colour to his thesis, Michel Lelart emphasises that a Eurobank has the power to enter on the liability side of its balance sheet a credit opened in favour of a borrower and, on its asset side, its own claim on that borrower, thereby apparently creating dollars *ex nihilo*:

> A Eurobank may lend to a client . . . without asking its correspondent in the United States to transfer dollars to its account. Instead, it will itself directly credit its customer's account. The customer will not thereby acquire a dollar in an account in the United States, the ownership of which passes to him from the lending bank; instead he will have a dollar in his account with this same bank . . . the bank has not lent a dollar which it already owned: it has lent a new dollar . . . it did not need to borrow before lending, it lent by indebting itself. We can no longer speak of a Eurodollar market, we should speak of a Eurodollar system capable of creating United States currency outside the USA without American help.[11]

But a savings bank can do exactly the same thing without having any power of monetary creation. There is nothing to stop it crediting its customer's account and entering amongst its assets its claim on that customer. Any economic agent has the same power. What matters is what happens when the bank in question receives a transfer order. If it is a non-bank, that is, a savings bank or a Eurobank, it carries out the order by means of funds it already has at its disposal, or which it obtains by borrowing. The power of monetary creation is not assessed by whether or not a bank can make simultaneous entries on the asset and liability sides of its balance sheet, but by whether or not it can issue claims on itself which have the payment function. (Apropos of this it is worth noting that in the statistics of Eurodollar liquidities simple lines of credit that represent potential but not actual loans are not included).[12]

It is not even certain that the Eurobanks do much to accelerate the velocity of money, which would have the same effect as an increase in the total money stock. Average annual transaction velocity of dollars is about 40, that is, there is an average interval of 9 days between two consecutive transactions. It remains to be proved that Eurodollar transactions are more frequent.

The fact that Eurobanks operate as non-monetary intermediaries also means that it is extremely unlikely that there will be any inflationary effects deriving from a supposed creation of new dollars. A depositor at a Eurobank abandons the title to goods and services he earned when he acquired the dollars he deposits. This title is transferred by the non-monetary intermediary — the Eurobank — to the final borrower, who uses it in his place. Let us, for example, consider the dollars deposited at Lloyds in London by the Arab oil producer. These dollars have been earned; they constitute a title to goods and services acquired by the oil producer in exchange for his oil. He abandons this right, and entrusts it to Lloyds instead. Throughout the entire circuit quoted earlier on, there was not one case of consumption of unearned items of production, in other words, things paid for with money created *ex nihilo*. At the end of the sequence, it is the BNP which, on Renault's behalf, holds the right to goods and services earned by the Arab oil producer in the form of a credit at the Chase Manhattan Bank. And if, finally, the bank in Rio mobilises the credit in dollars which it has made to Zaïre, there is no 'unearned' consumption over and above Renault's because the bank in Zaïre must get the dollars from somewhere else by borrowing or by drawing on its reserves. In other words, it too must get hold of an available earned right to goods and services.

Let us now suppose that Renault buys machine tools from a manufacturer in the United States or elsewhere and pays for them with dollars. Let us further suppose that the seller who receives the dollars keeps them in a bank in the USA, the Chase Manhattan for example, without depositing them in a Eurobank. Or, alternatively, let us suppose that Renault converts these dollars into francs and that the BNP then sells the dollars to the Bank of France, which deposits them at the Federal Reserve Bank of New York. In both cases, the dollars have left the Eurodollar system. In the case of the deposit at the Federal Reserve Bank, the money has done more than just leave the system, since money deposited at the Fed. is not included in M1, and thus counts as destroyed money. A withdrawal of funds from a bank in a national banking system puts into the hands of the person who makes the withdrawal a claim on the central bank in the form of bank-notes: a leak out of the Eurodollar system puts into the hands of the economic agent a claim on the US banking system.

Here, once again, we come across the equivalence of withdrawals through cash mobilisations and transfers, whether to a bank outside the clearing system or to a bank which has no other claims on the member banks of the clearing system. The three kinds of withdrawal — withdrawal of cash, transfer outside the clearing system and transfer to a bank with no obligations towards the other members of the system — have the same results in terms of what appears on the clearing chart. The 'owed by' column does not change, but the 'owing to's' decrease by the amount transferred outside the system. In the case of Eurocurrencies, the fact that the deposits generally stay in the Eurocircuit for a much shorter space of time than is the case in national banking systems helps to speed up leaks from the system.

It would thus be a serious mistake to add the mass of Eurodollars to the American M1, as Lelart recommends. This mass of dollars should be considered separately, in the same way as non-monetary deposits in dollars, such as deposits at Loan and Savings Associations are. But this does not prevent the Eurobanks from expanding their loan volume in just the same way as savings banks do. The original dollar can, as we have already seen, be lent, transferred and then re-deposited, bringing about, each time, a deposit when it enters an institution and a loan when it leaves one. This kind of process of loan expansion is only halted by the requirements of the reserves which any financial institution maintains in order to be able to cope with any possible withdrawals. Whilst there is not any reliable evidence to suggest that the Eurodollar system is responsible for an uncontrolled proliferation of payment dollars, it does not even seem to be proved beyond any doubt that it is responsible for making total non-monetary deposits denominated in dollars very much bigger than they would be if there were no Eurodollar system, that is if the multiplication of Eurodollar credit only took place within the United States and not outside them as well.

We now come to the last stage of the analysis: the question of liquidity and the monetary base. It is here that we can see, in the light of what has gone before, the consequences of the traditional doctrines in monetary matters. Michel Lelart considers that the central bank of the Eurodollar system is the entire American economy:

> Once the central bank is not a bank whose liabilities consist only of notes and deposits but an entire national economy, which includes other agents whose liabilities may be Treasury Bills, shares and bonds, it is logical that liabilities of this kind should be part of the central bank money or monetary base. While Eurodollars cannot be dissociated from ordinary dollars, the money stock we must take account of is the mass of all dollars, whether created in the USA or outside.[13]

So here we have, then, a dollar monetary base which is two or three times bigger than the one that the statistics deal with. This implies a power of monetary creation two or three times bigger than the one that is generally recognised. This seems odd, to say the least: is there not something, somewhere, that has gone wrong? Michel Lelart's reasoning is impeccable, his documentation is irreproachable and his style admirably clear. How, then, can he have arrived at such extraordinary conclusions?

The answer is simple: by starting from erroneous premisses. Here we have the great merit of Lelart's study: by arriving, through an unassailable process of reasoning, at unacceptable conclusions, he calls into question the fundamental data on which he bases his argument. Amongst these erroneous data there is the confusion of what is payment money and what is only a deposit denominated in money, and the failure to distinguish between what is a real payment instrument and what is only *potentially* a payment instrument. What is more, Lelart omits to make the very distinction between liquidity and money which he recommends himself: 'Whereas liquidity includes all those assets used as a store of value, money should be clearly distinguished from all those substitutes which, unlike it, are not means of payment.'[14]

The edifice of new money erected by the banking system on the monetary base of central bank money is like an inverted pyramid resting on a fraction of that base, which is the quantity of central bank money the banks keep in their reserves. The total amount of central bank money (M0) which the American banks may hold cannot exceed the total amount of money issued by the Federal Reserve Banks. Even if every single American were to mobilise all his assets, including bonds, shares and Treasury Bills, and deposit the proceeds at his bank, the total resulting amount of central bank money would not, *could* not, exceed what had been issued by the Federal Reserve Banks. But if, as Lelart maintains, the monetary institution that acts as central bank for the Eurodollar system is the entire American economy, then the total quantity of primary money in the system is no longer the money issued by the Federal Reserve Banks but rather the M1 money supply, which is far bigger and capable of expanding enormously if all Americans choose to mobilise their assets and deposit them in Eurobanks. If to this we add the supposed multiplier effect attributed by some writers to the system, we can easily imagine the potentially explosive process of monetary creation which the Eurodollar system could trigger off, and the devastating effect it could have on the world monetary system.

The, in my opinion, mistaken conclusions which Michel Lelart arrives at provide a good illustration of the sort of confusion that can arise from the use of heterogenous monetary indicators with imprecise meanings. The Eurodollar system is not without its faults, but they are not the ones people imagine. The most serious danger is that which is inherent in the nature of an extremely volatile mass of capital free to move in a matter of seconds from one financial centre to another, abandoning overvalued currencies in favour of undervalued ones. The very existence of such a mass of capital made the collapse of the fixed exchange rate system inevitable, and made equally inevitable the adoption of a suitably volatile mode of defence, namely floating exchange rates.

Another risk in the Eurodollar system is the result of the way the Eurodollar credits are arranged in long chains, each loan dependent on another, so that if one of the links of these chains should break through the failure of a bank it could bring the others down with it. Yet another risk is the absence of any moderating or protective device, such as a central bank represents in a national banking system. There is also a risk of an unbridled inflation of credits fed by abundant Arab capital and the American banking system. Such an expansion of loan volume, which would no longer be held in check by leaks out of the system, could lead to a collapse. None of the regulatory measures which the Eurobanks are at present obliged to adopt can prevent the multiplier from exceeding its present rate of about three times initial deposits. Finally, there is also the unsatisfactory nature of a system that gives to what is primarily a national currency the role of vehicle of international trade and main constituent of international reserves.

Against these dangers and risks, we should set the advantages that result from a system capable of transferring funds throughout the world with astonishing rapidity and flexibility, from where they are not needed to where they are needed. The Eurodollar market is a spontaneous creation which was planned by no one and which has never been organised or policed; in spite of that, it is a source of great benefit to the world economy.

Whichever way we look at it, the question of devising a new international currency leads to the conclusion that what is required is a new extranational, that is stateless, currency which would circulate outside states and not within them. If such a currency were created, a large number of the objections to the Eurocurrency system as constituted at present would be eliminated. This subject will be looked at in greater detail in Part 3 of this book.

NOTES

[1] There are exceptions. It is a matter of some satisfaction for those who refute the dominant doctrine in France to note that they count amongst themselves a monetarist, and one of the best, namely Jean Denizet. Mention should also be made of the banker and former university professor Fernand Colin.

[2] Michel Lelart *La multiplication européene des eurodollars*, *Revue Banque*, November and December 1976.

[3] *Eurodollars, the money-market gypsies*, Harper and Row, New York and London.

[4] Quoted by J. S. Little, op. cit.

[5] Let us just remind the reader that a bank functions as a Eurobank when it operates in currencies other than those of the country in which it is domiciled and takes in deposits and makes loans. A dollar received in payment by an Arab oil producer and deposited in his name at the Chase Manhattan bank in New York becomes a Eurodollar when this Arab oil producer transfers his claim on the Chase to Lloyds in London. The latter then lends the dollar to a Brazilian borrower and for this purpose gives a transfer order to the Chase, which transfers the money to an account which the borrower has opened in a bank domiciled in the USA.

[6] Michel Lelart, op. cit.

[7] J. S. Little, op. cit.

[8] Michel Lelart, op. cit.

[9] Published by Editions de l'Albatros.

[10] J. S. Little, op. cit.

[11] Michel Lelart, op. cit.

[12] Bank of France, Quarterly Bulletin, May 1975.

[13] Michel Lelart, op. cit.

[14] Michel Lelart, *Le dollar, monnaie internationale.*

9 Use of the three keys, third example–Investment on the basis of monetary creation

In 1975, monetary liquidities in France increased by 58,000 millions. This means that the holders of money suffered a reduction of 58,000 million francs, or almost a sixth, in the value of their total monetary assets, this being the difference between the money that was added and the money that was destroyed. This reduction in resources was the direct consequence of the fact that the first holders of the new money consumed or invested goods and services without having made an equivalent contribution in the form of new goods and services produced and earned, whereas the final holders of units of money before they were destroyed *had* made a restoration to total available resources, in order to earn the money, by producing *without* consuming.

The conclusion that follows from this is that the use that is made of new money and the purposes to which it is put ought to be the result of a deliberate choice, and that this choice ought to be decided on according to certain rules that take the general interest into consideration. The process of reduction is hidden. It is not perceived by those on whom it is exercised, but it is no less real as a source of resources than taxes, savings, money borrowed on the capital markets and retained profits. The resources obtained by monetary creation, just like these other resources, ought to be used for selected purposes, in terms of well-defined needs.

The state levies taxes. With the proceeds of these taxes it builds schools, manufactures arms, subsidises agriculture, pays civil servants and subsidises public services and loss-making nationalised industries. The public gets back (more or less) what it handed over to the state purse, in one form or another. Of course, the uses that are made of these resources and the efficiency with which they are put to use can be questioned; there is not one tax-payer in ten who thinks that he is getting his 'money's worth'.

But, all the same, there is a very evident circuit at work here, involving a withdrawal of resources in the form of taxes, and a subsequent redistribution.

New money is created by the state (primary money) and by the banking system (bank money). It is they who, by feeding the process of monetary creation, are responsible for the resulting reduction. The responsibility and the obligations incumbent on the state are well known, and, theoretically at least, firmly under the control of the representatives of the people. But the banking system creates more new money than the state, and therefore has particular responsibilities and duties when it comes to the question of attribution of new money through the granting of loans.

For a long time it was a dogma of financial orthodoxy that short-term commercial credit ought to be provided by the banks, whilst long-term investment ought to be supplied by the financial markets. Even today, this dogma still has a certain influence, and those who hold it tend to view participation by banks in long-term financing as a mere temporary expedient, which is the reason why medium-term credit is still granted in the form of renewable three month lines.[2] It is absurd that such a traditionally 'unorthodox' mechanism as that of medium-term credit should have functioned for so long and on so large a scale and with such evident success without anyone doing anything to accommodate to it the basic principles of monetary theory.

But first, the old moribund definition of money as representative of a commodity and dependent on a value backing must be abandoned and all net additions to the money supply must be recognised for what they are, taking due account, of course, of variations in the velocity of money — namely, withdrawals from the total wealth of the community. We should not look upon traditionally 'orthodox' banking activities like bill discounting and short-term credit as anything other than practical mechanisms which have the merit of being well tried and of providing the lender — i.e. the bank — with a certain security.

The principle on which banks do business is very special; it rests on certain assumptions — wagers, if you like — and certain probabilities. The assumption is that the borrower will be solvent and will repay the loan at maturity and, more particularly, that the depositors will not all withdraw their money at the same time. The probability generally is that this will be the case; if not, the bank runs the risk of being illiquid. The wager and the probability in turn imply that obligations should be entered into in predictable conditions and for a relatively short period of time. Discounting is an essentially short-term form of financing and one of its great advantages, from the macro-economic point of view, is that it works

automatically. When business is good and more money is needed, new
money must be created. Increased demand for money can be satisfied
more or less automatically by discounting bills and without the authorities
needing to intervene. Bills, moreover, are useful vehicles of refinancing at
the central bank or on the money markets. But all these undeniable
merits should not hide from us the realities that emerge from an analysis
of modern monetary systems. This analysis brings out the fungibility of
bank deposits, which overturns the traditional division into distinct
categories, according to whether deposits are current account deposits,
payable on demand, or whether they are savings or passbook deposits;
in fact, they all help to swell the reserves of the bank, and it is on the
basis of these reserves, that fiduciary money is created. Banks maintain
that they try hard to cover their long-term loans with 'stable' deposits,
but this is only an attempt to obtain additional security.

It would be wrong to conclude from this, however, as people sometimes
do, that a bank therefore has two separate compartments: one which
operates as a non-monetary intermediary and transfers savings to
borrowers and another which operates as a monetary intermediary by
creating bank money. The truth is simply that banks try to observe certain
rules of prudence. A long-term loan ties up liquidity, and so it is natural
that banks should try to balance this by attracting stable deposits. But a
one-for-one correspondence, if there is one, can only be fortuitous; it is
not, as is the case with a non-monetary intermediary, the result of a
direct relationship between the resources in question and the uses made of
them. When a businessman draws up his investment plans, he balances
his needs with his resources, including those which he has available and
those which he hopes to obtain. He adds up the total of his own resources,
including medium-term loans and loans from the financial markets. To this
he adds his discount ceiling and his overdraft ceiling. Each category of
resources is supposed to be matched by a well-defined category of needs.
This correspondence is closely adhered to in the document he shows his
bankers but this is not the case in his own mind, much less in his
treasurer's.

The money created specifically in order to satisfy the businessman's
(and his treasurer's) needs can be compared to money created for purposes
of investment. Money needed to finance trade is part of working capital.
Working capital is inseparable from the assets needed to ensure that a
company's business can be carried on, just like stocks and fixed assets
such as machinery and premises. The confusion of thinking between liquid
savings and stable savings, between money and near-money, between
resources ear-marked for the job of feeding growth and those needed for

everyday cash drawings, and the problems resulting from such a confusion, is all quite plain to see in the reports of the French National Plan on the financing of the economy. To be sure, the money supply is mentioned, but without any open recognition of the notion of 'transformation', or investment on the basis of monetary creation, the need for it and its benefits, and without thereby posing the problem of the allocation of resources produced by this process. It is still conventional wisdom to see a relationship between banks' savings accounts and long-term loans, whereas such loans are not in fact connected to savings. They are based on monetary creation, which is itself based on savings. Sooner or later, people are bound to realise that the people who put up capital for investment through banks are not only depositors who put money into savings accounts, but also, and even more so, those who work, receive a salary and then, after a certain lapse of time, spend. This must be so, because the provision of capital through monetary creation is based on reduction, and reduction operates on all holders of money.

As long as any doubt subsisted regarding the notion of the money supply the idea of reduction could not be recognised. But nowadays, the money supply has become one of the fundamental data of the economy. In practically all countries, the growth of the money supply is one of the factors which decide public policy. That is one achievement: another must be aimed at, namely the rational allocation of new money, deciding which proportions should be reserved for which sectors of the economy. The allocation of a larger proportion of a given quantity of money to investment causes a corresponding reduction in available liquidities for financing trade. Supposing, for example, that a manufacturer of barley-sugar has just made a delivery. He draws a bill on his confectioner customer and submits it for discount. The loan which he then receives from his bank in the form of a credit to his current account becomes part of the money supply, and thus helps expand it. If a larger proportion of the money supply is used for investment in the private or public sector, for example in telephones, there will be less available for loans to the barley-sugar manufacturer. This is the inevitable result of the redirection of funds. There is no miracle here: to attempt to finance investment and, at the same time, provide for the need for liquidity, would lead to an anarchic creation of new money.

But from the point of view of our interpretation of the nature of an increase in the quantity of money — i.e. a hidden reduction of a mass of monetary assets — there can be no objection to the liquidities resulting from the operation being used to finance telephones instead of being lent to the barley-sugar manufacturer. For a while he will suffer, but in the end he will benefit from it, as will all economic agents, because the new telephones, by contributing to economic growth, will bring new customers to the confectionery shops. The use to which new money is put will be all the more justified if the time necessary for the loan to be amortised is short, and the benefits, from the point of view of the general good, high. This is true of investment in telephones. It can easily be seen that the additional activity and the economies of time that the investment makes possible will compensate for the reduction and, in general, the expenses incurred for the investment. If the amortisation time is short or about equal to the time taken by the money to work through the economic system, the new money added is not inflationary, but rather conducive to increased production and therefore anti-inflationary.

The objection to that will be that such calculations are difficult to make, and encourage financial laxity. But this is the kind of argument one comes up against whenever one tries to replace traditional ideas, even when they are completely obsolete, by new ones which fit the facts better. How, in practice, can the allocation of new money be made? The banking system is the great provider of money; it should therefore be the banking system which allocates new money, guided by directives from the monetary authorities and backed up by measures designed either to encourage or to restrain lending, for which there is no shortage of instruments. The best known of these is simple credit control[3] – the 'corset'. The extra credit that each bank is allowed to make, over and above what it made the previous year, is calculated on the basis of certain formulae. The calculations could be weighted, the weight of each credit depending on its nature and the extent to which it promotes the general interest.

The retort will be that there is nothing new about this. For some time, the authorities have been making just such a selection and, by implication, encouraging or discouraging certain loans. Thus, for instance, certain credits are eligible for discount, others are not, whilst still others are exempt from the restrictions. This sectoral selectivity is not systematic: as often as not, it is bound up with a system of onerous subsidies, and is consequently inefficient. For example, savings for house purchases are intended to encourage future house buyers to save and put their savings in a bank. The Treasury pays the bank the difference between the preferential interest rate that will eventually be granted on loans to the holders of house savings accounts and the economic rate. These house savings are, like all the bank's resources, included in its assets, and are used to help make up the reserve on the basis of which it makes loans, and consequently contributes to the growth of the very M1 which the authorities wish to control. It is absurd to try to restrain with one hand the growth of the very thing one is subsidising, and therefore encouraging with the other. It would be much better to pay the subsidies to the owner of the house and ration the bank's loans using these data in the calculation of the credit quotas.

The banks have nothing to fear from the introduction of such measures — quite the reverse. By encouraging investment through monetary creation, they have helped the world economy make a great leap forward these last thirty years. It is entirely in the interest of the banks to demonstrate the mechanism and emphasise the great services it has provided. Contrary to a widely-accepted myth, banks do not make excessive profits; one could even say that they do not make enough profits. Bank financing is the very cornerstone of progress and growth. By reducing their profits, one eliminates them from an entire sector, the new business sector. They are thus confined to the most conservative sectors, those which run the smallest risks. People do not willingly play for big stakes if their pockets are empty. But if one has to lose, which happens from time to time, it is better that the sums at risk should be precisely calculated.

NOTES

[1] The notion of investment based on monetary creation — or 'transformation' as it is sometimes called — may help to resolve certain contradictions, which, in the eyes of the unitiated, may seem confused and even artificial, between the theories of Keynes, based on the 'propensity to save or consume' and those of the Chicago school, which take as their foundation the quantity of money in circulation.

One may well ask whether the traditional Keynesian idea which has been the guiding feature of economic policy for some time should not be called into question. In this respect, modern monetary theories merit some attention. By emphasising the role of money, neglected for so long, they may have much to contribute to the conduct of monetary policy. In any case, if one wishes to apply the principles of this theory, it is indispensable to understand properly the mechanisms which determine the formation of the money supply.
André Fourcans, *La politique de la monnaie*, Editions Economica.

[2] 'The distinction between short-term commercial assets, regarded as being by definition "healthy", and those assets that create false claims, has no economic foundation'.
Jean Denizet, *Monnaie et financement* (Editions Dunod).

[3] Credit control consists of limits imposed on the growth of bank lending. Thus, for every 100 distributed in 1977, the volume of credits

distributed in 1978 may not exceed 105 for banks whose total credits at the middle of 1977 were more than 6500 million, and 108 for those whose credits were less. Financing-loans at fixed rates granted for relatively short periods to exporting companies exporting heavy goods are excluded from the controls. (Another advantage is the preferential rate of 4.5 per cent charged by the Bank of France.) Building loans are also exempted. The total of exempted loans constitutes about 40 per cent of the total.

SUPPLEMENTARY NOTES

PAGE 31

(1) The nature of money

Henri Guitton asks 'Does money exist?'
For François Perroux, on the other hand (*Le Monde*, 27 June 1978), there is no doubt: 'Money... is the vehicle of the super-real, money, which is perhaps the ultimate symbol for the sociologist, is for us an introduction to the super-real: our food and drink, the roof over our heads, everything has to be bought or hired with money'.
Here we have two original thinkers who, to judge by appearances at least, are not in agreement: one is not certain that money exists, whilst for the other it is 'super-real'. In fact, however, the two are really in agreement, because Henri Guitton also says:

I'm afraid that in monetary matters pragmatism is still more important than mere theory. A line of approach or an experiment that has succeeded without anyone really knowing why, is immediately taken seriously. The thoretician is only consulted afterwards, so that he can give some rational explanation of the affair. If, on the other hand, it fails, it is soon forgotten. Are not discount-rate manipulations and open-market practices examples of successful experiments which have been retrospectively explained away by the theoreticians?

This book takes its inspiration from just such a line of thought. It is not concerned with the philosophical implications of the nature of money. Its aim is to discover that aspect of the nature of money which will help to understand the monetary mechanisms and their effects, and consequently help to improve what is conventionally known as 'monetary regulation'. It is from this point of view, and only this point of view, that the question concerning the nature of money at the beginning of this book is posed. The reply has two parts.
Firstly, let us admit that money everywhere takes the form of claims on various sorts of institution. But there are innumerable kinds of claim and innumerable kinds of institution, which naturally leads to another question: which claims on which institutions are really money?

At this point, I suggest that we abandon the traditional approach, which tries to define money by its fundamental functions of standard and store of value and medium of exchange. How, indeed, can one do anything other than abandon these three functions as criteria, given that nowadays money no longer properly fulfils more than one of them? In any case, it does not seem rational, when one is trying to define something, to trust to mere *properties*, no matter how important they may appear; the essence of a system is quite a different thing from its properties.

But Henri Guitton wonders whether one could not rely on the property that money has of

assuring the continuity of exchanges over a period of time, which gave rise to the expression 'Money is time'. Nowadays, we no longer deny this view, which was foreshadowed by Aristotle. In fact, it has been renewed and more sharply defined. . . Money is what is used to cancel, extinguish and liquidate debts; it provides payment today and tomorrow, it concludes exchanges, it completes and finishes them (is this not the etymological sense of the word 'finance'?). When it has been handed over, there are no longer any problems, arguments or worries. What a noble function!

But, people will also say, money is purchasing power, it is a claim on resources which needs to change hands . . .

Supposing a banker makes a loan to a customer by means of an over-draft. Here we have a claim on the bank which is put into circulation and which, having the payment function, plays the same role as money, just like a bank-note, and which, like the bank-note, gives the bank's customer a claim on goods and services that constitutes a drawing on the total available wealth of society. This process and its effects on the economy are worth analysing. This is why I think that, using the pragmatic approach recommended by Henri Guitton, we should prefer a definition which makes it easier to understand this particular process.

A unit of money is a transferable claim, the main function of which, the one that distinguishes it from all others, is to be directly exchangeable for goods and services. Of course, one can easily argue that in this process there is a discharge of a debt, since the supply of goods and services, as long as it is not paid for, causes the creation of a debt between supplier and purchaser. But this way of looking at things ignores the order of events. The claim which is to effect the payment and with which the holder will buy something anticipates this supply of goods and services. One cannot therefore say that its essence is to extinguish a debt. By granting an overdraft, the bank provides its customer with resources before he chooses to make use of them.

The nature of money, or, more precisely, the nature of *a unit of money*, is that of a transferable claim issued arbitrarily and artificially with an indeterminate exchange value and maturity. It goes from hand to hand and has the power of procuring directly, each time it is used, a certain

quantity of goods and services, until it is finally destroyed. Such is the
definition of money which we shall use here. This is the one that will
guide us, both in the critical parts of this book and in the constructive
parts (Part 2, Chapter 5, The search for a new monetary indicator; Part 2
Chapter 5, A new composite unit, the Eurostable). At the same time,
we shall ignore the other notions of money, which are all based on a
reason for its creation, such as a 'good' handed to an issuer in return for
existing goods or one or more functions of money (store of value etc).

PAGE 42

(1) The search for the final payment

It is only by looking for the final operation of transfer of a unit of
money or a claim that one can avoid errors of interpretation over whether
or not a particular claim has the payment function. Let us look at an
example.

X purchases an article from Y and pays for it with a £10 note. The
claim on the Bank of England represented by this note passes from X
to Y. X, instead of giving Y a £10 note, gives him a piece of paper on
which he has written 'I promise to pay the bearer ten pounds'. Y uses
this piece of paper to pay Z; the latter goes to X's bank and obtains
payment of his claim in the form of a £10 note.

The first payment from X to Y was made by means of an
acknowledgement of debt; the second was made by means of the £10
note remitted by X's bank. If we omit to look for the final claim that
effected the payment, we shall not be able to distinguish between the first
and the second transaction. The piece of paper signed by X will either
be considered a payment instrument, and in that case three transactions
will be registered instead of two (two through the acknowledgement of
debt and one by the note); or else it will not be counted at all, and in that
case we shall only count one (the £10 note given to Z).

X pays Y with a cheque drawn on his bank. He pays Z by giving a
transfer order to a savings bank. On the surface, it would seem that there is
no difference between the two transfers of claims. But if we look for the
final payment we can see that the commercial bank transfers a claim on
itself, which constitutes means of payment, whereas the savings bank gives
a transfer order to a bank where it keeps its funds. If we consider only
the operations involving deposits — which appear to be the same — we
omit from the analysis the final operation, that of the savings bank, and
we thus make a mistake.

X draws a cheque on bank A and gives it in payment to Y, who deposits
this cheque at bank B. The cheque does not effect the whole of the
payment. The search for the final stage shows that a fraction of the amount
of the cheque was not compensated for by cheques deposited at A and
drawn on other banks, but was paid by A in central bank money.

Can a composite or artificial currency constitute means of payment?
In order to answer this question we must look at what goes on in the bank

that carries out a payment order denominated in this composite unit, in what form the payment is actually effected and on whom the claim that ultimately effects the payment is drawn. If the payment is eventually made in dollars, the composite unit, in spite of appearances, was not used as a payment unit.

These examples show how the search for the final claim which effects the payment helps to clear up the confusion over what is money and what is not and at the same time provides a more accurate definition of the indicators. It also eliminates the frequent confusion by monetary theorists between monetary intermediaries and non-monetary intermediaries.

PAGE 73

(1) Analysis of the process of 'reduction'

The model used to study the way in which the creation of a new unit of money reduces the quantity of resources available to the holders of money may be adapted more closely to the facts by modifying and completing certain hypotheses. For example, the total volume of transactions is far higher in reality than the number of simple exchanges of produced goods into consumption or investment. In order to take account of this fact, all we need to do is to replace total production, P, by the addition made during an exchange, whatever its nature, whether this addition be a commodity which has already been produced, work or added value.

We also ought to bring in the different attitudes of economic agents, with their differing consequences. Let us suppose that one of them, more thrifty than the others, does not buy the goods that are offered for sale. In view of our basic postulate, that the sum of partial reductions must be equal to the value of the new unit of money, the abstinence of this frugal person means that the reduction effect affects fewer people. Once the equilibrium of exchanges has been reached and prices have stabilised, the economic agent who did not play his part on the market will suffer, along with everyone else, the depreciation of his assets in terms of units of account, although the reduction on his assets was not one of the partial reductions, the sum of which should be equal to the value of the new unit of money created. Thus, it may appear that the total of the partial reductions will be greater than the value of the new money.

This apparent anomaly can be resolved by bringing into the analysis the net addition to production by the frugal agent resulting from the fact that he consumed nothing during the process of 'restoring equilibrium'. This addition diminishes correspondingly the reduction in the total resources necessary to balance this new unit of money. Once prices have stabilised, the necessary addition to make up the total value of the new unit of money will be obtained for the reduction mechanism at the very moment the money belonging to the thrifty man leaves his bank account. When this happens, he will experience a partial diminution in the total resources he can command, corresponding to the difference between the

goods and services provided by him in order to obtain this money and the
goods and services he receives when he spends it. This partial reduction in
his command over resources completes the value of the new unit of money.

PAGE 76

(1) How to fight inflation: application of the notion of reduction

Curing a serious inflation without provoking a ruinous deflation is one
of the most difficult tasks that a modern government can be faced with.
No one knows with absolute certainty how to bring about the transition
from an inflation rate of 10−15 per cent, which is rightly judged excessive,
to a reasonable rate of the order of 2 or 3 per cent, without at the same
time slowing down the economy and increasing unemployment.

The classical recipe is austerity: curbing the growth of the money
supply, credit squeezes, high interest rates, tax increases, cut-backs in
public spending, etc. But all these measures slow down and hinder
economic activity, which is regrettable, as excessive additions to the
money supply can only be mopped up, in the end, through increased
output. All the elements of this traditional anti-inflationary therapy have
the opposite effect to the one desired.

The first thing to look at is the, as it were, mechanical factor, which we
analysed during our study of the phenomenon of reduction. Even if the
government has already launched an anti-inflation programme, nothing
can prevent the new money that was created before the programme was
launched from effecting the reduction, which is the inevitable corollary
of an addition of new money to the money supply in excess of the total
quantity of money destroyed. This reduction takes place at the expense
of the holders of money. If it is not compensated for by an increase in the
rate of production it inevitably causes a fall in the purchasing power of
money.

Restrictive measures designed to combat inflation contain within
themselves disruptive elements which frustrate the very policy the
government has adopted. Demand is curbed and trade slows down, which
increases the time necessary for the partial reductions to balance
out the money that was added previously. But beyond that, there
is another factor, namely the decision to invest and to undertake
business expansion. This is also hindered by making borrowing more
difficult and more expensive, by the uncertainty of the economic situation,
by deflationary expectations and by cut-backs in public spending.

Of course, after a time, which may be fairly long, the new money will
have completed its reduction and the inflation will be absorbed. But a
democratic system is ill suited to a period of prolonged austerity and it is
not surprising that such policies are rarely seen through to the bitter end.
Whilst recognising the courage of those who are brave enough to choose
such a policy, we should still look around to see whether there is not a
better way of beating inflation than putting millions of men out of work.

The very day that the decision is made to reverse the policy of soft
options in favour of discipline, non-subsidised prices and restrictions,

there remains a considerable price to pay. The new money created earlier, perhaps a few months or perhaps a few years before, has not completed its process of reduction which balances out the goods and services consumed by the first users of the money. This reduction must take place; there is no alternative. If there is not a sufficient rise in production, the statistics will continue to register month after month discouraging and indeed disconcerting inflation rates.

We shall look into the question of how a stable monetary unit could help this situation later in this book. By making it possible for money to be lent once again at low interest rates it would put entrepreneurs, and thus their decision whether or not to invest, out of reach of restrictive anti-inflationary measures and would thus help to offset the harmful effects such measures always have on economic activity.

PAGE 84

(1) The multiplier

Henri Guitton writes as follows about the multiplier:

> Since Keynes, this phenomenon of multiplication has been a source of ceaseless fascination for economists. They look for its effects in all areas, including employment and investment. The science of economics could almost be defined as the 'search for the multiplier'. The Physiocrats were probably the first to concern themselves with this phenomenon. For them the only really productive process was the process by which a seed multiplied itself, becoming an ear of corn by dint of its passage through the earth. Retailers were thus considered only capable of multiplying what Nature herself had already multiplied. (Note on the life and work of Emile Mireaux, published by Firmin Didot.)

It often happens that a new discovery is seized upon by the human mind as an excuse for not looking any further. I wonder whether this is not true of the multiplier. The mechanism of credit certainly involves a multiplier, but this multiplier does not necessarily create money in the sense of money as *payment instrument*, and yet this is what we are told by the contributor to a famous encyclopaedia.

> A bank, looked at individually, receives deposits and makes loans. It does not need to keep permanently available all the funds it accepts on deposit from its customers because depositors never come all at once to ask for their money back, except in quite exceptional times of crisis. On the other hand, the bank must keep a certain proportion of its deposits available or easily mobilisable in order to be able to cope with daily withdrawals. From time to time, especially at week-ends and at the end of the month, the quantity of this liquidity needs to be temporarily increased. In short, the bank may make use of a large proportion of the funds deposited with it for its own purposes and, in

particular, in order to make loans to those of its customers who ask
for them. Let us suppose that this proportion is 80 per cent. Thus, if
bank A has received £100,000 in deposits it will be able to make on
average £800,000 worth of loans and will have to keep reserves of
£200,000. Its role would be confined to that, i.e. it would remain a
simple intermediary without any money-creating powers, if it was not
part of a banking system involving other banks, its colleagues and
competitors, who act in the same way.

In a banking system, other banks than A receive deposits and also
make loans. The sums lent are held, in turn, totally or partially, in the
form of deposits by those who receive them. Let us therefore suppose
that a second bank, B, has taken in deposits just like bank A. Its initial
situation may be as follows, for example: deposits £2,000,000,
loans £1,600,000 (80 per cent deposits) reserves £400,000. The total
volume of loans made by the two banks is therefore £800,000 +
£1,600,000 = £2,400,000. If that sum is held entirely in the form of
deposits and if no cash withdrawal takes place, the banks have an
additional base of £2,400,000 on which to make further loans. These
will amount to £1,920,000 and will in turn constitute new deposits,
and, from loans to new depositors, the banking system will create new
bank money. This is what is meant when people quote the well-known
saying 'loans make deposits'.

It is true that money deposited at a bank can be re-lent, then
re-deposited and then re-lent, etc. In that case there is a multiplication of
credits and deposits denominated in money, but there is still no creation
of new means of payment.

Let us suppose, for the sake of simplicity, that the only payment
money in existence is gold. A gold coin is lent, deposited, re-lent, redeposited, etc. Each time, a depositor is credited, and he then has a claim
on the bank where he holds his deposit. There is, therefore, a multiplication
of such claims. But are these claims payment instruments? No, they are
not, because in order to make a payment the depositor must mobilise his
claim, i.e. he must go and ask the bank for a gold coin. In order to serve
its customer, the bank either draws on its reserves or borrows. If, instead of
mobilising his claim, the depositor gives the bank instructions to pay his
creditor, there is no difference. The bank carries out his instructions by
transferring a gold coin. There is only a creation of new money if the
bank pays by means of a claim on itself, which does not happen if the
issue of bank-notes is confined to the central bank and if there is no
system of clearing within the banking system.

Let us take another example. The gold coin is used to buy a bond.
Its new owner uses it to buy a share. The third owner of the coin uses
it to buy a case of wine, whilst the fourth deposits it at a savings bank,
which re-lends it. There is certainly a multiplication of claims and of
liquidity, but there is no multiplication of payment money.

The money supply continues to consist of all the gold coins in
circulation. That is all. It is only if a final payment is carried out by means
of a new claim that this claim is added to the coins in circulation to

produce an increased money supply. This is true of bank-notes, of endorsed bills (which, however, are negligible in quantity) and current account bank deposits, thanks to the clearing process.

Of course, those who argue in favour of the multiplier as a method of monetary creation will retort that the process of multiplication increases the velocity of money and the effect of this increase in velocity is the same as an increase in volume. But it is not because two *effects* are the same that it can be deduced that the causes are the same. The impact of a ten-ton lorry travelling at 30 kmph is the same when it hits a pedestrian as a car weighing one ton hitting him at 95 kmph. We would not conclude from this that the lorry is indistinguishable from the car.

The true importance of the multiplier is the fact that the proper working of the economy depends on this repeated movement of a unit of money from one hand to another. The number of times the money changes hands is increased, and with it there is a conversion of consumption into investment. This is the great and principal merit of the multiplier.

PAGE 83

(1) A few words on the 'liquidity quotient' of money

In his preface to A. Coutière's book *Le système monétaire français* (Economica), André Delattre writes:

> I should like to note *en passant* my friendly difference of opinion with Mr Coutière and with those who, like him, think that the extent to which the *Caisse des Dépôts* intervenes on the money markets justifies its being introduced into a description of the (banking) system. In my opinion, even if it has a great deal of liquidity at its disposal . . . the *Caisse* is not a creator of money, since it cannot discharge a debt by making a simple entry in its books.

The real cause of this friendly difference of opinion noted by André Delattre is to be found three pages further on, when one reads, from the pen of A. Coutière:

> From the point of view of non-financial agents, if the demand for money is analysed, various critical choices can be made regarding the most practical definition of money. It appears that a fundamental cleavage can be discerned in monetary and financial assets, according as their value can be realised or made liquid more or less easily. In the first analysis, we therefore separate the totality of liquidities making up M3, from financial investments (shares, life assurance policies etc.) and we can limit the monetary system to those institutions that mainly create the first category of assets. Thus we are led to restrict the field of analysis to the banking system, the *Caisse des Dépôts* and the *Trésor Public.* . .

The author then goes on to look at various definitions of money, and compares M1, M2 and M3. He adds, apropos of M1:

> To define thus the money supply would be to narrow even more the field of investigation to part of the banking system and the *Trésor Public*. . . From the point of view of the money supply, the mechanisms of the creation of money in the French system make it possible to justify very simply the choice of a broad definition of money corresponding to M3 (which includes savings bank deposits).

To define money in terms of what the author calls 'ease of making liquid', leads to uncertainty and contradictions. M3 includes savings deposits with maturities up to three years, for example, which have only an accidental 'liquidity quotient', but it does not include foreign currency or bills held by banks which may be mobilised at the Bank of France in a few hours, which is certainly much quicker than anything included in M2 or M3.

In fact, it is only by looking at the presence or absence of the payment function in the unit of money in question that one can clear up the confusion in which the notion of money is enveloped and, with it, monetary analysis. One cannot achieve this by taking as a basis the 'liquidity quotient' because this characteristic is one shared by many assets that are not included in the money supply and the mobilisation of which does not necessarily cause the creation of a new unit of payment, as André Delattre emphasises.

PAGE 87

(1) In his excellent book, *Or et monnaie dans l'histoire* (Flammarion), Pierre Vilar quotes Richard Cantillon and his *Essai sur la nature du commerce en général*, published in 1775:

> A banker will often be able to lend 90,000 of the 100,000 ounces of gold that have been entrusted to him and will only need to keep in his coffers 10,000 ounces, which is enough to cover occasional withdrawals. His customers are thrifty and opulent people; as often as one withdraws 1,000 ounces, another deposits 1,000 ounces. In general, it is enough for him to keep in his coffers a tenth part of the money that has been deposited with him. Some examples of this have already been noted in London. The result is that whereas the banker's customers might otherwise keep most of these 100,000 ounces in a safe all year round, the practice of depositing the sum with a banker means that 90,000 ounces are put back into circulation. So here we have the first lesson that can be drawn regarding the nature of this sort of bank: the bankers and goldsmiths help to accelerate the velocity of circulation of money by lending it out at their own risk, whilst still

being prepared to pay out specie at sight, on presentation of one of
their notes.

It is somewhat surprising to find in a book that is 200 years old the
same explanation of the multiplier as the one from the *Encyclopaedia
universalis* quoted on page 111. But Pierre Vilar is quick to add a
corrective. He tells us that what has happened over the last thirty or forty
years to change this picture is:

(1) the generalisation of the practice of setting payments by clearings in
bank money; (2) the systematic application of 'monetary policy' — the
attempt by states to control the volume of credit and the circulation of
money; and (3) since the end of the Second World War, the acceptance of
certain national currencies, especially the dollar, as instruments for international settlements.

Part Two
Monetary regulation and the monetary indicators

1 Nature abhors a vacuum

For almost five centuries, Rome governed the world, imposed her laws and maintained public order. To the barbarian peoples whom she conquered she brought discipline and civilisation, in a word, *pax romana.* So great was the prestige and influence of her power that long after the Empire had collapsed, its memory lived on. Fallen emperors and tribal chieftains, in the east as in the west, continued to dream of recreating the unity of the Roman Empire, of attempting to preserve or even rebuild the outward semblances, notwithstanding that the substance had long since crumbled to dust.

For thousands of years, men's minds were held in a similar kind of spell by gold, and then by the gold standard, the instrument of the Industrial Revolution of the nineteenth century. The great success with which gold functioned as a money and the fond memory people had of it, are the reasons why many refused to accept its disappearance and persisted in stubborn efforts to restore it and preserve mechanisms which had long ceased to have any meaning and which had degenerated into carefully maintained relics of a great tradition.

It is, of course, true that gold is a wonderful metal; no other commodity, except silver, has been able to rival it as medium of exchange because all the others involved greater risks of physical deterioration or of not being accepted elsewhere, of being difficult to transport, turn into coins and identify. Because it was thus such an incomparable *reducer of risks*, gold played a vital role in developing trade; it is not too much to say that is has been one of the great instruments of civilisation.

By using gold as a money, men tried to store up the right to goods and services that they had received in exchange for other goods sold or for services rendered. In order to do that they needed a commodity which could be bartered for other goods at an indeterminate time and place. In so doing they were avoiding the risks inherent in any future operation, which uncertainties of time and place made unpredictable; by using an inert metal they were eliminating the risk of deterioration over time, and by using a metal with the other inestimable advantage of being coveted and sought after everywhere they were eliminating the risk of place. There is no reason to believe that the fascination that gold has had for men over six thousand years will soon disappear or that it will cease to be a much prized store of value. But gold as a circulating medium of exchange is quite another matter, and the gold standard even more so.

The gold standard had the immense advantage of retaining the main merit which gold derives from its intrinsic value whilst eliminating its biggest defect, namely its rarity and its dependence on the vagaries of mine production. It is therefore not difficult to see why the system inspired and still inspires such respect. One can even understand the desire to recreate the gold standard system; it is harder to understand why people are so slow to recognise that the reintroduction of the gold standard, however desirable it may be, is impossible in practice because the very nature of the system, implying as it does a parallel circulation of paper and metal, also implies convertibility; that is, the option for the bearers of bank-notes to convert them at each and any moment into metal at a guaranteed rate. This is so because we can no longer do without bank money; no one, not even the late Jacques Rueff, recommends a return to a system of exclusive circulation of gold only. Consequently, we must also admit the need for convertibility, which is itself founded on a wager and a probability: the wager is that the holders of paper will not all come and ask for conversion at the same time, and if the system is to function properly the probability must be that they will not. This was the probability for more than 150 years, right up to 1914. It is no longer possible, in any country, because the situation has changed; the probability now is that at the slightest suspicion of trouble, all the holders of paper money would rush to convert it into a metal which has a genuine intrinsic value and which is certainly more reliable than a mere paper claim. This being so, the gold standard is finished. It is based on a form of confidence which it is in no one's power to recreate, because no one can eliminate from men's memories sixty years of their recent history.[1]

The real cause of the present paralysis *vis-à-vis* the monetary disorders of the world, the reason for the delay in the creation of a new system and the failure to make any rational progress, is a refusal to accept the truth, a stubborn preference for the past and defunct disciplines over the search for new doctrines and new paths, in a word, innovation. It is the fascination of the gold standard and its offspring, the Gold Exchange Standard, which is responsible for the limbo in which monetary thinking is stranded today. From conference to conference, from Bretton Woods in 1944 to the international meeting in Jamaica in January 1976 which finally confirmed the definitive abandonment of the gold standard, monetary history is nothing but a series of creaks and groans as the machinery of change reluctantly starts up, a system of pretences and compromises around a symbol which had become a myth and is now a mere chimera. Even after the official demise of the gold standard, which dates from 15 August 1971, when the United States abandoned convertibility, currencies and even the new Special Drawing Right (SDR) continued to be defined in terms of a weight of gold, although these definitions no longer had any relation to the real price of gold; gold had long since ceased to be used as a medium of exchange and convertibility had ceased to be guaranteed in any country.

The originality of the gold standard was that it complemented commodity money with claims on institutions and, in so doing, gave the economy the circulating medium it needed. Without this complement, economic growth would have been curbed, as it had been for centuries before, for lack of specie, a situation that was only partially alleviated by the debasements of various monarchs who clipped gold coins or arbitrarily altered their value in terms of units of account. At the same time convertibility tied down the purchasing power of money. The gold standard also had the property of guaranteeing internal monetary regulation through the velocity of money. Adjustment to a sudden influx of new money did not take place through a rise in prices but through a decrease in velocity, something which was less obvious to the public and sometimes rather brutal and liable to cause temporary crises. Internationally, gold had the great merit of constituting a currency common to all peoples, unhampered by frontiers and independent of the policies of individual countries.

The supposed regulatory powers of the gold standard in international trade are more open to criticism. The classical theory is well known: the deficit of the balance of payments is paid in gold and the metal flows into the banks of the country in surplus causing an increase in the money supply; this in turn causes a rise in prices which establishes a new trade equilibrium with other countries. It is a theory that no longer has any validity and is universally abandoned, except in certain university textbooks. Gold movements have many different causes and as many consequences, some of which can be dangerous. The inter-war period showed the dangerous aspect of these alternating transfers of gold, from central bank to central bank, and of the interventions by national authorities in order to slow down or accelerate them. On the other hand, it is beyond doubt that the gold standard imposed a healthy discipline on a government as regards the use of its privilege of issue.[2]

But these undoubted advantages were not purely fortuitous. The system could only work properly in very special conditions which happened to be brought about in the nineteenth country by a happy combination of circumstances. These were the discovery of new sources of supply and the subsequent opening of new gold mines in the United States, Brazil, Russia and South Africa, rapid growth in industrial production, social harmony and a kind of world central bank in the City of London. Thanks to these special conditions, the world was able to enjoy, for more than a century, the advantages of managed money and a more or less stable metallic standard of value.

The nostalgia for the gold standard and the refusal to admit that it is impossible to return to it have led over the years to irrational and bastard solutions to the problem, the Gold Exchange Standard being but one. Conceived in the immediate post-First World War period, it was intended to complement the ordinary gold standard in a restricted area of use, namely in the field of foreign trade, by substituting for gold fiat money, first sterling and the dollar together and then the dollar alone. The result was to confer on a national currency the role of key money and to make the economies of other states dependent on the internal policies of the United States. It was certainly a paradoxical solution to the problem to entrust the key to the gold standard system to a government which forbade its citizens to hold gold! No such paradox can last indefinitely; this one disappeared on 15 August 1971 when the dollar was declared inconvertible.

With the disappearance of the gold standard, other things have followed and the result has been to remove every vestige of discipline, to eliminate all the familiar landmarks and to open the doors to disorder of all kinds: the balancing of the budget, the defence of fixed exchange rate, the adjustment of the balance of payments — all these things imposed certain restraints and constituted useful safety devices for both governments and the governed. The budget is no longer anything but a tool which is allowed to go into deficit in order to stimulate the economy; exchange rates have become flexible in order to 'obey the law of the market'; international finance, both public and private, happily bridges the trade gaps of all countries, developed and undeveloped alike. But nature is not alone in abhorring a vacuum; societies do too. This is why, now that the vacuum is recognised and that governments are aware of it, they are turning, in spite of uncertainties and inaccuracies, towards other systems and other disciplines, and in particular towards the regulation and control of those monetary units which, potentially or effectively, constitute the means of payment.

NOTES

[1] 'The economic agent is not "in the market". He is not a choice of inputs and outputs in the neutral space of traded goods and services. His decision making is a function of the variables of memory and the variables of planning. It therefore cannot be completely expressed by a hereditary system, nor be assumed to be subject to an inexorable mechanism imposed from outside.' François Perroux, IESA, *Economie appliquée*, vol. XXVI.

[2] In 1814, David Ricardo wrote:

Experience shows that whenever governments or banks have had unlimited power to issue paper money they have always abused that power. It follows that in all countries it is necessary to restrict the issue of paper money and subject it to control; and no means seems more suitable to prevent the abuse of this issue than to oblige all banks that issue paper money to pay their notes in gold coins or in bullion.

Principles of political economy and taxation.

2 Monetarists and monetarians

Monetarists should not be confused with 'monetarians'. The former are those who study the way money works, the way it is created, the way it circulates, the way it is destroyed and its role in trade. They attempt to understand, to analyse and to explain — objectively. The 'monetarians', as I shall call them, are those who take sides and abandon their detachment; they believe in money as an instrument for the control and regulation of the economy; they argue that by regulating the creation of money and the way it circulates governments can achieve their main economic and even political aims.[1] (1)

Economists are very fond of these classifications. There are Keynesians and anti-Keynesians, quantitativists and anti-quantitatavists, Philippsists and anti-Philippsists (those who do and do not believe in the Philipps curve); there are fiscalists and anti-fiscalists, floaters and anti-floaters (as regards exchange rates . . .), auriphiles and auriphobes, 'costists' and 'demandists' (those who believe in inflation as being caused by costs or by demand . . . .); and finally, of course, there are the Marxists who would reconcile everybody by eliminating the free play of market forces altogether.

The undisputed leader of the monetarians is Milton Friedman. This brilliant man has managed, by the mere force of his convictions and his dialectical powers, to obtain acceptance for a fundamental concept: the concept of the money supply, both as a basic economic indicator and even, in the eyes of some of his disciples, as the principal instrument of regulation of the economy. In its edition of 2 July 1977, *The Economist* headed an article on the British economy 'All monetarists now?' and went on to say:

Five of the world's big seven economies now publicly practise monetary targetry. Two of them, France and Britain, have joined the club only in the past year. Even the OECD, bastion of demand management, gave its cautious seal of approval to the technique of announced targets for the growth of money supply after meeting in ministerial conclave last week. Revelation? A truce between Keynesians and monetarists? Fashion? Or desperation?

All four. Monetary targets have become the preferred economic lever of new conventional wisdom for several reasons.

Fast growth in money supplies . . . was followed by inflation in 1973–5.

Fiscal policy, in 1973–5, looked powerless . . . meanwhile interest rates, the conventional indicator of the stance of monetary policy, had begun to respond misleadingly . . .

The article goes on to say that the policy of control of the money supply is that of the hard currency countries, those that have managed to contain inflation and keep up employment.

This article reflects a genuinely new development.[2] It also illustrates a generalised confusion between the role of monetary indicators and the use of money as an instrument. The success that the monetarist doctrine has enjoyed in recent years must be attributed to the immense vacuum left behind by the disappearance of the gold standard. A monetary system cannot exist without a regulator. In its absence, the system becomes a 'non-system' and this is the description given to the world monetary system today. But such a system cannot last because the nature of man, the very essence of civilisation, is to create political, social and economic structures defining mutual rights and obligations.

For centuries, as we have seen, the prevalent system was that of metallic money. Then, up to the First World War, there existed the system derived from it, the gold standard system, after which, for more than sixty years, attempts were made, consciously or unconsciously, firstly to restore the gold standard and then to find substitutes for it. In the end, its demise had to be accepted with resignation and new disciplines sought elsewhere. But we are only at the beginning of this great change. Its first steps are uncertain; in some countries the experts are hardly aware of it and the public is quite ignorant of it; but the process of change is in motion.

The great merit of Milton Friedman is that he has proposed a different idea from the traditional one of money as an IOU for some commodity or other and another economic indicator than gold reserves, gold backing or interest rates. In 1973 in a book called *La vraie nature de la monnaie* I wrote:

No form of regulation of the means of payment has the slightest chance

of succeeding so long as the money supply has not been taken as an
essential indicator and, within this supply, the various instruments that
circulate, are used in trade and, taken together, give some idea of
demand as compared with supply.

One can better appreciate the services that such an indicator can
perform by looking at another, the GNP. The way it is assessed and the
uses to which it is put should guide us. The GNP dates from before the
last war, but its introduction into the management of the economy
only became generalised with the introduction of the National Plan.
The GNP incorporates all the goods and services produced by the
nation. Its rate of growth has become a fundamental element of
economic policy and it acts at one and the same time as a guide and a
landmark. The Plan, by making the growth of the GNP a fundamental
test, has earned the gratitude of those who have not forgotten the
sterility and impotence of the inter-war period.

But the GNP has another merit, that of being precise and self-
consistent. Starting from a target rate of growth in production derived
from a series of successive approximations, the matrix calculations of
the various committees make it possible to determine needs and
activity, sector by sector. I want to emphasise the example of the
GNP because the need that was felt for it and the reasoning that led to
it apply also in the case of money. The money supply is also an
aggregate that is still only partially defined, the components of which,
like the components of the GNP, are difficult to describe precisely. In
spite of these uncertainties the money supply is a parameter of
economic life and the adjustment and regulation of it are of the first
importance. But a proper understanding of the money supply
presupposes an improvement in statistical information . . .

At the time these lines were written, the French government was still
affirming its faith in the gold standard and its desire to see it brought back.
We had to wait for the arrival of a distinguished economist, Mr Raymond
Barre, at the head of the French government, to see the money supply
become an objective of policy, just like the GNP. Here is what Professor
Alphandéry said in an article in *Le Monde* of 27 September 1977 entitled
'A courageous turning in monetary policy':

The radical change in the doctrine on which French monetary policy
has been based since the war is one of the least understood aspects of
the Barre Plan, though it is certainly one of the most important. . . The
policy pursued since the war has been characterised by the deliberate

desire to provide cheap money for the economy . . . It is not difficult
to show that this policy tends to encourage inflation and that it is
probably the primary source of inflation in France . . .

This is no longer the case today because the French government
bravely changed the direction of its monetary policy in December
1976. Following the example of Germany, the United States and
Switzerland, it decided to couch its monetary policy in quantitativist
terms and not in terms of interest rates. It undertook to confine the
increase in the money supply in 1977 to 12.5 per cent. The government
has chosen a modern monetary policy in harmony with modern
economic theory.

As is often the case with an innovator, Milton Friedman has tried to
take his theories further and use his 'discovery' of the money supply for
wider and more ambitious purposes. In this way, he has ceased to be a
monetarist and has become a monetarian.

According to Friedman, the limitation of the growth in the money
supply to a fixed rate—he suggests 5—6 per cent annually—would be both
the principle and the instrument of a liberal economic policy which would
'automatically' achieve the twin objectives of a stable currency and steady
growth in the economy. In order to understand Milton Friedman's ideas, it
is important to remember that he is not only a great monetarist but also an
ardent defender and a formidable theoretician of liberalism, one might
even say of 'extremist' liberalism. In the eyes of a genuine liberal, the
quantity of money in circulation should not be at the discretion of
governments, who are too often tempted to resort to the 'printing press' to
solve their problems. Automatic systems which protect public finances
from demagogues and the weakness of politicians are thus to be preferred
to systems that rely on human discretion. This is the role of the growth of
the money supply.

In reality, however, monetary regulation is never completely automatic;
it is always more or less 'manual' because it results from decisions taken by
the authorities and the public, the government and the governed. It would
be better to admit as much rather than hide behind a false sense of
security. The mistrust with which the guardians of the public purse, and
with them the liberals, look upon politicians is understandable. The
severity, and indeed austerity, of public servants is not without a certain
grandeur; their rigour is often necessary to provide a counterweight to the
fatal tendency of politicans to seek the easy way out of a problem.
Nevertheless, it remains true that outmoded mechanisms which delude the
public make the task more difficult and the outcome less certain. It would

be better not to give too easy an alibi to those who are in power and admit openly that the so-called automatic mechanisms do not work, or that they work in reverse, and that automaticity must be replaced by some more deliberate policy. But even a policy of deliberate intervention cannot do without rules, guidelines and doctrines; this is why, whether one inclines towards the interventionist or the automatist view, two of Friedman's main ideas are worth looking into: the notion of the objective of a steady monetary growth and the notion of money as an instrument of downstream control of the money supply.

In order to grasp the basic ideas better, we should distinguish the two main themes of Friedman's theory. First he proposes a fixed growth rate of the money supply as an essential indicator, if not as an objective in itself. This idea is widely accepted nowadays; it has been sucked into the vacuum created by the disappearance of the gold standard. Milton Friedman's other thesis is more debatable:[3] should we and can we regulate the addition of new money to the economy so as to keep the growth in the money supply within immutable, pre-established bounds? The classic image always quoted here is that of the doctor who advises a patient to lose weight and, instead of forbidding him certain foods and urging him to get more exercise, prescribes that he should wear tight clothing and not be allowed to slacken his belt. The patient consequently runs the risk of stifling; more probably, he will split his clothes at the seams and burst his belt and perhaps his braces too! There is no doubt that regulation of the money supply downstream by means of an invariable rate of money-supply growth may very well strangle production. This happens, for example, when the price rise has an exogenous cause, other than the addition of new money to the money supply.

The analysis carried out in the chapter dealing with reduction gives an almost mathematical demonstration of the truth of this, and experience confirms it. In the spring of 1968, during a dramatic meeting with union leaders, the then prime minister, Mr Georges Pompidou, granted an overall wage rise of 14 per cent. He really had no alternative; the entire economic life of the country was paralysed. Once the so-called 'Matignon Agreements' had been signed, the trains began to run again, the shops opened and everything returned to normal. Within a few months production had more than made up the losses of the two months of strikes and disorders.

Once order had been restored through the wage rises, the return to prosperity was due to the wisdom of the finance minister, Mr. François-Xavier Ortoli, who turned on the money tap in order to adapt the money supply to the new price level. He deserved some praise for so doing because all the high priests of traditional finance, the guardians of orthodoxy, were all talking about the need to 'mop up liquidity' and prevent the creation of 'false claims'. How could Mr Ortoli's policy have been reconciled with a regulation constant growth of the money supply?[4]

In support of Milton Friedman, however, we ought to admit that, in certain circumstances, a downstream curb may produce a salutary effect upstream: a businessman will be less inclined to yield to excessive wage demands if his banker is unwilling to give him more credit. It can also be argued that the patient whose doctor trusts to tight clothing as a remedy will be less inclined to eat in order to be able to carry on wearing the clothes. This is perhaps true in certain cases, but then it is a more or less accidental secondary effect. On the other hand, the Friedmanites are right to maintain that an excessive increase in the money stock, by inflating demand, can be considered directly responsible for a rise in prices. In this case it is not a secondary effect but a primary effect.

The only conclusion we can draw from this is that the mechanisms in question are complicated and subject to reactions and inter-reactions which are entangled with psychological effects, anticipatory effects, sectoral influences and other factors and that in such matters it is very imprudent to try to be too systematic. But let us try to summarise the points on which there is a certain consensus:

(i) It must be admitted that an excessive increase in the money supply causes a rise in prices and that an insufficient increase can curb economic activity. There ought, therefore, to be an optimum growth rate, but in the present state of knowledge we cannot accurately calculate it, much less get people to respect it.

(ii) We nevertheless need reliable monetary indicators, which are to the flow of money what the GNP is to activity and production. It is possible to calculate them and interpret them properly.

(iii) The growth of the money stock should be monitored and subjected to 'regulation'.

After this, however, differences of opinion arise.[5] (1) Some people opt for upstream regulation, such as prices and incomes policies, others for downstream regulation, which, if necessary, will include credit control. There are also those who prefer a purely automatic regulation and an adjustment of needs to available money according to the level of activity, by means of the discount rate, ultimate arbiter of the distribution of credit.[6] If we wish to make progress in this field we must begin at the beginning and understand the way the monetary mechanisms work, by analysing them carefully. Only then can we hope to create reliable indicators, mechanisms for intervention and guidelines for action.

NOTES

[1] Monetarism' is usually seen as an economic 'system' opposed to
other 'systems'. It is therefore proposed in place of 'Keynesianism',
'Budgetism', 'Consumerism', etc.
I must say that I have some difficulty in grasping these 'systems'.
Happily, however, that is not the aim of this book. From our point of
view, monetarism is only the study of a mechanism, the mechanism of
money. Medicine, like economics, can be divided into several disciplines.
In economics, there are perhaps even more disciplines. They are all valid
objects of study, which does not necessarily imply any striking of
attitudes or creation of 'systems'. Why should it be otherwise with
'monetarism', one of the most important departments of economics?
It seems to me that it is in this sense that the very interesting text
by Serge-Christophe Kolm on monetarism (see page 192) should be read.
[2] 'It is not surprising that monetary policy should have been long
regarded with hostility and that even now it should often be suspected of
being, to say the least, less than efficacious. Post-Keynesian economics,
concerned much more with the explanation of the economy in terms of
its simple physical elements, naturally directed policy towards control
of incomes, expenditure, salaries and taxes. At the most, monetary policy
remained an escape and almost a diversion for thinkers and political
parties who were frightened by the idea of economic organisation and
planning.'
Valéry Giscard d'Estaing, preface to *Monnaie et financement* by Jean
Denizet (Editions Dunod).
[3] 'The authorities may aim at not letting the money supply vary
excessively from a growth rate defined in terms of long-term development
aims. This is rather what the position of French planners is when they
consider the growth rate of the money supply as a "warning light". But
the difficulty is to define these guidelines and safety devices.' Sylviane
Guillaumont Jeanneney, *Politique monétaire et croissance économique en
France* (Editions Armand Colin).
[4] 'It is absurd to let wages and salaries rise by a rate several times greater
than the increase in productivity and then try to fight the resulting
inflation by raising interest rates and applying credit controls. The decline
in liquidity in the economy will then coincide with a rise in companies'
cash needs. . .
It is also absurd to let the external current account balance of payments
deteriorate and then try to make up for it by attracting foreign capital
through a policy of keeping interest rates higher than is compatible with
the internal balance of the capital markets. If interest rates are too high,
investments are inhibited and production costs are increased, and capital
flows attracted by this device are generally extremely unstable . . . '
Jean Marczewski, *Vaincre l'inflation et le chômage* (Editions
Economica).
[5] No real progress in economic policy can be made so long as there is no
general consensus on monetary policy, which is the heart of economic

policy. This is what constitutes the main interest of the thesis put forward by Emil-Maria Claassen and Pascal Salin in their book *L'Occident en désarroi, turbulence d'une économie prospère* (Editions Dunod) to which F. Boyer de la Gironday, J. Garello, H. G. Johnson, N. Krul, A. Lindbeck, R. McKinnon and D. Pilisi have also contributed). Some remarks on this matter will be found on page 193.

[6] This was the late Jacques Rueff's point of view. Coming as it does from one of the best known defenders of economic orthodoxy and the salutary disciplines of the gold standard, this attitude may appear surprising, since it seems to open the door to an unbridled creation of money. The reason seems to me to be the fact that Rueff overlooked bank clearings. Before clearing became a generalised banking technique, banks usually functioned (contrary to what the textbooks say) as non-monetary intermediaries. They certainly lent a more or less large proportion of the funds they received on deposit, but a payment made by a depositor using a cheque or a payment order was *ultimately* paid in central bank money, and not, as is the case today, largely by means of mutually clearing claims on the banks themselves. It was, therefore, reasonable to suppose that the central bank had control of the circulation of money (as regards volume, if not velocity) since the money it had issued was the ultimate payment instrument.

3 The uncertainties of monetary regulation

Now that the inevitability of the regulation of the money supply and the government's responsibilities in the matter are no longer in doubt, the poverty of the means at the government's disposal, the vagueness of the indicators and the defectiveness of the available instruments have all become apparent; proof, if further proof is needed, of the uncertain state of knowledge on these matters.

> We cannot identify within the mass of money transactions the respective roles played by the quantity of money and prices, nor can we distinguish in the mass of payments the role of money from that of its velocity of circulation so that we have no short-term stability, largely because of the volatility of the monetary behaviour of banks, companies, households and foreign holders of francs. . . It is because of our ignorance of these matters that the Monetarist School teaches, with some justification, that monetary policy should never be adjusted in the short term to fit the short-term economic situation. . . But if this advice, like advice urging that the budget should be balanced, is not lacking in practical virtues for our political and monetary masters, it indicates the limits of our knowledge of monetary mechanisms. . . Which way should we move in order go beyond this purely pragmatic approach?[1]

This quotation takes us right to the heart of the problem of monetary regulation.[2] What we generally call 'regulation' is the adjustment process by which an organism adapts to changing circumstances. All organisms that are not completely static have such mechanisms. Problems of regulation arise, for instance, in industry, biology, sociology and also in monetary matters. The process may be spontaneous and natural, that is it may be triggered off by the phenomenon on which it acts; or, on the contrary, it may be deliberate and result from conscious decisions which anticipate what is likely to happen or which try, retrospectively, to correct their effects. Knowledge of the way regulation works is essential for anyone who wishes to be in control of a process. Choices of methods, instruments and decisions all depend on it. The goal at which we should aim, in the conduct of public or private affairs, should be that of substituting for natural regulation, which is sometimes harmful and often brutal, a form of deliberate, planned regulation which would prevent the unpleasant aspects of a process of natural adjustment.

A system of regulation should make it possible to transmit orders efficiently; it should be gradual and it should obey specific laws, a necessary condition if the effect produced is to be predictable and renewable. The controls should be selective and the response should be rapid and reliable. Unfortunately, present-day monetary regulation does not comply with these requirements. The instruments used are mere makeshifts, most usually turned to purposes for which they were not intended; the response is irregular and uncertain and the secondary effects are unpredictable. Sterilising banks' reserves in order to control their powers of monetary creation constitutes a good example. Freezing part of a bank's liquidities in central bank money aims to lower the illiquidity threshold and thus diminish the quantity of liabilities that it can take on, and consequently the amount of money it can create.[3](1) Banks rely on the probability that their depositors will not all withdraw their deposits at the same time, and that actual drawings will not exceed the liquid or semi-liquid reserves that they keep. A system like this, which is based on the dispositions and whims of the public, is bound to be precarious. The chain reaction that a bank failure might set off would have incalculable consequences, which explains why, though on the one hand the monetary authorities deliberately increase the risk of illiquidity, on the other they will not hesitate to take steps to remedy it in the event that it should materialise. It is irrational to base a system of discipline on such an aggravation of the risks.[4] The erection of a high voltage wire which threatens the imprudent with electrocution in order to bar access to a precipice merely causes potential trespassers to look for ways of getting round it, and at the same time imposes on the owner of the land the moral obligation to provide help. This is what has in fact happened: national and international money markets and mutual support agreements amongst the banks have brought the banks closer to the well known textbook example of a banking system with only one bank, which can create as much money as it likes without any risk. The central banks, for their part, are obliged to keep a watchful eye on the banking system and be prepared to intervene as lenders of last resort.

There are other, subtler instruments of regulation than increasing risks, but they muddle just as much, if not more, the orders from the authorities. This is true of bank refinancing, the cost of which is controlled by the central bank through the rediscount rate and through purchases and sales of government paper and bills on the money markets. By raising its rediscount rate, the central bank causes interest rates on the markets to rise, which increases borrowing costs for a bank, but also increases its income because the rate it charges on the loans it makes to its customers rises at the same time as the rediscount rate and the money market rate. A policy like this, based on the manipulation of interest rates, is so full of contradictions that one wonders how anyone can trust to it. The logic of such a policy leads, in France at least, to exclusively restrictive measures.[5] (1) Thus, the inflow of foreign money consequent on a balance of payments surplus causes an inflation of internal liquidities through sales to the central bank, which justifies restrictive measures designed to slow down the inflationary tendencies that result from an excessive quantity of new money. But the resulting interest rate rise causes foreign money to be sucked in even more, and increases still further the balance of payments surplus. In the case of an outflow of funds, the defence of the exchange rate also causes a rise in interest rates so that foreign capital is attracted or retained. Domestically, these interest rate variations inevitably have harmful repercussions: is it reasonable that a young couple who are borrowing in order to buy a house should suffer the consequences of a forward market discount because of international speculation on the Deutschemark?

To the imperfections of the regulatory instruments we should add the deficiencies of the indicators and the faulty interpretation of the lessons they teach. The consequence may be the kind of 'monetary accident' described by *The Economist* in its edition of 3 May 1975, in a discussion of British monetary policy between 1971 and 1974. The situation was as follows. In November and December 1972, the authorities began to be alarmed by the growth in the money supply. New compulsory deposit requirements were imposed. The two indicators of the money supply had begun to diverge: M1 (notes and current account deposits) had begun to grow much more slowly than M3, which includes, in addition, time deposits and negotiable certificates of deposit. But M3 was the wrong indicator at that time because it was distorted by large scale arbitrage operations. In fact, the money supply, properly understood, was not growing so fast. At the end of 1973, the monetary authorities nevertheless continued to ignore the evidence of M1 and insisted on tightening interest rates. Everything gave in November, and made the crisis inevitable. Credit control had been too efficient. The rise in interest rates had achieved its aim, but very few people realised that it was M3 that had caused the mistake. The result was too abrupt an application of the brake to the economy and a serious banking crisis.

This monetary accident is worth looking at closely, because it highlights some worrying and harmful weaknesses in the interpretation of the basic monetary indicators. What exactly had happened? M3, for which the authorities had prescribed a fixed growth rate, includes, as *The Economist* reminds us, certificates of deposit, whereas M1 only includes payment money (current accounts and notes).[6] Monetary regulation was concentrated on M3, but the borrowers and the bankers were oblivious of M3; they were following their own policies. It was obviously in the borrowers' interests to take out overdrafts and convert the money thus obtained into certificates of deposit, for which the interest rate paid by the banks was higher than the rate they were charged on their overdraft! This was the inevitable consequence of the banks' obsessive desire to 'remain liquid'. The result was a gradual inflation of banks' long-term liabilities and corresponding claims, whilst the reserve requirements on the deposits also grew, thus diminishing the quantity of central bank money available to the banking system. As a corollary, the amount of money available for lending diminished, whilst the competition amongst the banks for deposits and the needs of the public borrowing requirement caused a spectacular disruption of interest rates. This monetary accident had a pernicious effect on economic activity and prices. If the authorities' understanding of banking and monetary mechanisms had been better they could probably have prevented it.

In the United States it is M1 that is called into question. The reason why M2, which also includes savings deposits, is preferred, is that companies are now allowed to open interest-bearing savings accounts, which results in transfers from their current accounts, which bear no interest, to their savings accounts, and a consequent diminution of M1 without a corresponding fall in the total volume of transactions. The companies draw on their savings accounts instead of drawing on their current accounts when they want to make payments, which causes an increase in the velocity of money.[7] It is well known that the velocity of money takes on two forms: income velocity and transaction velocity. The first is the ratio of the GNP to the money supply, M1 generally. It is a simple statistical coefficient which indicates the number of times that the money supply is 'turned over' in order to 'produce' the GNP. The second, the transaction velocity, gets closer to the nature of money in its role of medium of exchange. It is defined as the number of transactions, i.e. changes of hands, in which a unit of money participates during a specified period, which is then annualised. On page 197 some details of the statistical techniques used by the Bank of France in its calculations of the velocity of money are given.(1)

In the United States, the transaction velocity only registers movements in bank current accounts measured in terms of the ratio of debits on these accounts to average credit balances during the period under investigation. A representative number of banks are asked to provide the statistical information. The graphs on page 201 give the changes in transaction and income velocity of M1 for the years 1919 to 1968. More recent graphs give, in percentages, the accelerations and decelerations, i.e. the changes in the income velocity, of the various indicators: V1 for M1, V2 for M2, V3 for M3. etc.

One of the first things we can conclude from an examination of these graphs is that the income velocity of M1 grows at a regular annual rate of 3 per cent. This can easily be explained in terms of a gradual improvement of transfer techniques and more efficient management of their cash resources by companies, who reduce their liquidities in favour of interest-bearing accounts. A second conclusion is that it is important to take account of the growth rate of the income velocity of M1, which reaches more than 1/5 of the rate to which the monetary authorities claim to keep the increase in the M1 monetary liquidities, which implies that a policy of control of the growth of the money supply should take account of the velocity of money. Another point to note is the long-term stability of V2, which explains why certain monetary experts prefer to concentrate on M2.

In 1975, when the Fed., yielding to the pressure—or, as some would put it, the fashion – of monetarism, adopted the policy of 'targetry' or the choice of a conscious target for money supply growth, it chose 7.5 per cent for M1, a rate which took due account of the expected rapid acceleration of the velocity. This rate was severely criticised by certain experts, whose econometric models predicted a slowing down of velocity and not an acceleration, largely because of the fall in interest rates. But the experts were wrong. The velocity of M1 increased by 8.8 per cent in a year, i.e. 3.2 per cent more than the rate observed during a comparable period of emergence from recession. The error of calculation in the model was equivalent to 20,000 million dollars! In the light of such things, it is understandable that a stabler aggregate than M1 should be chosen for the 'targetry'—hence the choice of M2. Nevertheless, the fact remains that M2 can only be justified as an intermediate target if it can be shown, empirically or by means of pure reasoning, that there is a constant correlation between the growth rate of M2 and economic activity and prices. In the present state of knowledge it would be extremely risky to prefer one indicator rather than another. All that can be said is that they should be properly interpreted.[8](1)

Monetary regulation can only be a manual system, which is precisely how those who are responsible for it understand it, and they make a sharp distinction between

indicator statistics,
intervention techniques,
intermediate targets,
final objectives.

A lorry driver checks the instruments on his dashboard; the speedometer, oil pressure gauge and thermometer are all *indicators*. The *intervention technique* which he uses consists of affecting the supply of petrol to the carburettor by applying more or less force to the accelerator pedal. The *intermediate target* is the speed of the vehicle. The *final objective* is to transport a certain quantity of goods from *A* to *B* in a given period of time.

In the case of the monetary regulator, the indicators are M1, M2 and M3, and their various velocities. The intermediate targets are, in the case of the Germans,(2) the monetary base, M0 (notes, to which banks' liquid reserves are added); whilst for the monetary authorities of the United States it is M2, and for Britain it is M0, complemented by external account balances. The intervention techniques are open-market operations, the rediscount rate at the central bank, freezing of a part of the reserves, in the case of the French authorities, and fixing a ceiling on new credits in the case of credit control. The final objectives are economic activity, measured in terms of GNP growth and prices, measured by the indices. If the intermediate targets, the intervention techniques and even some definitions of the indicators differ from one country to another, *the ultimate aim*, nevertheless, remains the same, namely the control of economic activity as measured by the growth of the GNP, and the price level as measured by the index numbers. This is what one might call the 'monetary effect'.

One article, amongst many others, in the *International Herald Tribune* of 22 August 1977, shows how the question of the money supply in the United States has ceased to be just a matter of economic theory and has become instead a subject of everyday discussion.

The Fed. is trying to put the clamps back on the money supply. . . At

the regular monthly meeting on 19 July, the twelve-member Open
Market Committee decided that the money supply should grow within
a 3.5–5.7 per cent annual range in July and August. By 4 August,
according to the minutes, it had become apparent that the money
supply had exploded and had grown in July at an annual rate of 18.5
per cent. Immediately, the members of the committee decided to
apply the brakes. But opinions were divided as to the cause of this
explosion of the money supply.

Every week, the Federal Reserve Board publishes the latest figures for
M1, M2, M3 etc. In some people's eyes, M1 is not growing fast enough;
for others, it is exploding.[9](1) The problems of monetary regulation are
nowhere more obvious to the observer than in the United States; nowhere
do people trust more willingly to the money supply to deal with those
fearful maladies, unemployment and inflation, which are gnawing away at
the vitals of modern economies. This is the reason why the man in charge
of monetary regulation, the chairman of the Federal Reserve Board, is
always in the news. Constitutionally irremovable and appointed for four
years, this regulator-in-chief implements a policy which is not necessarily
that of the President, or even of Congress.
      Differences of opinion generally concern the choice of growth rate for
the money supply. Some people maintain that an excessively restrictive
policy on the part of the Fed. throttles activity, hinders expansion
and prevents a return to prosperity, and that economic activity needs
more money in order to compensate for the decline in the purchasing
power of the dollar. In the opinion of others, however, the growth in
the money supply is too fast, and feeds inflation by excessively inflating
demand. It is here that the question of interest rates comes in.[10] In order
to soak up liquidities, the executive committee of the Federal Reserve
Board is obliged to sell through the Federal Reserve Banks state funds
(Fed. funds), which act as a reserve for the commercial banks. The result
is a rise in money market interest rates. This rise in rates has
repercussions on credit and curbs an already feeble investment rate. It
also hinders the Treasury in its recourse to the financial markets, which
is forced on it by the enormous budget deficit. On the other hand, it is
in line with the policy of defence of the dollar on the exchange markets
(which does not, however, stop it weakening). An expansionary, not to
say, inflationary, policy would consist of buying up Fed. funds so as to
inject new money into the economy and thus lower interest rates, and
help the Treasury.(2)
      The confusion in which monetary policy is floundering means that

people do not merely not know what it ought to be — they don't even know what it is. As *Business Week* remarks in its 7 November 1977 issue:

> During the last six months, short-term rates have risen by two percentage points, enough to stop the recovery, whilst at the same time the money supply has increased by 9.7 per cent, a rate likely to seriously aggravate inflation and well beyond the upper limit of the margin chosen by the Fed. (6.5 per cent). The use of the money base in order to control monetary creation and, indirectly, economic development, presents two potentially serious difficulties. On the one hand, the relationship between the growth of the base and the money supply is not very stable, and on the other a policy concerned exclusively with controlling the money base risks leading to an intolerable and dangerous instability of short-term interest rates.

The Fed. admits that there is something artificial about this policy, which is supposed to ensure prosperity and contain inflation through manipulation of the money supply. It is no more capable than any other monetary authority of dictating the behaviour of the public, or correcting the sluggishness with which the economy reacts to stimulation or efforts to curb activity. We have already seen, in the chapter on Reduction, that the effects of a creation or destruction of money took months, perhaps even years, to work their way through the system. A stop–go policy, at the mercy of public opinion and dependent on weekly statistics, is inefficient and dangerous. The table of monthly variations in the money supply in the United States, given on page 148 demonstrates this.

In an article published in *Le Monde* on 8 December 1977, Paul Fabra shows up the dilemma of monetary regulation carried out through the manipulation of the money supply:[11]

> The money supply is not an immediate datum of the economy: it is invented by statisticians, who are obliged, in order to produce a more or less coherent series of statistics from month to month, to make a certain number of adjustments to allow for variations in the velocity of money, etc. . . . These variations, or corrections, represent something like 30 or 40 per cent of the final figure. To found an economic policy on fluctuations which can be more justly said to be 'reconstructed' than real, is reminiscent of the sterile games of those who, not so long ago, used, in all seriousness, to think that economic policy consisted in choosing between a growth rate of 6 per cent and

one of 7 per cent because the 1 per cent difference was smaller than the margin of error!

As far as indicators, and more particularly monetary indicators, are concerned, various problems arise. First of all, there is the question of the unpredictability of the phenomena under examination, an unpredictability which makes it impossible to draw any firm conclusions in the short term. At certain times of year, for example during holidays, when taxes fall due and when rents have to be paid, the demand for money and the velocity of circulation increase, which leads the statisticians to make seasonal corrections of doubtful validity. Another problem is the *accuracy* of the data: some are known very accurately, such as the total quantity of notes that have left the presses of the Bank of France, corrected to allow for losses. This could also be true of other components, such as deposits, since the authorities are in a position to compel banks to reveal details of their figures. Others are less certain, for example the velocity of circulation of money. It is only necessary to compare the total number of debits in a given period with the total positive balance in order to find out the velocity of circulation of deposits. But this does not mean that each economic agent can be ordered to give precise information on his payments and receipts in cash.[12]

Uncertainties regarding the *definitions* are of another kind, but just as troublesome. Thus, in the United States, the income velocity, or ratio of the GNP to the money supply, registers on the numerator the contributions to the GNP which are of federal origin, whereas M1 excludes government deposits. The experts never stop arguing about it but they can never agree. Ignorance regarding the *uses* to which money is put is even more serious: the *monetary effect* is different according to the nature of the operation to which the transaction is applied. The conversion of final production into consumption, such as the purchase of a car, has a different effect from the purchase of a second-hand car or a transfer from account to account, but both are counted as identical transactions.[13]

But there remains an even more intractable problem: how should we interpret the figures and what should we deduce from them? That is the heart of the matter. Almost all the other problems are soluble: definitions can be agreed on, more or less accurate figures can be arrived at by means of polls, surveys and systematic collection of statistics. But what lessons can be learnt from this? How is one to interpret these data? It is a major misfortune of our times that the management of money should be plunged into such uncertainty. The annual reports of the central banks of the world reflect this uncertainty and the annual report of the Bank for International Settlements sums it up:

> As regards the monetary norms and their application, although the authorities are in fairly broad agreement on the long-term inflationary consequences of excessive monetary expansion, they diverge considerably in their fundamental ideas regarding the nature of money, not to mention the extent to which they do in fact control the circulation of money.

The state and the banking system share the responsibility of creating new money. As regards the creation of money by the state, everything, or almost everything, has been said. Its power of monetary creation, with some exceptions, is obvious to everyone. Thus, through the mechanism of open-market operations, the state can obtain short-term money, whilst at the same time apparently respecting the rules of strict financial orthodoxy. The Treasury issues bills which the banks buy and which they then discount against central bank money at the Bank of France. Everybody is happy: the Treasury has been able to tap the market; the banks have improved their liquidity ratios; on the asset side of the Bank of France's balance sheet there is a solid asset to balance the new money on the liability side. As for the 'printing press', it is not used in the case of loans to the state, which proves once again the necessity of subsuming within the same quantity of money all genuine instruments of whatever origin and making this quantity the essential indicator for monetary policy. Whatever one thinks about inflation, 'stagflation', and the merits of budgetary and fiscal policy, one cannot deny that monetary creation ought to be controlled, and no longer left to chance and the whims of economic agents. Throughout history, the sovereign has always claimed the prerogative of the issue of money. No one doubts this; even the ultra-liberals accept it and merely recommend external restraints, such as may counteract the effects of a policy designed to go no further than the next elections. This privilege is nowadays delegated by the state to the banking system, which creates the lion's share of new money (two-thirds of the total of M1). Bankers prefer not to talk about their power of monetary creation and the public is largely unaware of it. It nevertheless remains true that there can be no monetary regulation without the exercise of some control by the state over the use which the banking system makes of the privilege that has been delegated to it. Apropos of this, the national authorities in various countries differ, as regards both the choice of instruments and their efficacity. According to Mr Renaud

The essence of monetary regulation is control of the mass of means of payment, which presupposes that the particular monetary aggregate that is to be regulated should be precisely defined and that the right monetary indicator should be selected.

By choosing an indicator that included all bank deposits (M3) and consequently confused units with the full payment function with those that had none, in 1974 the authorities in the United Kingdom allowed M1 to shrink dangerously, causing, in the opinion of *The Economist*, a serious liquidity crisis.

This accident serves as an illustration of the prevailing confusion with regard to the meaning and interpretation of the monetary indicators. It is a grave mistake to confuse within the same definition units of money that can be used directly to effect payments with those that cannot. It is another, equally grave, error to take as a criterion of what is money and what is not the 'liquidity quotient' of an asset. Those units of money that have a direct transaction function (M1), the monetary features of which are volume, velocity and the extent to which they cause the conversion of production into consumption or investment, should be rigorously distinguished from those units that can only be classified in terms of their potential effects on M1, its volume and velocity.

A MONETARY ACCIDENT IN THE UNITED KINGDOM

Graph showing the divergence between M1 and M3 at the beginning of 1972.

First half 1969 = 100

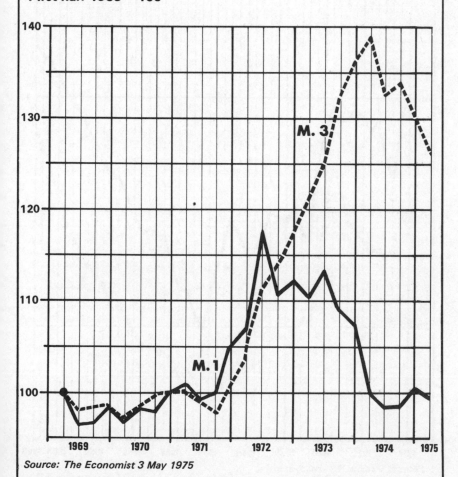

Source: *The Economist 3 May 1975*

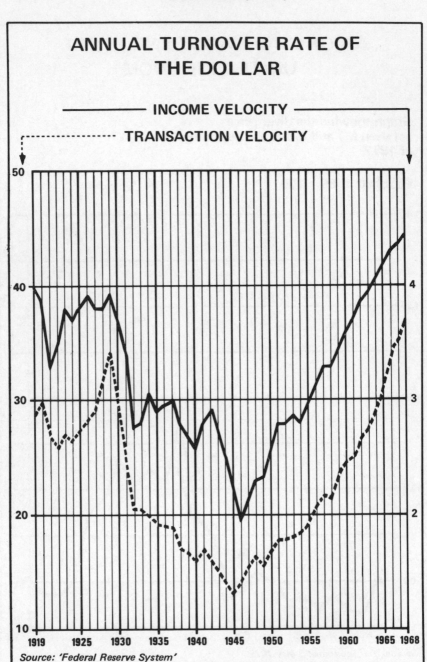

ANNUAL TURNOVER RATE OF THE DOLLAR

—— INCOME VELOCITY ——

---------- TRANSACTION VELOCITY

Source: 'Federal Reserve System'

de la Genière, deputy governor of the Bank of France: 'With the instruments at our disposal at present we can more or less control the growth of the money supply in the medium term. We have the means to regulate, according to our taste, the different counterparts of this quantity of money.' He then goes on to say: 'but is what we are doing correct from the point of view of monetary policy? People may consider that it is either too lax or too restrictive. . . .'

The principal means of regulation of the money supply in France today is credit control. The other instruments already mentioned, such as freezing of reserves, money market intervention, etc., are not considered efficient enough. J. H. David explains to us that the effect of these indirect measures is very different, according to the country, and the way its banking system is organised. Thus, in France, freezing reserves has different effects according as the banks get their resources from the money markets (some banks refinance in this way 90 per cent of the loans that they make) or from customers' deposits. The bank money created by the former ends up as deposits at the latter. What is known in professional jargon as 'liquidity rationing' by the central bank does not affect the wholesale banks but weighs heavily on the money-market banks. This is why, in France, the financial administrators have adopted the apparently Malthusian practice of credit control, or credit rationing.

This technique of regulation calls forth bitter criticisms — and not only on the part of the ultra-liberals — because it makes no distinction between the sheep and the goats, the enterprising and the unenterprising. But credit rationing is, in itself, only the consequence of the shortage of regulatory instruments. No one can deny that the authorities have the right and the duty to control the quantity of new money introduced into circulation.(1) The state may delegate some of its privilege of issuing money to the banking system, but this does not mean that it thereby abandons it. If the system of regulation turns out to be deficient, it is reasonable that, in the absence of adequate instruments, the right to issue money should be limited and measured. Nevertheless, this is only a *pis-aller*, as Mr Renaud de la Genière confirms:

> Credit control ceases to be a suitable technique for the management of monetary policy once it becomes more or less permanent. The problem is a very simple one: over the last four or five years, have we in this country had any other effective way of limiting the expansion of the money supply? The answer is no. There was none, because we have been through a period of rapid inflation. In such cases, only quantitative restrictions on credit can ensure that that growth of the money supply which we consider acceptable will be adhered to.

Two units of money that each effect one transaction in a lapse of time, *T*, have together the same monetary effect on economic activity and prices as a unit of money that carries out two transactions in the same space of time. This is why it is just as important to analyse the *dynamics* of money as it is to analyse it quantitatively.

The transaction velocity registers all the changes of hand of payment money, that is, M1. The income velocity, on the other hand, only registers transactions that promote a conversion of production into consumption or investment (one in eight, on average, of all transactions).

Looked at, therefore, from the point of view of the velocity of money, analysis of monetary phenomena cannot rest on classifications that put under the same head those units of money that are free to circulate (M1) and those that are not (M' = M2 − M1, M" = M3 − M1). As long as the indicators are not defined with more accuracy, we cannot expect any rationality or efficiency from attempts at monetary regulation.

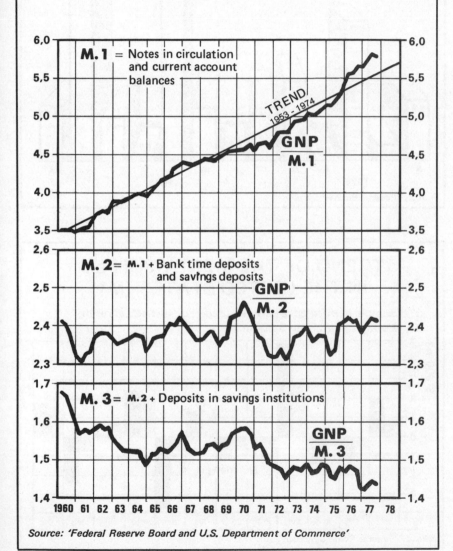

THE TREND OF THE VELOCITY OF MONEY IN THE UNITED STATES
(INCOME VELOCITY)

M.1 = Notes in circulation and current account balances

TREND 1953 - 1974

GNP / M.1

M.2 = M.1 + Bank time deposits and savings deposits

GNP / M.2

M.3 = M.2 + Deposits in savings institutions

GNP / M.3

1960 61 62 63 64 65 66 67 68 69 70 71 72 73 74 75 76 77 78

Source: 'Federal Reserve Board and U.S. Department of Commerce'

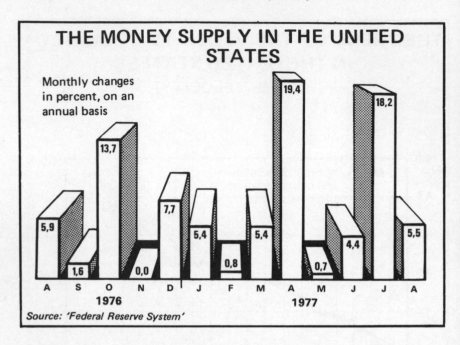

THE MONEY SUPPLY IN THE UNITED STATES

Monthly changes
in percent, on an
annual basis

Source: 'Federal Reserve System'

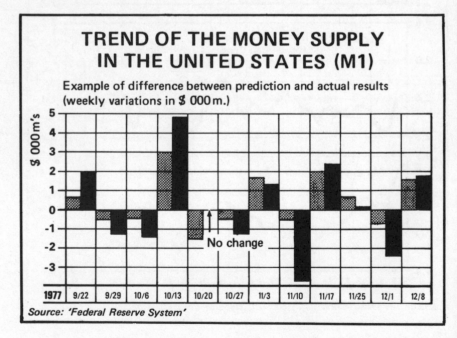

TREND OF THE MONEY SUPPLY IN THE UNITED STATES (M1)

Example of difference between prediction and actual results
(weekly variations in $ 000 m.)

Source: 'Federal Reserve System'

The banks submit to the disciplines of credit rationing because they know that the alternative is total control by the state, withdrawal of their privileges: in a word, nationalisation. The main objection one can make to credit control is that such a system, which takes no account of the uses to which new money is put, i.e. to the nature of the credit, is extremely inflexible. This has already been pointed out in the chapter dealing with investment on the basis of monetary creation. It is not enough to say that certain sorts of credit, such as credits for housebuilding and exports, i.e. 40 per cent of the total, shall be outside the scope of the restrictions, and then restrict all the rest. Instead, we ought to weight things so as to orientate the capital withdrawn from the public in the form of monetary creation towards uses that are most likely to serve the general interest.

Jacques-Henri David sums up, very conveniently, in an article in *Banque*, October 1977, the uncertainty of monetary regulation and the problems it raises for the authorities:

> If it is true that in 1977 there are not very many economists who will deny the existence of a link between monetary creation, growth and inflation, there is no real consensus regarding the exact nature of this link and its causes. The conduct of monetary policy, even now, is still inspired by extremely pragmatic methods, and success or failure in this field are generally attributed to a greater or lesser degree of skill on the part of the authorities.
>
> Just like singers, finance ministers and governors of central banks aim to get to the top of a kind of 'hit parade' of the art of money management, which is charted by a small circle of initiates like themselves. But like all 'hit parades', this one does not just reflect the qualities of those who appear in it; it also reflects the conditions in which they exercise their talents. The conduct of monetary policy is, in fact, an attempt to control the liquidity of the economy, that is, the volume of monetary creation and the velocity of circulation of money. But monetary creation is the business of the banks and the velocity of circulation depends on the behaviour of those who hold money. Any attempt to control the behaviour of money can be frustrated by the banks or by the public.

In the face of such uncertainty, some people may be tempted to give in, ignore the indicators and abandon any attempt at monetary policy. To do so would be to return to that fatal pre-war policy which was unable to avoid either inflation or deflation, and which plunged the world into depression. The regulation of payment instruments is inevitable. No

The rate of interest has been one of the great topics of traditional monetary theory, which presents it as an instrument of monetary regulation for the authorities and an important factor in any decisions taken by businessmen and investors.

This was probably the case when there was more or less consistent monetary stability. But the wild oscillations of the interest rate in real terms, which these curves traced by Alain Cotta demonstrate, clearly serve to show how remote from reality traditional teaching has become

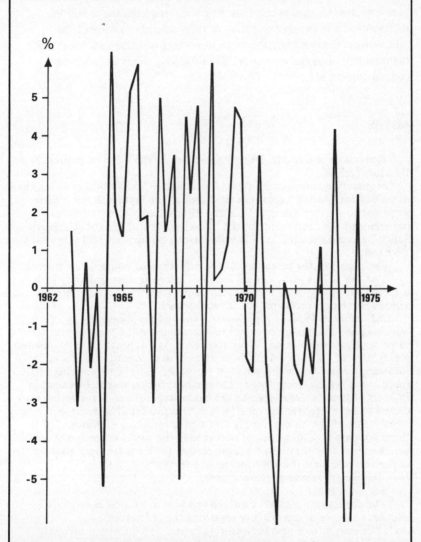

REAL INTEREST RATE TRENDS IN THE UNITED KINGDOM

Source: 'Taux d'intéret, plus-value et épargne en France'
(by Alain Cotta – Edit. P.U.F.)

government can abandon its responsibilities in this respect, for the obvious reason that money, its creation, its uses and its circulation are fundamental to the economy, and constitute the very precondition of progress. It is not the need for regulation that we should call into question. What we should do is try to correct its deficiencies by trying to solve the problem in its three aspects: first the indicators, then the means of intervention and finally the guides or rules suitable to control the intervention instruments. The most important of these indicators is M1, the quantity of payment money. The following pages will therefore concentrate on M1.

NOTES

[1] Renaud de la Genière, Deputy Governor of the Bank of France, 7 December 1976.

[2] Monetary economics is subject more than other disciplines to a degree of uncertainty which transcends time limits. The layman is not a little surprised to see, for example, that the differences of opinion which preoccupied the proponents of the 'Banking School' and the 'Currency School' around the middle of the nineteenth century are still very much alive today.

[3] See page 194 for an *exposé* of the principles of compulsory reserves.

[4] The risk works just as much for the bank as against it. In any case, it means that the system becomes fundamentally unstable and creates serious regulation problems for the authorities.

'In November 1957 . . . the government and the monetary authorities were engaged in a policy of credit restriction intended to overcome the balance of payments crisis, which was reaching its climax. This manoeuvre was frustrated by an accident. In consequence of various unauthenticated rumours, a panic broke out amongst the general public concerning 10,000 franc notes, which, according to the rumour, were going to be called in. Holders of these notes rushed to the banks to get rid of them before they ceased to have legal-tender value, which caused a rapid increase in the bank money part of the money supply and a corresponding diminution of the fiduciary part. . . This influx of notes made the banks exceedingly liquid, which meant that they could escape central bank control and make loans at the very moment the government was trying to stop them'
Jean Denizet, *Monnaie et financement*.

[5] See page 197.

[6] *The Economist* uses M3 to describe what, in France, is called M2 – another example of uncertainty regarding the indicators.

[7] 'The search for a new indicator' (Chapter 5) is intended precisely to take account of this ease of passage between current and savings accounts, as well as of the velocity of circulation.

[8] The strong currency countries in the West today are Germany and Switzerland. Their monetary policies are cited as exemplary, and yet the

uncertainty regarding the indicators, their definition and meaning is no less important there than anywhere else, as the two passages on pages 207–8 show.

[9] On page 208 there is an interesting comment by a member of the Board of Governors of the Fed., Mr Philip Coldwell. In particular, this passage shows the problems of the definition and meaning of the indicators and interest rates. There is also a warning about the danger of short-term and short-sighted monetary policy, which is vulnerable to the 'gut' reactions of the public.

[10] Businessmen and company treasurers have some difficulty in following the traditional arguments on the subject of interest rates. The reason is probably that now that inflation seems to have become a permanent aspect of economic life they view the question of interest rates from a different point of view from the one they had before the war, since the whole question is now falsified by expectations that have no connection with logic or academic predictions.

In his book *Taux d'intéret, plus-values et épargne en France et dans les nations occidentales* (PUF), Alain Cotta gives quarterly curves showing nominal and real interest rates as they can be deduced from statistics on the money market and the inflation rate (see table). How could such irregular movements set off 'propensities', 'preferences' and 'trends', all of which are in fact without any semblance of rationality? As Alain Cotta puts it, 'the interest rate, after having been the main variable of economic analysis has now been put on the rubbish heap of intellectual history.'

See on page 211 a further quotation from Alain Cotta.

[11] Paul Fabra's perplexity when faced with ambiguous and heterogeneous aggregates is understandable, as are his doubts and his sarcastic comments on the accuracy of the statistics. The Fed., for example, announced at the end of March 1978 that the growth rate for M1, published in January, had, after correction, passed from 7.2 per cent to 8.6 per cent on an annual base, whereas the contraction noted in February was only 1.1 per cent instead of the 3.3 per cent that was announced. The Fed.'s errors of approximation derive above all from the fact that a large number of banks are not members of the system and that they do not give regular returns for the totals of their current accounts which make up M1. But the total of these accounts amounts to a quarter of all sight deposits in the United States! The revised growth rate of M1 for 1977 is 7.8 per cent, instead of 7.4 per cent. As for M2, it was changed from 9.6 to 9.8 per cent.

Having once recognised these facts, inaccuracies and uncertainties, as well as the imperfections of the system of monetary regulation, one still cannot ignore the money supply and its growth for the simple reason that there is nothing else that can be put in its place, both as indicator and as instrument of what constitutes the very essence of the economy — activity and prices.

[12] When it calculates the transaction velocity, the Fed. takes no account of the movement of notes, which is equivalent to admitting that the velocity of notes is the same as the velocity of bank deposits, or more precisely that the variations of velocity (because it is the variations that count) are the same as those of bank money.

Nothing is less certain. According to Garvy and Blyn of the New York Federal Reserve Bank: 'Fiduciary money in the hands of the public is, on average, equivalent to one fifth of the mass of the means of payment. This fraction has varied and there is no reason to think that the efficiency with which fiduciary money is used by its holders has increased as much as the efficiency of bank money. In fact the contrary is certainly true.'
The velocity of money, Federal Reserve Bank of New York.
This supposition is confirmed by the graphs of the Bank of France. Given a base of 100 in 1958, the velocity of circulation of notes went from about 93 on average in 1967 to about 110 in 1970, whereas the velocity of circulation of bank demand deposits, which was lower than 80 in 1967, had exceeded the velocity of circulation of notes by more than 10 points in 1970. If we assume that the changes in velocity of bank and fiduciary money are the same in the USA as in France, the error committed by the Fed. in not taking account of the movements of bank-notes is likely to be considerable.
[13] Mention is sometimes made of the 'float', or delay between the crediting of a cheque to a depositor's account and the debiting of the account of the drawer of the cheque, as a possible cause of error in monetary statistics. This delay may be as much as ten days in the USA, whereas the average period for which a unit of money remains stationary before moving on to its next transaction is nine days. The result of this is an important distortion between the totals of liabilities announced by a bank and the claims on that same bank which are effectively at the disposal of the public. But this cause of error disappears if one brings into the calculation, along with the mass, the velocity of circulation, which proves the need not to rely only on static statistics, but to complement them by dynamic ones.

4 A flaw in monetary thinking

There exists a fundamental flaw in contemporary monetary thinking which invalidates interpretations of the indicators, causes wrong decisions to be taken, disrupts the mechanisms and paralyses monetary regulation, or causes it to work in reverse. This flaw consists of a failure to discriminate between those categories of assets that are used as means of exchange and those that are not, those that have a definite payment function and those that do not, those that may be transformed into money or cause the creation of money and those that *are* money.

This confusion is so general and so widespread that people are rarely aware of it. Most writers do not mention the problem of defining what should be understood by the term 'money', although this fundamental defect undermines their arguments from the start. A great deal has been written on money, on its circulation, how it is created and so on. Whether they are discussing inflation or deflation, slumpflation or stagflation, whether they are attacking the Phillips curve or income distribution, whether they are urging the merits of growth, floating exchange rates or the monetary 'snake', writers inevitably refer to the money supply, its growth and even, sometimes, its contraction, but without apparently taking any trouble to define accurately, much less justify, the indicators upon which they rely.[1]

Never before has the money supply been the object of so much discussion; never before has monetary policy occupied the attentions of governments so much. In the United States, Congress asks the chairman of the governors of the Federal Reserve Banks to establish fixed targets for monetary growth, to justify them, and to say how the Open-Market committee expects to achieve them as well as to explain any discrepancies. Each week, the government publishes the latest figures for M1 and M3. The Stock Exchange rises or falls as a consequence, whilst the experts from the Fed. protest that the growth of the money supply can only be interpreted in the long term. In Germany, in England and nowadays even in France, the test of sound economic policy is as much the growth of the money supply as the growth of the GNP.

The aim of this book is not to take sides on this issue: the important thing to notice is that nowadays both monetarians and antimonetarians attribute a significant role to the money supply. The disagreement between them is not over the use of the money supply as a test but over the more or less *exclusive* use of the money supply as an instrument of economic policy. One might, therefore, at least expect economists to agree about what they are discussing and what the object of their discussions is, but this is not the case. The money supply ought, above all else, to be *precisely* defined, and yet its exact meaning, what should be included in it, how it should be calculated and how its growth should be interpreted, are all factors that are ignored. When people do talk about it, the tendency is, if anything, to abolish all distinctions between the different categories of what is called money. This is understandable: when one is surrounded by uncertainty it is easier to put everything under the same heading than to try to discriminate.

In every respect, the definitions given to the different categories of money supply diverge, some being very general and some narrowly specific. These differences are indicative of the uncertainties of present-day knowledge and the urgent need for a re-examination. If and when it is finally undertaken, such a re-examination can only restore a little order to thinking on these topics. In Germany the Bundesbank no longer takes M1 (notes and current account deposits) as its operational target; nor does it take M2 (M1 plus deposits with maturity of less than 4 years), nor even M3 (M2 plus savings deposits). It also ignores 'freely usable liquid reserves' and concentrates instead on the 'QBNC', which is the quantity of notes in circulation and the total of compulsory reserves on resident current and savings deposits, the reserve coefficient being constant and January 1974 being taken as base date.

In England, what counts now is the DCE, or Domestic Credit Expansion, which adds the balance of external payments to the money supply, defined as the total of resident current and deposit accounts. In France there are the so-called 'monetary liquidities', which correspond more or less to M1; the money supply proper (M2), which adds to the monetary liquidities near-money, defined as bank assets likely to be easily transformed into cash, as well as savings managed by the banks and the Treasury. Finally, there is the liquidity of the economy which includes, in addition to the money supply, savings bank deposits and Treasury Bills (M3). The American definitions are given in the table on page 159.

An airline pilot needs to know whether his altimeter is graduated in yards, feet or metres but he doesn't know whether the zero on the dial corresponds to sea-level or to the top of Big Ben. Our monetary pilots, even when they seem most self-assured, are no better off. The self-assurance which they evince in public is only a façade hiding an uncertainty fraught with incalculable consequences. The monetary accident in England described in the previous chapter had pernicious consequences, but it could have been avoided through a proper understanding and interpretation of the indicators. The error in this case was to fail to distinguish between those bank liabilities that have the payment function and those that do not. The cause of such fundamental errors is muddled thinking, due to the fact that the basic phenomenon, which is the passage of a unit of money from one agent to another, is neglected, and trust is put in data that are essentially static, whereas the process in question is dynamic. Messrs Garvy and Blyn of the Federal Reserve bank of New York say, in their authoritative work *The Velocity of Money*:

We concentrate on the narrowly-defined money supply. Our preference for a definition of money limited to notes and current account deposits is rooted in our conviction that an identification of money with the means of payment gives the best tool of analysis. The line of demarcation should not be between all the deposits at a bank and other moneyable claims, but rather between current account deposits and all other deposits, including financial assets, savings bank deposits etc.

In the opinion of Garvy and Blyn, therefore, there is, on the one hand, means of payment, i.e. notes and current account deposits, because notes and current account deposits are used to make payments; on the other hand, there is everything that is capable of being turned into money, or which can bring about the creation of money, the list of which is evidently not exhaustive and certainly not confined to near-money. Of the three functions traditionally assigned to money, that of standard of value that of store of value and that of medium of exchange, the money that is created with such gay abandon nowadays is only capable of honestly fulfilling the last one. But this function is of the first importance, because economic activity and prices both depend on it, and it is economic activity and prices that constitute the principal aims of economic policy and even of politics in general. It is, therefore, all the more surprising that this role of medium of exchange should be neglected or, more exactly, that the indicators should reflect it so badly.

THE DEFINITIONS OF THE MAIN MONETARY INDICATORS IN THE UNITED KINGDOM AND GERMANY

The Bank of England definitions

M1 = notes and coins in circulation and current account balances held by the private sector (whether interest-bearing or not)

M2 = (obsolete)

M3 = (a) 'Sterling M3', defined as M1 plus time deposits held by the private sector, plus all sterling deposits held by the public sector

= (b) a wider definition still, consisting of sterling M3 plus deposits in foreign currencies held by residents

These definitions call for a few comments. The first thing to note is that the monetary aggregates in England include deposits with every kind of banking institution — commercial banks, merchant banks, foreign banks, consortium banks etc. — with the following exceptions:

(a) Building societies,
(b) The Trustee Savings Bank and the National Savings Bank,
(c) The National Giro.

Furthermore, deposits held by non-residents are not included.

The separation of M3 into two different indicators was the result of the 1976 sterling crisis, which forced the government to turn to the IMF for help. The main condition of IMF support was a 'letter of intent' from the Chancellor of the Exchequer, in which he formally undertook strictly to limit the growth of the money supply. At the time, there were considerable sums held by authorised companies and individuals in accounts denominated in foreign currencies and as it was felt that this foreign currency overhang posed a constant threat to the money supply the decision was taken to create a new definition of M3 which would be called 'sterling M3' and which would exclude these foreign currency deposits. It was the growth of sterling M3 which the government undertook to control in its letter to the IMF.

The Bundesbank definitions

M1 = notes and coins in circulation, plus demand deposits

M2 = M1 plus time deposits having a maturity of less than four years

M3 = M2 plus savings deposits having the legal maturity of three months

In Germany, no distinction is made between the various kinds of banking institution. Commercial banks, merchant banks, savings banks and mortgage banks are all included in the Bundesbank statistics and no distinction is made between resident and non-resident accounts.

The wide differences between what the Bank of England understands by M1, M2 etc and what the Bundesbank understands, and the arbitrary way the definitions have been modified by the Bank of England to suit the needs of the moment will, perhaps, give the reader some idea of the uncertainties in present-day knowledge of monetary matters which the author of this book has been at some pains to point out.

Money stock measures and components United States of America, March 1979

in billions of dollars, averages of daily figures, not seasonally adjusted

	Types of assets considered as components	Measures of money stock						
		M.1	M.1+	M.2	M.2+	M.3	M.4	M.5
1	Currency (bank notes and coins) outside the Treasury, the Federal Reserve Bank, and vaults at commercial banks	99	99	99	99	99	99	99
2	Demand deposits at commercial banks other than interbank deposits and United States government deposits, less cash items in process of collection, and Federal Reserve Float	255	255	255	255	255	255	255
3	Foreign demand balances at Federal Reserve banks	0	0	0	0	0	0	0
4	Savings deposits at commercial banks	—	217	—	217	—	—	—
5	Various other accounts subject to transfer by check or equivalent draft or order (NOW savings accounts, credit-union share-draft accounts, demand deposits at Mutual Savings banks)	—	3	—	3	—	—	—
6	Savings deposits at commercial banks	—	—	217	217	217	217	217
7	Time deposits open account, and Time CDs other than $100,000 or more at weekly reporting banks	—	—	307	307	307	307	307
8	Thrift deposits at mutual savings banks, shares in Savings and Loans associations and at credit unions	—	—	—	—	639	—	639
9	Large negotiable CDs of $100,000 or more	—	—	—	—	—	98	98
	Total	354	574	878	1098	1517	976	1615

Source: *Federal Reserve Bulletin*, Vol. 65 (May 1979), p.A.14.

Since economic activity and prices are the direct results of money in its role of medium of exchange, it is this latter function which ought to be isolated and analysed. The factors that determine it are numerous; it is not just a question of the quantity of money but also of the velocity and the purposes for which money is used.[1] But the truth is that the attention given in monetary analysis to other factors than quantity is minimal. The most commonly mentioned velocity — though even this is rarely mentioned — is income velocity; it gives no indications regarding the transaction function since it looks at money in its action of converting finished goods into consumption (non-productive consumption or investment). Such a conversion is only set in motion, on average, by one transaction out of every eight. The other seven also affect activity and prices; they concern the supply of goods and services for *productive* consumption (salaries), acquisition of goods that have already been produced, simple transfers etc. but they are not included in the income velocity, which is only a statistical coefficient, and not a real measurement.

It is true that statistical classification of transactions according to type is difficult and imprecise. But it is also true that modern statistical methods have made immense progress. In any case, the difficulty of making accurate measurements does not excuse muddled thinking, and to argue that savings deposits managed by banks are the same as current account deposits, simply because they are both more or less interchangeable and can be easily mobilised by their holders, is very muddled thinking indeed. (1) As Michel Lelart puts it: 'The assessment of total liquidities is made difficult by the confusion between money proper and long-term claims. One cannot repeat too often what a source of problems such a confusion is.'

Of course, it is easier to count masses than measure velocities or estimate acceleration, so it is justifiable to attempt to devise heterogenous aggregates based on surveys, hypotheses and probabilities, but on one condition only, namely that the propositions should be supported by solid reasoning or experimental evidence. But here we come back to the basic fallacy discussed at the beginning of this chapter: the monetary indicators do not stand up to a test seeking to establish a correlation between them and what they are supposed to measure, namely transactions seen from the point of view of their monetary effects.[1]

If we want to calculate and anticipate the effects of motor cars on traffic, pollution, accidents, energy consumption and the balance of payments, we must count the number of registered vehicles. But these factors are dynamic, whereas the census method applies only to static factors: a stationary vehicle consumes nothing, does not pollute anything, does not knock any pedestrians over and causes no traffic jams. But we

know experimentally the connection betwen the number of registered
vehicles and the effects they have. We therefore draw the appropriate
conclusions.

It can also be worked out deductively: in order to amortise the
cost of a lorry, one must drive the vehicle for a certain number of miles,
which produces statistics regarding fuel consumption and wear and tear
that can be expressed in figures. In the matter which concerns us here,
there is no reasoning, or rather there is a false train of reasoning, namely
that if a claim on a bank *may* be converted into payment money or *may*
cause the creation of payment money, in consequence and *for this reason*
it is the same thing as a unit of payment. This is not so. A certain degree
of comparability could be admitted if it was proved that there was a
correlation, but there is no such proof. There are many kinds of claim
that can cause a creation of money but which are not included in
the money supply — this is true, for example, of discountable bills drawn
on the Bank of France or the foreign currency holdings of banks — whereas
other claims, such as deposits with a maturity of five years, will probably
remain sterile for a long time but are nevertheless included in the broadly
defined money supply.

There can be no hope of sorting out this confusion as long as no attempt
is made to get to the heart of the matter, which is the process of *payment*;
at the same time, it is imperative to try to define, rationally and experimentally, appropriate indicators which will reflect, as faithfully as possible,
the dynamic factors which we are trying to measure. The difficulty of
measuring these velocities and, over and above the question of velocities,
the question of assessing the different kinds of transactions and payments,
which have varying monetary effects, explains the fruitless attempts which
some monetarians have made to show that velocity is always constant.
Such difficulties also explain the tendency to turn to heterogeneous
aggregates. But such aggregates would still need to be defined in such a
way as would reflect as faithfully as possible the dynamic nature of the
money flows. (1)

Let us come back to our example of motor cars. Let us suppose that we
wish to take the analysis further and appreciate more precisely the 'traffic
effect' of the cars. Would we therefore add to the number of vehicles duly
registered those kept in stock by the manufacturers and those they plan
to make in the near future? Surely not, because the question of 'traffic
effect' obviously does not apply in the case of stocks or vehicles which
have not yet been manufactured; in the same way, the monetary effect
does not apply to long-term or savings deposits. But we can take account
of certain factors which affect the traffic by classifying cars in different

categories with different traffic effects. We could, for example, register the number of taxis in use. If a given taxi travels, on average, five times the distance travelled by a car registered in the same town, we can work out an indicator which will give an approximate measure of the traffic effect, by adding to the number of registered vehicles, M, four times that of the taxis, equivalent to m. The total traffic effect will then be equivalent to $M + 4m$.

Monetary indicators may be defined in the same way. M1 for example, the total of notes and current account deposits in circulation, the most representative indicator of the quantity of means of payment, may be complemented by a variable which represents the incidence of acceleration of circulation of a loan or the withdrawal of a savings deposit. Let us take, for example, a savings bank. The proportion of M1 deposited at the savings bank, and then put back into circulation when the bank makes a loan, is accelerated. Passing through the books of the savings bank does not modify the quantity of M1, but it does modify the velocity, generally by speeding it up; more precisely, it has the effect of bringing forward in time the moment when the monetary unit lent to the borrower is used to convert a unit of production into consumption (non-productive consumption by householders, or investment). This same conversion set off by the unit of money would have taken place later if the unit had remained in the hands of the original economic agent and had been spent by him, instead of being deposited at the savings bank and lent by it to someone else. Similarly, the withdrawal of a savings deposit — and, assuming total cash deposits remain equal, its replacement by another deposit — has the effect of accelerating exchanges, by bringing them forward in time. These anticipations can be assessed approximately; they depend on certain factors which are easily measured, such as the turnover time of deposits and loans. The resulting monetary effect is the same as if one had added to M1, which is supposed to remain at the same velocity, a certain quantity, m, of units of payment.

Long-term deposits and savings deposits [2] deposited with monetary intermediaries, and, generally speaking, all deposits not used directly as payment instruments, should not be included in the money supply, even in the form of near-money. When a bank-note or cheque is deposited in a savings or time deposit at a bank, its payment function disappears. The money is destroyed; it is withdrawn from the mass of payment instruments. In its place, there appear one or more new units produced by the bank in proportion to the reserve of liquidities to which the initial deposit, now defunct as money, has contributed (bank reserves are not included in M1). To add deposits which have ceased to have the payment function, as is the case with near-money, to those that still have it, is equivalent to assessing the population of a country by adding up the number of living and recently dead, and calling the latter 'semi-living'. But the reasoning used for non-banks can also be applied to banks; a complementary term can be added to the mass of M1 in order to take account of the accelerating effect of loans and withdrawals on the units of money which the bank puts into circulation. The units of money created by a bank are, in practice, disconnected from the deposits hidden in the same liquidity reserve, which makes no distinction between their different origins (time deposits, savings deposits, current account deposits etc.). The probability is that the money created by a bank and lent to a borrower has a monetary effect in the form of a speeding-up of transactions, an acceleration which causes a conversion of production into consumption over and above what there would have been if the same money had simply carried on circulating like other payment units, without having been the instrument of a loan or a withdrawal of savings. The same reasoning as that used about loans made by non-monetary intermediaries would lead one to take account of this speeding up by adding to M1 a corrective factor calculated in the same way.

Besides M1, there are all the other aggregates. We cannot do better than quote Mr Renaud de la Genière on this:

> We have hitherto justified adopting broader definitions of the money supply, M1, M2, M3 up to Mn until all debts and claims are included. But now we can see that this enlargement, which helps understanding of the phenomena, their place in the economic system, their influence and the influences they themselves undergo, causes them to lose a large part of their meaning, because of the growing heterogeneity of the masses in question. In order to understand their economic role, we must look at them in isolation and consider the particular function of each one.[3]

In order to clarify monetary analysis, the best thing would be to put on one side those forms of money that have the payment function, and on the other all assets which may be transformed into payment instruments or give rise to them. Though we should be careful not to mix up the two, this does not mean that they should not both be attended to. The attention paid to M1 does not mean that the other sorts of money that may become payment money, or cause it to be created, should be ignored; on the contrary, they should be counted and classified according to their degree of 'moneyness'. But such a transformation is only an eventuality, and eventualities ought to be assessed in terms of their probability and their likely consequences, which means, in turn, that care should be taken to distinguish eventualities from events. Near-money is an *eventuality*; the withdrawal of a deposit included in near-money and the corresponding issue of a new payment instrument is an *event*. An insurance company will take due account of the degree of inflammability of anything which it agrees to protect against fire risks. Such risks, and the consequences in the event of a fire, are not the same for a concrete building as for a barn or a petrol station. Nevertheless, the insurance company does not confuse what *may* catch fire with what is already on fire.

This error, of confusing what *is* money with what may *become* money, arises from the neglect of the fundamental criterion, namely the payment function. If the possibility of a direct exchange for goods and services received is not taken as the criterion for distinguishing different kinds of money, it is impossible to avoid the conclusion that all the deposits in a bank are money. How can we differentiate a current account deposit from a time deposit on the sole criterion of duration, when the customer of a bank can mobilise his time deposit whenever he wishes, either because he gets this concession from his bank manager, who is anxious to accommodate his customer, or because he goes to the secondary market? And how can one refuse a deposit in a savings bank, which can be withdrawn at any moment, the same role as a similar deposit in an ordinary bank? The current account credit and the savings account credit in a bank are interchangeable. A transfer from one to the other does not alter, in the slightest, the bank's liability profile, the more so as the bank uses for the same purposes resources deriving from demand or time deposits. It is not on the basis of such criteria as maturity and availability that a bank's liabilities should be analysed from the monetary point of view, but according as they have or have not the payment function.(1)

The muddled thinking that leads people to attribute to a Euromarket bank a power of monetary creaton identical with that which it has in its own national banking system – i.e. the banking system of the country in which it is domiciled – is due to the confusion between *money* and what I shall call *deposits denominated in money*, which is not at all the same thing but which is bound to be confused if no attempt is made to look for the payment function. Such a confusion can only lead to people attributing to all and any deposits, including the 'deposits denominated in money' which a savings bank holds, the same function as to money proper; this in turn leads to the error of attributing the power of issue to any establishment that takes deposits and makes loans. The question is not a matter of scholastic interest only. It is the foundation of monetary policy and even of economic policy.[4] (1) It is also the basis of the disciplines which monetary authorities in all countries wish to impose on the Eurobanking system, a system of several hundred billion dollars which makes up the bulk of international financial flows.

Promotion of economic activity and price stability are the very *raison d'être* of monetary regulation. The three problems that this raises are, first of all, the quest for reliable indicators, secondly the search for intervention instruments and finally the search for a doctrine. So far, we have shown that the present indicators do their job badly and we have also explained why. The following chapter will show how M1 could be corrected so as to give information on the main object of this quest: the monetary effect of the mass of circulating means of payment.

NOTES

[1] 'Money is normally considered to be a stock existing in the economy at a given moment. The concept of the money stock has no meaning, since for the most part, all money is produced for a specific period of time after which it is destroyed.'
Michelle de Mourgues, *Economie Monétaire* (Editions Daloz).

[2] Apropos of the images used here to describe money, its creation, its circulation, its dormancy and its destruction, see the explanation given in Chapter 4 of Part 1.

[3] A lot has been written about the 'propensity to save', the 'propensity to spend' etc., and on the different functions of money, on the 'desire for cash', 'liquidity preference', 'transaction intention', the 'will to consume or invest', etc. The result is to eliminate all precision from the analysis of monetary mechanisms.

On page 215 there is a comparison between the functions of money seen from the traditional viewpoint of the 'propensity' of the holder and from the point of view — which is also the point of view of this book —of what actually happens in the institution on which the unit of money is a claim.

[4] On page 216 there is an interpretation of the measures adopted by the Swiss authorities against the rise of the Swiss franc on the exchange markets.

5 The search for a new monetary indicator

The search for a new monetary indicator is not so much intended to provide better information on which to base monetary policy as to make it possible to get closer to the real nature of the mechanics of money by bringing into the equation a parameter which is rarely taken into consideration, namely the *nature* of money transactions and the *uses* money is put to. To this end, the main tools of national accounts — production, consumption and added value — will be used. This search demonstrates the monetary effect of a payment unit and confirms the special nature of M1, which sets it apart from all the other monetary aggregates. At the same time, it gives some idea of the mistake people make in indiscriminately including all the aggregates within the same definition of the money supply.[1]

The first responsibility of those who decide monetary policy is to be well informed, and for this they need properly-defined indicators. The main indicator is the mass of cash liquidities, M1, i.e. notes and current account deposits, because they are the instruments of exchanges of goods and services, which are the very factors that determine economic activity and prices. But M1 is a static indicator which only registers quantities, whereas the velocity of money and the varying uses it is put to have just as significant an effect on activity and prices as quantity. These factors — velocity and uses — depend on movements of deposits and loans in credit institutions, whether banks or non-banks. This is why a more accurate reflection of the 'monetary effect'(1) is likely to be obtained by adding a corrective factor to the purely quantitative M1, so as to reflect the incidence of credits and cash withdrawals on the velocity of money, and the purposes for which it is spent or invested. This proposed corrective factor is

$$\frac{1.5}{V} \Sigma MR$$

M is the volume of savings or credit registered per category of institution, no distinction being made between banks and non-banks. In the case of banks, freely transferable deposits that have the payment function, i.e. current account deposits, are not included. *R* is the annual turnover rate of the category, and *V* is the transaction velocity of M1 (annual turnover rate). The monetary effect may be defined either as the effect of money on activity and prices, or, alternatively, as the effect of activity and prices on money.

Economic activity fundamentally consists of exchanges of goods, or trade — the provision of a product or a service by *X* to *Y* in return for a claim on an institution. As for prices, they are the very essence of money in its role of measuring instrument, bringing all values under the head of one common denominator. Prices are also the result of trade; without trade there can be no economic activity, no prices and no monetary effect. But to speak thus of monetary effects is not to espouse the cause of the quantitativists, nor even the anti-quantitativists, but simply to look at money at work. Money does its work when goods or services change hands; economic activity follows and a price is determined. This is what the 'monetary effect' consists of. The way the economy works, just like the price level, is something that is also inseparable from money. Monetary analysts need indicators which will provide information on the object of their researches. What we are trying to measure, or at least perceive, is this monetary effect. Having said that, however, we must admit that this particular effect is very difficult to isolate. It would be otiose to try to formulate too precise a relationship between the factors which determine it; it is better simply to recognise the existence of the monetary effect without bothering too much about its definition.

In many disciplines, such as biology, physics, politics, medicine and psychology, it often happens that an undeniable relationship between phenomena is noted without anyone being able to provide concrete proof of the exact causality, much less quantify or formulate it. This is also true of the monetary effect, which connects activity and prices with money in its aspects of quantity, velocity and uses. But if the effects of money are refractory to exact formulation, they are, nevertheless, of variable intensity, and this, in the end, is what we are trying to get at. It is easy to see that a transaction which registers the consumption of a product (buying petrol at a garage, paying for a meal) has a more intense monetary effect than the purchase of a piece of second-hand furniture, which requires no additional production by anyone. The same is true of a transfer of money to a solicitor, preparatory to a payment (both are included in M1 and in the transaction velocity).

Of course, it would be useful if one could accurately graduate the different degrees of intensity of various sorts of transaction from the point of view of their monetary effect. But, in fact, it is not possible, and we must be content to divide transactions into only two categories: those whose monetary effect has nil intensity, and those which have a full monetary effect. Let us take, for example, the case of a transfer of funds. A man sends a certain sum to his solicitor in the form of a cheque, which the solicitor deposits at his bank, preparatory to making the payment which his client desires. The transfer is included in the transaction statistics but its monetary effect is nil. But if we take the case of a restaurant bill which a customer pays, we have a transaction with a significantly different monetary effect. There has been a conversion of a certain quantity of production into consumption, which cannot be repeated without a new provision of goods and services, i.e. new production, and this takes time. Alternatively, let us take a workman receiving his wages. Unlike the previous case, there is no conversion of production into consumption, but the time factor does intervene. If the transaction — the payment of the man's wages — is to be renewed, the workman will have to work a certain number of hours. Another case in which the production factor in terms of time disappears would be when a motor car, which its owner had bought new, is sold once and then a second time. The transactions in the second-hand market may be repeated; they do not presuppose fresh production, nor do they involve the passage of time. Their monetary effect can therefore be considered as nil.

These distinctions, and the search for a classification of monetary effects corresponding to different kinds of transactions, lead us towards the definitions used in government accounts, the methodology of which we shall borrow. According to official accounting practices, *final production* is intended for non-productive consumption, to which are added investments and the balance between exports and imports. This transition from production to non-productive consumption or investment is what is called a *conversion*, or change of state; in one case (non-productive consumption) there is a disappearance; in the other (investment) there is a change of state. Household consumption and consumption by the government or by financial institutions is called non-productive. On the other hand, productive consumption is used for the creation of new goods and services and constitutes a step towards the ultimate objective, which is final production for non-productive consumption or investment. All consumption by industry of goods and services is productive consumption.

Having looked at these government classifications of production, let us now look at transactions, or changes of hand, made with units of money, and let us try to connect the different kinds of production. In the first category we shall put transactions corresponding to conversions or uses — i.e. those transactions which lead to non-productive consumption, by householders or government bodies — or investment (changes of state). These transactions, for purposes of conversion, mark the final stage of a process of production, at each stage of which value was added. The process is complete when the finished product is consumed or used. If it is consumed, there is a disappearance; if investment is made, there is a change of state; in both cases there is a process of conversion with a full monetary effect. In the second category, which we shall call the category of simple transactions, we have all those transactions that do not come into the first category. They include, first of all, transactions corresponding to productive consumption, such as supplies to industry, salaries etc, which do not correspond, unlike their predecessors, to a process of destruction or change of state but simply to a transformation for the purposes of production. In this second category, we shall also put transfers of funds, transactions involving purchases of goods that have already been produced, and government income.

Having thus shown the connections that exist between the categories set up by the government accounting services and individual transactions, we shall use their statistics to work out the volume of transactions in each category, and calculate their monetary effect. The volume of the first category, that of conversions, is the same as the volume of final production, since it corresponds to the definition given of final production. The volume of the second category of transactions is worked out by calculating the difference between the total volume of all transactions and the volume of transactions in the first category.

The total volume of transactions can be arrived at using statistics relating to bank account transactions; information relating to bank-notes can be obtained in the same way. Given these factors, we can introduce into our calculations the quantity of payment units included in M1. It is known that the total annual volume of transactions in the United States is more or less equal to forty times M1 (transaction velocity), whereas final production is more or less five times M1 (income velocity). From this it can be deduced that the total volume of transactions (both simple and for conversion) is eight times that of final production. The volume of transactions of the first category (conversion) being equal to the volume of final production, by deduction, the second category (simple transactions) can be seen to be equal to seven times the volume of the first.

So the volume of the two main categories into which we have divided transactions is as follows: in one year, the first is equal to five times M1, whilst the second is equal to thirty-five times M1. Now we must decide whether the transactions in each category have full or nil intensity. The category of conversions, or non-productive consumption by households, the government and investors, has, as we have seen, a full monetary effect. Each transaction in this category represents the elimination of an item of production or a change of state; a certain lapse of time and a process of fresh production are necessary for them to be repeated. The transactions in the second category, on the other hand, are more complex. Some have full intensity, others have nil intensity.

The first flow of transactions, those which create added value, has a full monetary effect. In contrast, the second flow (factor costs, i.e. payment of suppliers, etc.) has a nil effect. This flow moves in and out of a company without adding anything; it is a mere by-product of the process of production. But a monetary effect is, above all, the resulting effect of a given transaction on economic activity and prices. Economic activity is already accounted for by the value added over and above consumed factor costs; the latter are, by definition, the same at the beginning as at the end (the price of semi-finished products included in the production of a motor-car is exactly the same as the price that is paid by the manufacturer to his suppliers).

From this, it follows that transactions involving consumed factor costs have a nil monetary effect. The full effect, in the second category of transactions (simple transactions) must be limited to simple additions of value. So, in other words, transactions included in the first category (final production) have a full monetary effect, as do those second category transactions that create added value through fuelling productive consumption, e.g. payment of salaries. All other transactions are considered to have a nil monetary effect.

We shall now make use of government statistics to estimate the volume of transactions that have a full monetary effect and those that have none. The volume of first category transactions is equal to the total of final production as it is registered by statistics. In the second category (simple transactions), only added value has a full monetary effect, all the other transactions counting for zero in this respect. But the total volume of added value is also equal to final production. From this, it can be deduced that the overall monetary effect of the first category is the same as the overall monetary effect of the second. In other words, the overall monetary effect, E, of a given unit of money can be divided equally between conversion transactions and simple transactions. The problem

we face now is that of finding a corrective factor to add to or subtract
from M1, the mass of payment money (current account deposits and
notes), in order to take account of the slowing down or speeding up
of these units of payment money through identifiable or countable
intermediate operations, such as the opening of a credit, the making of a
deposit or the withdrawal from a savings account.

These speeding-up or slowing-down effects have, themselves, a certain
monetary effect, which is added to or subtracted from the monetary effect
that this same mass of units of payment would have if these transactions
had not taken place, or, in other words, if this unit of money had passed
from one person to another in the process of current transactions other
than deposits, withdrawals or loans. In one case, a bank-note may be used
for the purpose of a purchase; in another, it may be deposited in a savings
bank, which lends it or uses it to pay a depositor who wishes to withdraw
cash. The result of these operations is to modify the use that is made of
the bank-note and, therefore, its monetary effect; static counting of the
components of M1 takes no account of this. The note is included in the
mass of payment units, whether it circulates or not, whether it is spent
or not, whether it is used for a purchase or not. Even when the velocity
is carefully recorded, the uncertainty concerning the uses to which the
money is put remains and, with it, the uncertainty regarding the monetary
effect of the transaction. A transfer of funds or a payment from account
to account are both included in the transactions and are there under
the same head as payments for the purchase of a new car, although
their monetary effects are different. The simple process of comparing
the volume of transactions and final production (a ratio of 8 to 1)
is enough to demonstrate the uncertainties regarding the monetary
effect of a transaction. It is this uncertainty which the preceding study
was intended to correct.

Let us now try to find a corrective factor to be added to or subtracted
from M1 so as to take account of the resulting monetary effect of

    making a loan

    depositing money in a savings account and then withdrawing it,

whether the institution in question is a bank or non-bank (in the case of
a bank, only deposits or withdrawals included in the stock of near-money
are noted). These operations — the granting of a credit, the making of a
deposit or a withdrawal — speed up or slow down the succession of
transactions and modify their nature. The resulting monetary effect is
the same as if a certain imaginary quantity of units of money, m, were
added to or subtracted from M1 whilst the rate of M1 transactions remains
constant. It is this term m that we shall attempt to calculate by following

the movements of one payment unit; we shall consider as payment units only those that are used for exchanges, that is, in practice, notes and current account deposits.

A bank-note is a claim on the central bank which circulates from person to person. A current account deposit is a claim on the banking system which also passes from person to person and fulfils the same functions, but the institution on which the claim is made changes as the institution where the cheque is deposited and the identity of the payee both change. Units of money are created, come to life, pass from person to person, cause transactions and then are destroyed. The creation of a unit of money may have different causes, for example, the purchase of a quantity of gold or foreign currency by the central bank. The issue of a new unit of money by the banking system takes place when a cash deposit is made (credit to a current account) or when a loan is made (credit to the current account of the borrower), or when savings are withdrawn.

Once it has been put into circulation, the unit of money passes from one person to another. It is destroyed when it returns to the central bank or when the bank receives a repayment of a loan, a deposit in cash or a transfer order to a savings account, or a time deposit.

Let us follow the career of a single unit of money, from the moment someone uses it to buy a loaf of bread; this constitutes the first transaction;

2nd transaction: the baker pays the retailer for the flour
3rd transaction: the retailer pays the miller
4th transaction: the miller sends a cheque to his co-operative
5th transaction: the co-operative pays the farmer who sold it the corn
6th transaction: the farmer buys a machine
7th transaction: the manufacturer of the machine makes an inter-bank
                     transfer
8th transaction: the manufacturer pays his workers' wages
9th transaction: the worker uses part of his wages to buy a loaf of bread;

and so the cycle recommences.

The unit of money has thus taken part in nine transactions, of which three (1, 6 and 9) can be included in the first category (conversions for purpose of non-productive consumption or investment). The other six belong to the second category (simple transactions). The series of transactions in which a unit of money takes part may be represented on a graph. The transactions are represented on the abscissa XY by alternating dots and spaces, the length of the spaces being proportional to the amount of time that has elapsed. The transactions in the first category (conversions) are represented by black dots and the transactions in the second category (simple transactions) are represented by white dots.

We have seen that during the course of a year, a unit of money effects an average of forty transactions (this is the transaction velocity) and that the income velocity, the ratio of final production to the mass of payments, is around five, from which it can be deduced that a unit of money takes part, on average, in five first-category transactions — the black dots — and that there are, on average, seven white dots — simple transactions — for one black dot. Having established that, how do we distribute the white dots and the black dots along the time abscissa?

Units of money are fungible; taken together they are involved in an immense number of transactions. The annual number of transactions involving an American nickel (5 cents), for example, is approximately 3×10^{14}. If we assume that distribution of the white and black dots is not systematically influenced by any one factor and is only the product of chance, the distribution of the dots corresponds to the one given here. The spaces between the dots, expressed in terms of a fraction of a year, are equal to $1/V$ (V being the number of annual transactions, i.e. about forty). The spaces between the black dots are $8/V$ (five black dots per year). The graph will make it possible to show how the granting of a loan alters the frequency of exchanges.

Let us take, for example, an operation by a non-monetary intermediary, such as a savings bank. (We shall see later that there is no difference between operations by non-monetary and monetary intermediaries from this point of view). We have seen that a non-monetary intermediary (e.g. a savings bank) does not increase the money supply. The money deposited with it is simply re-relent: the depositor abandons the right to goods and services represented by these units of payment, in favour of a borrower. But the process of passing through the books of the intermediary causes a redistribution of transactions; more exactly, it brings forward the moment when the unit of money lent to the borrower is used for purposes of a conversion (black dot). This same process of conversion which the monetary unit sets in motion would have taken place much later if the unit had remained in the possession of the original owner and had been spent by him instead of being deposited at the savings bank and then lent by it.

The process is represented graphically as follows. Let there be, for example, on abscissa XY two transactions for purposes of conversion, A_1 and A_2 (black dots). Between these black dots there are seven white dots, equally distributed, which represent simple transactions (this is the average distribution). If there are no deposits at the bank, the monetary

A unit of money is created, starts to circulate, takes part in a number of transactions and is then destroyed. These transactions can be divided into two categories: those that effect a conversion of final production into consumption or investment (the black dots) and those, called simple transactions (white dots), that fuel a productive process, represent a transfer within the system of production (factor costs) or which simply pass from account to account without any productive effect. Only productive transactions that create added value have a monetary effect on economic activity and prices.

Since total added value is equal to final production, the overall monetary effect of the black dots is equal to the overall effect of the white dots. Given a transaction velocity of forty and an income velocity of five, there are seven white dots for one black dot and eight intervals $1/V$ between two black dots. Transit through a financial intermediary (whether bank or non-bank) causes the temporal distribution of the black dots to be changed, but has no effect on the white dots. It brings forward by three intervals $1/V$ the black dot that follows the passage of a unit of money through a financial intermediary. This produces an increased monetary effect represented by the expression

$$\frac{1}{2} \times \frac{3}{V} = \frac{1.5}{V}$$

The corrective factor to be added to M1 to take account of the monetary effect of repeated passages through financial intermediaries is

$$\frac{1.5}{V} \times \Sigma\, MR$$

in which M is a category of loans or savings, R the annual turnover of the category and V the average annual number of transactions. This is taken as being 40 in the case of the dollar, which gives an interval of nine days $(1/V = 360/40 = 9)$.

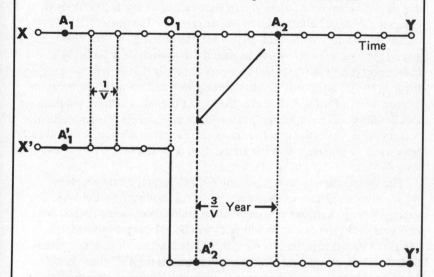

DIAGRAM SHOWING TYPICAL CIRCULATION OF A UNIT OF MONEY

o = Simple transaction (e.g. a payment)
● = Conversion of production into consumption or investment

XY Transaction *not* involving a financial intermediary

X'Y' Transaction involving a financial intermediary (cash balances remaining constant)

— deposit and loan

　or

— deposit and withdrawal

　or

— repayment and use for new purpose

　or

— repayment and withdrawal

V = annual number of transactions (e.g. 40)

unit effects the transactions represented by the series of black (conversions) and white dots (simple transactions) at the rate represented on the abscissa XY. At O_1 there is a deposit then a transfer by the bank of the unit which has been deposited with it to a borrower (total credit volume being supposed to be constant), who then puts it back into circulation. The movement of the unit thus transferred is represented on the line $X'Y'$ drawn underneath XY. The loan operation O_1 may be placed in the middle of A_1 and A_2. There is in fact no reason why this dot should be nearer A_1 than A_2, in the absence of any factor likely to exercise a systematic influence in one direction or the other.

Let us now follow the unit on its new trajectory, $X'Y'$. The first use given to it by a borrower when he uses it for a purchase is probably a conversion (black dots). In fact, the probability is that he will not keep for long the liquidity that he has thus acquired and on which he is paying interest without using it. It is also likely that the use which he will make of this liquidity will be either an investment or an example of non-productive consumption, operations that are classified as conversions. It is therefore reasonable to represent the first transaction after the loan O_1 by a black dot, A_2.

The anticipation in time represented on the graph by the segment $A_2A'_2$ gives some idea of the monetary effect produced by the loan. The average interval between two consecutive transactions being (in fractions of a year) $1/V$, the extent to which A_2 has been brought forward, measured by the segment A'_2A_2 is three intervals, i.e. $3/V$, which means that there are, in one year, $3/V$ more conversions on $X'Y'$ than on XY. In order to translate this increase in conversions into a monetary effect, we must come back to the previous demonstration, from which it resulted that the total monetary effect, E, of a monetary unit was divided into two equal fractions, one produced by conversions (black dots) the other by simple transactions (white dots). The effect of the anticipation due to simple conversions (black dots) is therefore only half what it would be if all the sections were brought forward. It is therefore only

$$\frac{1}{2} \times \frac{3}{V} \times E = \frac{1.5}{V} \times E.$$

We have now looked at the credit operation proper. The process of mobilising savings follows the same pattern. The mobilisation of a deposit with a non-monetary intermediary, assuming cash balances to be constant, has the same effect as that of a loan: the depositor withdraws a unit that has been deposited by someone else. The deposit made by this latter depositor figures in O_1. The use the customer of the bank puts this unit to after he has withdrawn his asset is represented at A'_2. It is probably a conversion (black dot), as in the previous example. The advance is the same as if it had resulted from a loan.

The operations described above are typical of non-monetary intermediaries; the case of monetary intermediaries — ordinary commercial banks — looks somewhat different, but the result is the same. When a note is paid into a bank, or a cheque is deposited in a savings account or a time deposit, the payment function disappears; the unit of money is destroyed and it is withdrawn from the mass of payment units. It is followed by one or more new units created by the bank on the basis of its reserves, to which the initial deposit, which has now disappeared, has contributed (bank reserves are not included in M1). At the moment a credit is opened or a savings deposit is withdrawn by means of a transfer to a current account, a new unit of money with the payment function, namely a current account deposit, is created and put into circulation. The argument that has just been used for a non-bank can be adapted to the case of a bank, and used to define a complementary term to add to the mass of M1 in order to take account of the acceleration which credit operations or savings withdrawals give to money put into circulation by the bank. The probability is that the unit of money created by a bank and lent to a borrower has a monetary effect in the form of an anticipation or speeding up of the flow of transactions; this causes a certain conversion over and above what the same monetary unit would have caused if it had simply circulated like other payment units, without being involved in a loan or a withdrawal of savings.

The same line of argument as that which was used for loans granted by non-monetary intermediaries leads us to take account of this anticipatory effect, by adding to M1 a corrective calculated in the same way:

$$m = \frac{1.5}{V} \Sigma \, MR.$$

In fact, the preceding formula applies to all loan operations and to all withdrawals of savings, without distinction between banks and non-banks. Savings deposits include all deposits which have no payment function and which need to be mobilised, i.e. exchanged for other units, such as notes or current account deposits, in order to be used for payments.[2]

Now we must look at the validity of these hypotheses and, if necessary, estimate the corrections that need to be made to the formula and the likely margin of error. It is certain that there is an element of arbitrariness

in the preceding distinctions; for example, to deny that there is any
monetary effect deriving from transactions involving articles that have
already been manufactured and which have already entered into the
cycle of consumption, may be questioned. Let us take, for example, the
case of a picture bought by a collector just after it has been finished, and
thus 'consumed' (non-productive consumption, a first category
transaction). This picture changes hands several times, and eventually it
reaches 100 times its original value. It can be argued that these
transactions do have a monetary effect, to the extent that the term
'monetary effect' can be understood as producing an acceleration of
exchanges and an increase in production. Continued reselling of works of
art at ever increasing prices may encourage the production of further
works of art and cause assets that would otherwise have remained
unproductive to circulate through the economy.

   This is true, but if we had to take account of all the effects of a change
of hands our analysis would get bogged down from the start. The
complexity of the problem and the multiplicity of its many aspects are
the reasons why statisticians usually ignore the dynamic phenomenon
of *transactions*, although transactions represent the very quintessence of
the phenomenon we are trying to understand. There is no doubt that the
monetary effect occurs, above all, in transactions representing additions
to productivity, in the form of goods and services effectively produced,
additions whose end result is either a conversion, i.e. non-productive
consumption or investment, or an addition of value in the process of
production. The other transactions may also have some effects, but they
are likely to be small compared with the others.

   Another possible objection centres around the nature of the
transactions which a unit of money takes part in after the granting of a
loan. If the borrower leaves the money in his account, or if he uses it for
a repayment and, more generally, for a simple transaction, there is not,
as we have supposed, a drift to the left in the rate of conversion (black
dots). The calculations we have made would then give an excessively large
result. Nevertheless, the probability is that most of the transactions
effected after the granting of a loan are conversion operations (black
dots). The margin of error is therefore sure to be small.[3]

   Over a year, the monetary effect due to credit operations or savings
withdrawals is expressed by the formula

$$\frac{1.5}{V} \Sigma MR,$$

in which V is the transaction velocity, or number of rotations per year, of the mass of means of payment, M is the volume of a category of savings or loans (bank and non-banks) and R is the annual turnover rate of this category. Here is an example: the cash in a savings bank equals 100 units. The average velocity of turnover of deposits in this bank is two years, that of loans, five years.[4] The complementary term to be added to M1 to take account of acceleration of the 100 units is

$$\frac{1.5}{V} \times 100\left(\frac{1}{2} + \frac{1}{5}\right),$$

which equals almost three units ($V = 40$).

If, instead of 100 units, cash volume in the bank had been N, the corrective factor added to the M1 money supply, to take account of the acceleration of these N units, is $0.03\,N$. The money supply total, thus modified, is then M1 $+ 0.03\,N$.

Let us now take the case of a bank, the average life of whose loans is four months (annual turnover = 3); cash volume = 100. The average life of deposits other than current account deposits, i.e. near-money, is six months, and their annual turnover rate is therefore 2 and the cash balance is 50. The corrective factor to be added to M1 is

$$\frac{1.5}{40}\,(100 \times 3 + 50 \times 2) = 15.$$

These figures should be compared with the total of near-money (50). They show how big is the error arising from including these time deposits in the money supply, and in thus attributing the same monetary effect to these different components. They also reveal the even bigger error which would be made if we were to add deposits in savings banks to M1.

In traditional monetary statistics, near-money and time and savings deposits at banks are considered to be constituents of the money supply, whilst deposits at savings banks are not. It would be more logical to add to the mass of units which actually have the payment function (M1) a corrective factor which would take account of the effects on the velocity of circulation and on the uses of the money exerted by loans and savings withdrawals carried out by both monetary and non-monetary intermediaries. M1 would always be a composite indicator, but its components would all be representative of a common characteristic, namely the monetary effect. Apart from this modified version of M1, the other aggregates, M2, M3 etc. would be similarly redefined so as to reflect trends and possibilities which could be graduated in terms of the likelihood of their causing the creation of units of payment money, just as a banker assesses the differing degrees of liquidity of his various kinds of asset. Indicators of this sort would give monetary analysts and those who are in charge of monetary regulation a more accurate and more faithful picture of the relations, both actual and potential, between the money supply, economic activity and prices.

NOTES

[1] This search may also be seen as having a bearing on the inflationary effect of non-monetary intermediaries from the viewpoint of Gurley and Shaw. See also page 217.

[2] All the credit operations carried out by a bank, whether as monetary or non-monetary intermediary, but not all the deposits, are included in the formula. Credits to a current account that have the payment function, i.e. that are readily transmissible to another economic agent and which have legal tender power, are *excluded*. Deposits in current accounts answer this description.

The reason for this exclusion is that such a deposit is, by its very nature, a transaction instrument. It cannot, therefore, be included in a measurement which takes account of purpose and origin in connection with savings operations, deposits, withdrawals, credits and reimbursements.

Here the reader will find once again the observations already made concerning distinctions and classifications based on mere accidents of nomenclature, categories of banking establishment and presumed motivations. The only thing that is taken into account here is the nature of the claim acquired by the depositor: either it is transmissible and has legal tender power or it isn't and hasn't. In the first case, it is a transaction instrument; in the second, it is a savings instrument. It is only on the basis of a criterion of this sort, free of all subjectivity, that a coherent 'mechanics of money' can be founded.

[3] V may be taken to have a constant average value (40—50). Its variations, from one year to the other, are less than 5 per cent.

[4] It should be pointed out that this reasoning is only valid in the case of constant balances. According to this theory, withdrawals and loans balance deposits and reimbursements; it may be said, if one distributes them, that deposits balance out new credits. If the balance of the bank is 100 and if the total of sums deposited is 200, the annual turnover frequency of deposits is 2. If the amount of credits granted and reimbursed during the year is 500, the average annual turnover of loans is 5.

In fact, the flows in question vary in time, but this does not invalidate the conclusion. Over a short period of time, the flow equilibrium is the one given. The proof in this case is based upon instantaneous measurement: when it is said that a vehicle has a speed of 72 kmph, that means that in a very short space of time, 1 second for example, the distance covered is 20 metres, i.e. 72 km on an hourly basis. The reasoning used for the monetary effect of savings is similar.

6 Monetary creation and inflation

The money supply, even when those elements that are not payment instruments have been removed from it, and even when it is confined to notes and current account deposits (M1), is not a reliable indicator of the monetary effect resulting from financial exchanges; and yet this is the very purpose for which it is intended and the reason why it was devised. We have seen that it can be improved and made more representative by means of a corrective factor, which allows for identical monetary effects to those that derive from the quantity of money but which are caused by the velocity and the nature of the transactions in which money is involved. Credit cards provide an example of the mistakes that can arise if one neglects these last two factors.

A man makes a purchase with a credit card. After a certain time the shopkeeper is repaid and the purchaser is debited by the company that issued the card. What is the monetary effect of this transaction? The corrective factor to be added to M1 in order to take account of the monetary effect of a loan or a withdrawal of savings is, as we saw in Chapter 5

$$\frac{1.5}{V}\sum MR$$

In order to make use of this formula, we must first of all adapt to the case of the credit card the classic operation which we used in the previous chapter to work the formula out.

The shopkeeper can be considered to correspond to the depositor. He lends the price of the goods to an imaginary bank, which immediately re-lends it to the shopkeeper's customer. The withdrawal of funds by the shopkeeper takes place when he gets back the sum he has lent, from the credit card company. At the same time as it pays him, the company debits the account of the shopkeeper's customer. Just as in the operation which we used to work out the formula, we have here, simultaneously, a deposit

and a loan, followed, after a certain time, by a repayment from the
borrower (debiting the customer) and a withdrawal by the shopkeeper
(depositor). But the hypothesis of a speeding-up of the process of
conversion after the withdrawal of funds by the depositor does not hold.
There is no reason why the shopkeeper should put the money he receives
to any particular use (say, a conversion instead of a simple transaction).
What was counted as two operations for the purpose of working out the
formula counts as only one here. On the other hand, as far as the customer
is concerned, the hypothesis we have advanced may be maintained; the
money he borrows from the shopkeeper is used for the purposes of a
conversion. So in the formula $1.5/V$ ΣMR, we should only take into
account the money borrowed by the customer and not the quantity of
'deposits'.

The volume of annual credit card transactions in the United States
has been estimated to amount to \$375,000 million. If we suppose that
during one year the volume of credit card transactions expands by 10
per cent the corrective factor to be added to the indicator M1 is $(1.5/40)$
x 10 per cent of 375,000 million, i.e. about 1,500 million dollars. If,
during the same year, M1 has increased by 30,000 million dollars, the
corrective in relative terms for the increase in credit card transactions is
1.5/30, i.e. 5 per cent. This line of argument and these calculations show
how one can use statistics in order to improve the definition of the first
of the monetary indicators, M1, and the interpretations that can be made
of it.

The accusation most commonly levelled against the Eurodollar system
and, in general, against any form of international, non-national currency
(such as the SDR would have been if, as was originally intended, it had
been developed into an international currency) is its supposedly
inflationary nature. The question is an important one. The faults of the
international monetary system are well known, and the need for a neutral,
stateless currency grows as time passes, and there is reason to believe the
IMF may well gradually develop into a world central bank. The
reconstruction of the world monetary system necessarily involves the
creation of a new international payment unit, and it is just as inevitable
that this should raise many questions. The first and most pregnant is the
one that always arises apropos of monetary creation, namely the inflation
it may cause.

In order to settle this question, we must first of all decide what sort of
an inflationary impact an international money would have. Inflation is in
fact a complex, many-sided phenomenon. There is no way that we can
reach any definite conclusions if we do not distinguish between the

different kinds of inflationary effect which are caused by or involve financial transfers from one country to another. We must exclude from the analysis domestic inflation in national currencies, even if it is caused by international capital movements. This internal inflation is the result of a large number of factors, which are partly autonomous and partly under the control of the monetary authorities in each country. There is no doubt that the extreme fluidity of the international capital market is a factor leading to disorder. But it is not this aspect of inflation that people fear in the case of the creation of a new international payment unit. What people do fear is monetary inflation caused by the introduction onto the monetary markets of payment units created *ex nihilo*. These units give those who use them for the first time a title to goods and services which they have not earned, i.e. which have not been balanced by a corresponding supply of goods and services. This is the very essence of monetary inflation as it is usually understood: it is the acceptation we shall use here.

The foregoing analysis will help us to understand the matter better and, in particular, to distinguish between the different kinds of inflation according as they arise within a state or outside it. Let us take the simplest case, that of a stateless currency not circulating within the borders of any state. This would be the case of the SDR issued by the IMF in its role of world central bank. The currency units would be created *ex nihilo* and then introduced into circulation by means of loans to central banks or to commercial banks. They would not be used for payments within the state in question, but would circulate in that monetary no man's land that exists between the frontiers of states, being used as the vehicle of payments by one state to another or by an inhabitant of one state to an inhabitant of another. They would therefore be isolated from internal markets by exchange offices, where they would be converted into national currencies at a given rate.

Let us now suppose that this neutral international money is in existence. The world central bank makes a loan in this currency to a national central bank which, in turn, lends it to a commercial bank. An importer wishes to buy, from an exporter residing in another country, goods which he intends to consume and which will be paid for with the borrowed money, that is, with 'unearned' money. This appears to be a classic example of inflation caused by monetary creation *ex nihilo*. But if we take the term 'unearned consumption' in its strictest sense, we cannot say whether or not there will be monetary inflation, because of the fact that other currencies, that is the national currencies of the states where the importer and exporter are resident, are involved. In fact, the intervention of foreign exchange offices, functioning as a sort of air-lock, radically alters the situation.

We shall use the concept of reduction, and the way this reduction is distributed amongst the different economic agents, as a guide, and we shall also make use of the calculations used to work out the corrective factor defined in the previous chapter. Starting from the fundamental principle that unearned goods and services must be provided by someone, and that in consequence there must be a corresponding reduction somewhere, at some time, we shall be able to find out where, how and when the monetary inflation arises that accompanies an *ex nihilo* creation of new payment instruments outside frontiers.

Let us now get a bit closer to reality by taking a concrete example: the IMF issues X units of international currency and lends them to the Central Bank of Brazil, which re-lends them to a Brazilian importer via a bank in Rio. The importer purchases machines from an exporter in Hamburg; he 'consumes' the machines but he does not pay for them with his units of international money; he pays for them in cruzeiros, which his bank exchanges for international currency at the Central Bank of Brazil. The origin of the cruzeiros will help us to locate the monetary inflation at this stage in the sequence of exchanges.

These cruzeiros, though they have been used for the purchase of the German machinery, are no different from other cruzeiros being used for domestic transactions in Brazil. They may have been created *ex nihilo* or may also have been transferred without any corresponding new creation of money, like all the other cruzeiros in the hands of Brazilian residents. It can even be argued that, in that narrow aspect of the operation under consideration, monetary inflation proper does not exist; the effect is rather one of deflation, since cruzeiros have been removed from circulation by the importer and returned to the Central Bank.

The international monetary units which the German exporter has received either remain in his account at the bank in Hamburg or are exchanged for marks at the Bundesbank. To the extent that, as is the case in Germany, the growth of M1 is controlled by the authorities, i.e. kept below a certain ceiling, there is no particular monetary inflation attributable to the changing of cruzeiros into marks. The marks paid to the bank in Hamburg are either marks removed from circulation and not created for this purpose, or they are in fact created, but in that case there must be other marks which would have been created and have not been, because the total of marks created nevertheless remains below the ceiling. Looked at from the narrow viewpoint of the creation of national currency within the two countries, the creation of extranational monetary units, in other words, of artificial liquidity, does not cause any monetary inflation.

The formula $1.5/V \ \Sigma MR$, however, is inapplicable. It illustrates the way a loan speeds up transactions that cause a conversion of final production. But the transaction set off by the loan from the IMF in international currency does not cause any conversion of production into non-productive consumption outside the countries in question, simply because there is not really any production or consumption, properly speaking, but only the transition from one currency, the international currency, to another, the national currency, within the walls of an exchange office.

Let us now look at the situation, not inside but outside the countries. The Central Bank of Brazil is in debt to the IMF, whilst the Bundesbank, or the bank in Hamburg, has claims on this same institution. This means that the goods and services provided by Germany have been consumed by Brazil without having been 'earned' by it. This contribution by the Germans has been removed from the German economy, more exactly from the holders of money, by means of the national currency, i.e. the mark, and not through the extranational currency. Reduction is only operative, for obvious reasons, within the confines of a state. The instrument of this reduction is the national currency, which ignores extranational currencies. The latter remain neutral in such operations; it is not by means of the variations in purchasing power, as the unit changes hands, that reduction takes effect. This shows that it is possible to equip a new extranational currency with a special property, which would be eminently desirable, namely a constant purchasing power, independent of the price level and exchange rates.

It might be supposed from this example that our imaginary world Central Bank, the IMF, would be free to create as much liquidity as it wished. This is not the case, because in that case other considerations than those we have looked at above would have to be taken into account, among them the question of confidence and expectations other than the, as it were, mechanical parameters which we cited in the previous analysis, Nevertheless, we ought to bear in mind the very special neutral character of an extranational currency which gives it a broad area of issue and which, above all (and this is the most important thing), means that it can be equipped with this remarkable property — constant purchasing power — thanks to which it would constitute the stable standard of value which has been lacking for so long. This constitutes the subject matter of Part 3.

7 The taboo of inconvertibility

The concept of backing, in terms of precious metals or other commodities, long dominated monetary thinking and also influenced the notion of fiduciary money. It led people to identify the unit of money with the commodity it represented and define it in terms of the very thing that acted as its guarantee. This idea obscured the true nature of money and distorted its mechanisms. These distortions can plainly be perceived by comparing the interpretation of money from two separate points of view: from that of a commodity backing and that of the transaction (or 'exchange') function.

As regards the commodity guarantee, what counts for the holder of a title acquired in return for a supply of goods is the security of being able to make use of this title and thus receive something in kind, wherever and whenever he likes, in exchange for the goods he has supplied. As regards the transaction function, as was revealed in chapter 5, debt money is seen as the essential instrument for the conversion of production into consumption or investment. The search for some kind of security may help a monetary system to function smoothly and efficiently, but it cannot be regarded as the essence of such a system. If we want to understand the monetary mechanisms, we must first of all consider the exchange and conversion function, because it is fundamental. We must also resist the temptation to see, in the search for a guarantee or commodity backing, anything more than an ancillary operation, the means of which may, moreover, vary, and the role of which should be assessed only to the extent that it promotes the proper use of money in its conversion function.

The origin of money is not to be found in barter; its true role is much more of a fiduciary nature. In return for the article he had supplied, an animal skin or a flint axe, primitive man attempted to create a claim which he could use later somewhere else, and which could also, if necessary, be used for the purpose of obtaining another commodity, different in kind from the one he had sold. In order to do this, he needed some sort of security, a guarantee both for the continued validity of the claim and the opportunity to make use of it at another time, in another place and for another thing. Men soon found the security they were looking for in the shape of precious metals, which fulfilled the necessary conditions thanks to their durability and their intrinsic value, which made them universally recognised and coveted assets.

But the identification of money with precious metals, however remote in the history of man, should not deceive us. If we look at things in chronological order, we can see that the search for a backing to money is posterior to the recognition of the existence of a *claim*, and is only one manifestation of one of the most powerful impulses which have at all times governed the actions of men — the search for *security* and the attempt to *reduce risks*.

The duality inherent in the function of metallic money, which was at once representative of a claim and the material security for this same claim, is reflected in the separation which persisted up to the eighteenth century of the metallic object which constituted the guarantee (*Louis d'or, écu*, etc.) from the exchange value of this same object expressed in units of account (pounds) on the faces of coins. It also explains how governments, whose fiat determined the connection between coin and unit of account, have been able, from time immemorial, to make abusive use of this privilege.

For centuries, kings took advantage of this inherent ambivalence in order to fill their own coffers, and at the same time supply the specie needed to keep the economy functioning smoothly. But, in fact, they were only partially successful; the shortage of specie, even more than the chronic deficits of public finances, was what hampered economic development from the Middle Ages to modern times. It was only in 1720 in France, at the time of the banking revolution of John Law, that the unit of account was first visibly marked on the currency units, first on the notes and then on the coins, and that the pound ceased to be a mere abstract unit of account.

The identification and assimilation of money and its guarantee very soon resulted in credit and the issue of the circulating medium being based primarily on the guarantee. The development of money and the introduction of the abstract unit of money, in the form of a claim on an institution, was not the result of a logical process of reasoning but was only the consequence of the risks which experience led lenders to take, *vis-à-vis* this same security.

The first banks, in the Middle Ages, kept all the specie that they received from their customers, in their coffers. Later, they learnt to lend what had been deposited with them. The next stage was to put acknowledgements of debt into circulation, and to use them as money, in parallel with the specie which had been deposited and then lent. Thus it was that the problem of risk, which dominates money and credit, arose. The main risks bankers faced were the insolvency of a borrower, the risk of cash withdrawals in excess of available reserves and the risk of abuse by the government of its privilege of issue. It is not, therefore, hard to understand why the desire for a guarantee in the form of a commodity backing should have so obsessed people as to ensure that the idea should persist right up to the present day in the conceptions people have of the nature of money.

Like many human institutions, the idea of commodity backing has sometimes been useful, and sometimes pernicious. The gold standard system, epitome of the system founded on the idea of backing, was useful while it lasted because it managed to retain the merits of a backing as an anchor for the value of the money and a natural regulator, whilst at the same time correcting the restrictive nature of the system by means of a parallel circulation of fiduciary money. But beyond that point, the search for a backing has caused mechanisms which might have been useful to become harmful; it has led people to trust to mere appearances of security and to justify, on the basis of these appearances, excessive monetary creation.

From the beginning of the eighteenth century up to the present day, monetary history has been criss-crossed by attempts to replace, at first partially and then entirely, precious metals, in the role of payment instruments, by debt money, this debt money being based on a backing, which has itself varied in nature over the centuries. At the time of the French Revolution's *assignats*, it was the confiscated property of the *émigrés* and of the church that was taken as backing. Seventy-five years earlier, John Law[1] (1) had realised that the shortage of circulating medium, which at the time was limited to specie, was curbing economic activity and impeding growth. But he, like all his contemporaries, could only conceive of paper money in terms of its backing. That is why, instead of confining his activities to that of founding a General Bank — later transformed, by royal charter, into Royal Bank — he thought he ought to give it, as a foundation, powerful, profitable and prosperous business, such as the *Ferme des Tabacs*, the *Compagnie des Indes, de la Louisiane et du Mississippi.* In the belief that he was giving his bank a solid foundation, Law in fact sowed the seeds of its ruin.

In his impressive study, *La Banqueroute de John Law*,[2] Edgar Faure says:

> Here we come to the essential point: a claim which is payable on demand
> cannot be backed by a security which is not completely liquid; one
> cannot make something which is excessively mobile (paper money)
> out of something which is highly immobile (property). Money being
> inclined by its very nature to circulate, it cannot be exchangeable for
> a form of wealth which can only change hands slowly. . .
>   The logic of Law's analysis ought to have led him to the notion of
> a currency backed by a security, but inconvertible. But why back it
> with land rather than with national wealth? In fact, his mind was
> already moving in this direction, but he was never to rid himself of the
> taboo of inconvertibility. That is why he later settled for the
> intermediate formula of share-money. But he did not notice the fault
> in this system, namely that a share considered as money is based on a
> security which cannot easily be mobilised, which is scarcely more
> tractable than land, because though it is represented by documents
> which can easily be passed from hand to hand, it still runs the risk of
> a collapse in market rates[2] . . .

The fault in Law's system was not the fact that convertibility was
difficult and uncertain: it was the fact that convertibility was relied upon
at all. The primary function of a monetary claim is to promote trade and
the conversion of production into consumption or investment by passing
from hand to hand. There is, as we have already seen, no natural
connection between this function and the security that guarantees the
money or the commodity it is supposed to represent. Faure goes on to
say:

> In the absence of an absolute value and an empirical solution, namely
> precious metals, what comes closest to it is neither land values (the
> illusion of Law and, later, Bernard Cornfeld and many others) nor
> baskets of commodities, as recommended by Pierre Mendès-France:
> it is, quite simply, the credit of the state backed up by a prosperous
> economy. Moreover, this was what Law's mind was moving towards
> during his period of intellectual vagabondage. To this extent he is the
> real father of modern economics.

But a country may be prosperous and the government quite capable of
paying its debts while the currency may be far from stable. Deflation,

which increases the purchasing power of money, often weakens the economy.

Law dreamt of a currency which would be free of the variations of value inherent in metal. The perfect currency, he thought, ought to be based on the supposedly constant value of an economically profitable good, which is why Law remained attached for so long to the notion of paper money, and subsequently touched on the idea of share-money, to which he was later to return. His researches took him towards a currency which would be backed by the entire economy, as the SDR is today . . .

Edgar Faure gets close to a conclusion which could be very fruitful, but he hesitates to put it in so many words and to recognise that convertibility is only a security and that it cannot constitute a general basis for a monetary mechanism.

How could convertibility, which is already very difficult to respect in the case of a share-money, become easier when it is based on the 'entire economy'? By replacing, in the role of backing of precious metals, land and shares by the 'entire economy', we do not get away from the idea of a backing on which the currency is founded. We have simply replaced one term with a precise meaning (gold, land, shares) by another which is much less precise. Edgar Faure certainly understands the artificial aspect of the mechanism of convertibility, but by saying that 'the heart of the matter is that the economic function of money is not to produce interest but to represent capital', he has let slip the occasion he had so carefully prepared of denouncing the mistaken notion of a money supposedly representing a good (or, as he says a capital), and at the same time pointing out the dangers of basing money on often deceptive securities which, in any case, have no chance of providing the economy with its means of exchange and conversion, the essential functions of money. As for the SDR, it is not based on the 'entire economy'. It is made up of a basket of national currencies in immutable quantities and it is only worth what these national currencies are worth. Like them, it is affected by that universal evil, inflation, or erosion of purchasing power. Moreover, the SDR is not even a currency, it is simply a right − hence its name − which entitles the country holding it to obtain fixed quantities of the national currency of another country.

Until very recent times, governments have preferred to trust to mechanisms based on so-called securities, rather than try to evaluate and maintain rationally and pragmatically the volume of debt money in circulation at an optimum level. This is the reason why, after the unfortunate attempts of the eighteenth century, people have tried to base money on a metallic cover, then on claims representative of a commodity (discounts), and finally, generalising more and more, to justify and guarantee it by means of 'claims of the economy'.

The great crisis of the 1930s was not caused by defective monetary mechanisms but it was aggravated and prolonged by a lack of comprehension of these mechanisms.[3] The movements of gold from central bank to central bank, the chain-reaction collapses of banks, the resulting deflation and the breakdown of all economic activity, marked the end of a series of ardent but wrong-headed efforts to recreate the securities on which money had traditionally been based. At the same time, Adolf Hitler, having thrown overboard the traditional rules of monetary orthodoxy and broken the constraints of metallic backing, set the German economy in motion again, gave work to five million unemployed and turned the Third Reich into an island of prosperity in a sea of unemployment.

It is understandable that the idea of a backing or a security should have dominated monetary mechanisms which were themselves all based on various kinds of probability. This fact also explains why, in the absence of adequate knowledge and statistical information, there should have been a transmutation of what was only a single cogwheel in the mechanism (i.e. the notion of reduction of risk) into a kind of revealed truth, which in turn brought about the transformation of the mere commodity — the security — into the monetary unit which it represents. Modern methods of statistical analysis should make it possible to reject such an out-of-date notion, which has since become pernicious, and take money for what it is, namely a simple claim, created arbitrarily and equipped with an important role, which is to facilitate a process that is the very essence of economic activity: the conversion of production into consumption. Only then can we hope to establish the rules of a rational management of money.

NOTES

[1] The Bank of England owes its existence to another Scotchman, William Paterson, who founded it somewhat before Law founded the *Banque Royale*. Just like John Law, Paterson dreamt of colonial exploits and the fabulous riches of the Americas. His colonial enterprises led to a disaster in which his wife and daughter perished, but the government of England was wise enough to keep the Bank of England and the Gulf of Darien Company separate. The Bank of England confined itself to distributing

negotiable bank-notes in exchange for cash deposits which it lent to the Royal Treasury. Very soon, it provided the Treasury with supplementary resources, by lending to it in the form of bank-notes. Fiduciary money had been born, and with it all the tremendous advantages and dangers that such a form of money involves. It was the 'Bullion Committee', in which Ricardo played a dominant role, which, in 1810, and subsequently, once peace had returned with the fall of Napoleon, set out to find the causes of the weakness of the pound sterling *vis-à-vis* gold and the rise in the cost of living.

It is from this period that we can date the restrictive system known by the name of the gold standard, destined to prevent financial laxity and, in particular, the issue of notes to cover budge deficits. What was originally only an instrument designed to eliminate risks was subsequently transformed into a dogma, the dogma of money as representative of a commodity.

[2] See page 188.'The monetary lessons of John Law's system,' as revealed in Edgar Faure's book *La banqueroute de John Law.*

[3] 'What is really lacking is not will-power, but knowledge. The crisis of 1930 was not foreseen and for a long time politicians were paralysed and impotent because the economic theory of the time could not tell them how to deal with the situation . . . Because they were not properly understood and because they were not under control, monetary events helped to plunge the world, 36 years ago, into a serious crisis and subsequently, during the last twenty years, into inflation. This is a warning which those in positions of authority should always bear in mind.'
Valery Giscard d'Estaing.

SUPPLEMENTARY NOTES

PAGE 124

One view of monetarism
(1) 'Finally, monetarism does have its excesses and exaggerations, its tendency to oversimplify, its unproved assertions, its appeals to the lay public — and, what's more, to reactionary sentiments of doubtful validity concerning free enterprise — even demagogy. Nevertheless, by calling into question a theory which had become just a little too well established, by giving currency to ideas which, even if they have still to be tested empirically, have a certain degree of plausibility, by putting forward alternative solutions, by compelling everybody to think more clearly and sharpen their analyses on many points, it has had a very positive role to play. No person and no idea can be sure of being able to emerge unscathed from a confrontation with monetarism; but there is a good chance that everyone stands to gain intellectually in the end. The shock of its onslaught has brought with it progress in the field of economic forecasting in short-term dynamics (particularly period analysis), the effects of budgetary and monetary policies and the evaluation of price flexibility.'
Serge Christophe Kolm, SEDEIS, April 1971.

PAGE 129

(1) Towards a consensus?
The immediate cause of inflation is always an excessively rapid growth
of the money supply compared with that of production . . . The basic
proposition that inflation never occurs without creation of new money
would appear to be one of the most solidly founded statements in the
science of economics. It is so often and so regularly confirmed by events
that it is astonishing that people should still doubt it. . . It is important
to repeat once and for all: the only way to halt inflation is to limit the
growth of the money supply.
Emil-Maria Claassen and Pascal Salin.

In the opinion of Mr J. L. Guglielmi, however, in an article that appeared
at about the same time as the above quotation, in the *Revue d'Economie
Politique*; 'Once again, in 1976—7 the claim that the economy can be
controlled through the money supply, without taking any account of
production and the formation of capital appears to be nothing but an
illusion'.
  At first sight, it looks as if the antagonism between monetarians and
anti-monetarians is as strong as ever, and that the categorical assertion of
Claassen and Salin is taking us even further away from the consensus
we so earnestly desire. The anti-monetarians have no difficulty in showing
that the economy is threatened with strangulation if a general rise in the
wage level in excess of growth in production is not accompanied by a
parallel increase in the money supply. This, in fact, is what experience
shows us, and an almost mathematical proof of it can be provided (see
Chapter 6 of Part 1).
  Where then, do the two theses meet? In the assertion — which no one
can doubt — that inflation is rendered so complicated by reactions and
interreactions, influenced by so many psychological factors, inflationary
anticipations and other forms of 'contagion', that we can only hope to
understand it and, *a fortiori*, control it, if we take the only element
common to it in all its forms, whatever the cause, namely the excessive
proliferation of means of payment compared with production. Inflation
affects the price level and the price level results from the interreaction
between the money supply and production. As Claassen and Salin go on
to say:

Inflation is a continuous process in which different variables play in
turn the roles of cause and effect.
  These variables are very numerous and they change according to
time and place. Only the monetary variable is always there. A monetarist
explanation of inflation means that one can assimilate elements that
have a more partial bearing on the course of events. . . If the behaviour
of unions or companies or the level of import prices exert inflationary
pressures, the latter can only develop to the extent that the monetary
authorities ratify these price rises by an appropriate creation of new
money. From this point of view, the old distinction between cost-

push inflation and demand-pull inflation should be abandoned. . . .
Whatever the individual causes of a given inflation, at a given moment
all inflations have one thing in common: an excessive growth of the
money supply. It matters little whether this phenomenon is the ultimate
cause or, as in most cases, the permissive cause . . . Monetary policy is
the easiest lever to work; it alone is completely under the control of the
government.

In short, in the absence of the traditional disciplines, such as the gold
standard and fixed exchange rates, the best guide for monetary policy is
the one that gets closest to the desired objective — control of economic
activity and the price level and the only one that does get close to these
objectives is the money supply. Only governments have the power to
affect the factors that influence the money supply, but in a democracy,
the government is nothing more than the expression of the will of the
voters. The public must, therefore, be made aware of the relationship
between its desires as regards wages and the effects of those desires on the
price level. The rate of growth of the money supply is the only way the
public can understand this cause and effect relationship. Only then shall
we see the emergence of that political will without which there is no cure
for the disease of inflation, for, as our authors say, 'The problem is not
that of deciding how to stop inflation but rather that of deciding how to
find the political will to stop it. We can be cured of inflation, but have we
got the political will to be cured?'

Put in this way, a so-called monetarist policy does not prejudge the
relative merits of the various instruments of intervention on the money
supply which may be exercised upstream or downstream and may even
be other than monetary (e.g. intermediate targets).

These suggestions might perhaps reduce the differences between the
various schools.

PAGE 133

(1) Compulsory reserves

The system of compulsory reserves is derived from the mechanisms
developed in the United States and Germany to control credit expansion
through bank liquidity. This system obliges the banks to keep assets in
non-interest bearing accounts at the central bank in proportion to the
volume of deposits that they have taken in from the public. Since 1
April 1971, the reserves are no longer calculated simply as a proportion
of total deposits but also as a proportion of total loans made. Reserve
requirements have since been extended to financial institutions.

Originally, the reason for obliging banks to keep reserves with the
central bank was to ensure that they would always be liquid, and thus
protect the interests of the depositor. It was only subsequently that the
monetary authorities began to use this measure as a way of controlling
and checking the creation of new money by the banks.

In fact, any granting of credit and consequent creation of new money by the banking system creates a need for reserves, given that a part of the bank money thereby created escapes from the monetary circuits managed by the banks. This is so when the bank money is converted into notes or transferred to the Treasury, Post Office Giro accounts or accounts with savings banks, or even exchanged for foreign currencies. To these leaks, which affect the whole of the system, should be added those that may result from transfers to another institution in order to pay the balance of the day's clearing. The banks must therefore be sure they have enough bank liquidity or find the means of raising it. At the same time, however, it should be noted that these leaks become less important as the percentage of bank-notes in the money supply becomes smaller. In France, this percentage had fallen to about 12.5 per cent at the end of 1976, whereas it was 25 per cent in 1968 and 35 per cent in 1962.

In the most commonly used system of reserves against deposits, the constraints imposed have a relatively general justification; they are applied, whatever the factors that caused the creation of money. For this reason, the banks do not normally establish any direct link between their responsibilities as providers of credit and the volume of additional reserves that they must accumulate when their liabilities grow. They have even less reason to do so, given that, if in theory it is true of the banking system as a whole that credits and deposits grow in parallel, as regards the individual bank this is not in practice the case. There is no obvious connection between the making of loans and the taking of deposits, or, in other words, between a bank's role as creator of money and its role as money manager. Reserves against loans may cause banks to establish this relation of causality by affecting directly the main source of the growth of bank deposits. At the same time, financial institutions, which contribute indirectly to the expansion of the money supply to the extent that a large proportion of the loans they make to householders and to companies must be refinanced by the banks, have also been obliged to make reserves against their deposits.

Manipulation of reserve ratios, which has been used fairly frequently in France as the requirements of the short-term economic outlook dictate, provides a means of affecting the liquidity of the banks directly and quickly, so as to modify in the appropriate direction the expansionary or restrictive effect of those autonomous factors that affect banks' reserves.

But the reserves have their main effect on the cost of credit. In France, where the banking system as a whole is permanently in debt and where the availability of central bank support is not strictly limited, any variation in the level of reserves brings with it a parallel increase in the volume of refinancing. The need for reserves makes itself apparent in each bank's trading account.

The reserve ratio on residents' current account deposits reached 17 per cent in 1974 and then fell to 2 per cent in 1976. It was 33 per cent on cash deposits in 1974 and 0.5 per cent at the end of 1976. Bank of France Information sheet No 35, December 1977.

COMPULSORY RESERVES

Monthly averages 1972–7 (all figures FF 000m's)

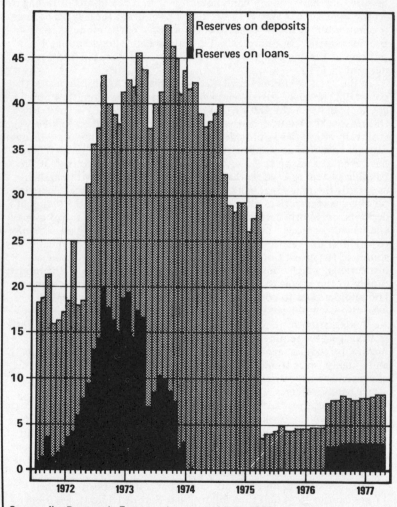

Reserves on deposits

Reserves on loans

Source: 'La Banque de France et la monnaie' Edit. 1978

PAGE 134

(1) Interest rates
Apropos of the manipulation of the interest rate as an instrument of
monetary regulation, Pierre Berger, former head of the Research
Department at the Bank of France, writes as follows (*Monnaie et
Balance des Paiements*, Fondation Nationale des Sciences Politiques).

> The monetary authorities . . . are led to apply restrictive credit policies
> when money comes into the country because they are afraid of the
> repercussions this influx of liquidity will have on the money supply.
> Thus they are tempted to try to combat the supposed ill effects of the
> balance of payments surplus on the money supply whilst
> underestimating the close ties that exist between the different sources
> of monetary creation.
>   But when they are faced with outflows of money, the monetary
> authorities are still inclined to take restrictive measures because out-
> flows of funds, as everyone knows, are a sign of inflationary pressures.
> The desire to fight price rises and to attempt to right the balance of
> payments leads them to impose a credit squeeze. Thus they are forced
> to adopt a perpetually restrictive credit stance, whether the balance of
> payments is in surplus or in credit.

Apropos of credit policy, Pierre Berger adds:

> Two positions, at opposite extremes, are imaginable: the first is a
> fatalistic one. If funds leave the country we should not be surprised to
> see the quantity of loans rising at the same time, since the country's
> needs in money must be satisfied. We must therefore let loans replace
> currency as stimulants to the money supply, which leads naturally to a
> certain laxity. But one can also argue the other way round and adopt
> a position of extreme severity since at one time or another economic
> agents will need a specific quantity of money and a check on loans will
> prevent outflows of funds and may even encourage an inflow. Such a
> line of argument would lead to an extremely tight credit squeeze. . .

What can one conclude from this, if not that the most important
thing lacking in monetary regulation policies is a coherent body of
doctrine?

PAGE 136

(1) Measuring the velocity of money: the Bank of France's approach
Measuring the velocity of circulation of money poses various problems.
In France it is measured on the basis of two different approaches:
transaction velocity and income velocity.
  To use the *transaction velocity* may appear complex methodologically,
but it is the most satisfying approach because it gives quick results. It

consists of attempting to count payments themselves, both cash payments and cheque payments, and compare the result with the appropriate money-supply figure. Data concerning the circulation of fiduciary money are obtained on the basis of movements of bank-notes as they are observed at certain banks. In the case of cheque payments, which are debited to the accounts of non-financial economic agents, the ratio debits/positive balances is calculated. These various items of information have been collected regularly by the Bank of France since 1958. After having weighted the information thus obtained, the statisticians work out a synthetic indicator for the velocity of circulation of M1 monetary liquiditites. The main inconvenience of this method is that it is impossible to differentiate, within the mass of payments, between non-financial transactions and financial transactions. In spite of this difficulty, the development of the resulting index of the transaction velocity makes it possible to form a reasonably accurate idea of the behaviour of holders of money. This approach is supplemented by working out the turnover coefficients of savings book accounts in banks and savings institutions according to the ratio debits/balances of pass book accounts.

The *income velocity* has been defined as the ratio between a particular aggregate of national accounting representing production and national income and the M1, M2 or M3 money supplies. The aggregate that was first taken in order to make this comparison was gross national (later, domestic) product: subsequently, in order better to reflect the actual expenditure of economic agents, it was the gross domestic expenditure which was preferred as term of reference for the calculation. This way of working out the income velocity leads, from an accounting point of view, to results corresponding to the opposite of the liquidity rates of M1 or M2 or M3/GNP or GDP. The approach via the income velocity at present raises practical difficulties, especially because of the need to make short-term economic observations during the course of the year.

Nevertheless, the two kinds of indicator complement each other rather conveniently. In particular, the monthly indicator of M1 transaction velocities usually reflects fairly well the trend of the income velocity of M1 and has the advantage of being more rapidly available than this latter indicator. The progression of the income velocity, which can only be studied in the long term, using annual data, has been analysed in the examination of the liquidity rate, which for accounting purposes may be considered the opposite of this velocity.

The transaction velocity index is particularly useful when the aim is to analyse the effects of monetary policy on the demand for money and the velocity of circulation. This is particularly the case during periods of credit control. More detailed knowledge of the incidence of credit control has been obtained thanks to the comparison of the transaction velocity of M1 with a synthetic indicator intended to show the extent to which credit control 'bites' and which included, as regards the banks and the users of credit, objective data (growth of credit, premium on loan exemption from credit control, quantity of unreimbursed securities etc.)

and subjective data taken from surveys carried out by the Bank of France involving company directors and banks. If we examine this indicator, its movements seem to prefigure those of interest rates at the beginning of the period when the credit control comes into force, and it shows a close relationship between the growth of the credit control constraints and an increase in the velocity of money.

Thus it appears that, because of the greater mobility of otherwise inactive cash balances velocity increases very significantly during periods of restrictive monetary policy (e.g. from 1968 to 1970 or in 1974), whereas, on the other hand, it diminishes at the end of a period of credit control or during periods of expansionary monetary policy (e.g. at the end of 1970 and at the beginning of 1971, or during the second half of 1975). Calculated as an average throughout the year 1976–7, the index of transaction velocity of M1 increased by about 10 per cent; the income velocity of M1 calculated using annual accounting data increased by about 3 per cent, whilst its opposite, the liquidity ratio M1/GDE diminished – at the same rate, of course.

In order to work out the average period during which economic agents hold certain financial assets and thus calculate the degree of liquidity and stability of these assets, a comparison between debits and cash may be made. The turnover coefficient, equal to the ratio

$$\frac{\text{debits during the year}}{\text{annual average of end-of-month cash balances}}$$

represents the intensity with which the assets have been used during the course of the year. The period of use of the assets during a given year is expressed by multiplying the number of months or days in the year by the ratio

$$\frac{\text{annual average of end-of-month cash balances}}{\text{debits during the year}}$$

The information available derives from the two sorts of savings banks (national and ordinary) as well as from a sample of big banks. They only concern certain categories of assets. Moreover, they can only be used to obtain average results, without any details concerning, for example, the distribution of deposits in passbooks according to their effective turnover rate.

Thanks to our knowledge of the average time-spans during which assets are held, it is still possible to make a classification of financial assets according to their degree of 'moneyness'. Comparison between 1976 and 1977 confirms that in the case of bank demand deposits the transaction velocity of the total of financial assets measured by the synthetic velocity index increased, whilst at the same time the tendency for passbook deposits to turn over more rapidly continued.

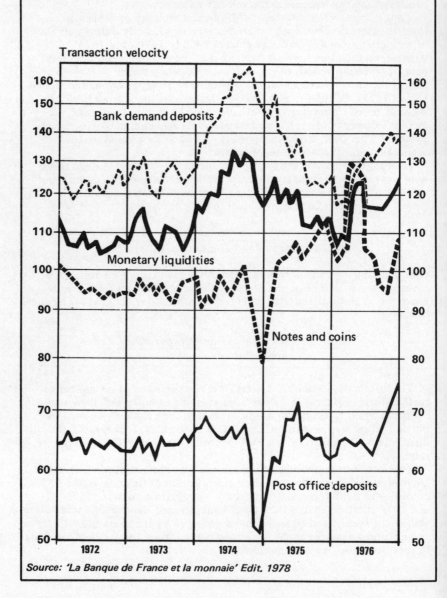

THE VELOCITY OF MONEY

(1958 = 100) (seasonally adjusted data averaged over three months) 1972—76

Transaction velocity

Bank demand deposits

Monetary liquidities

Notes and coins

Post office deposits

Source: 'La Banque de France et la monnaie' Edit. 1978

THE VELOCITY OF MONEY

TRANSACTION VELOCITY

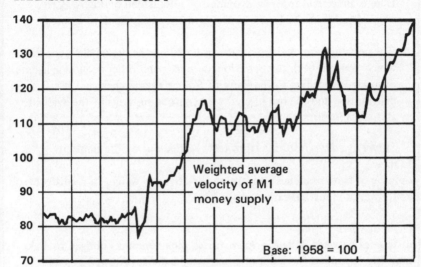

Weighted average velocity of M1 money supply

Base: 1958 = 100

INCOME VELOCITY

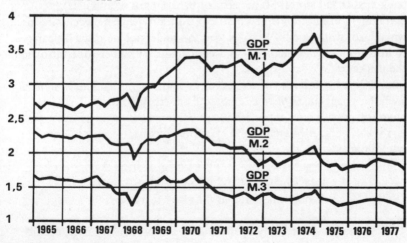

$\frac{GDP}{M.1}$

$\frac{GDP}{M.2}$

$\frac{GDP}{M.3}$

Source: Banque de France

This synthetic index is of great interest. It is the result of a serious effort
to obtain condensed, reliable, easily understood information and a more
reliable guide than the present purely statistical indicators. It has an
additional interest, inasmuch as it can be used in support of a particular
policy, that of credit control. This policy is controversial but it fits in with
present trends in the attempt to control the money supply.

Here is an extract from an explanatory note issued by Pierre Barre,
General Manager of the Research Department of the Bank of France.

The construction of the indicator is based on the use of different data
which concern both the behaviour of banks and other economic agents,
estimated according to the Bank of France's researches, and the
distribution and the use of credit understood in terms of the available
statistical information.

Subjective data, resulting from tests carried out by the Bank of
France:
opinion of bank branches concerning the effective weight of credit control;
condition of industrial cash reserves.

Objective data:
difference between balances noted for all member banks obliged to make
monthly returns to the Bank of France and balances allowed as part of
the system of supplementary reserves (70 per cent of total registered
bank credits and almost 50 per cent of bank credits of all kinds);
premium of exemption from credit control: difference between rates used
when loans which are likely to exceed the guidelines are made by banks
to institutions benefiting from unused margins *vis-à-vis* credit control, and
the market rate;
total of loans in foreign currencies to residents by the banking system as
a whole, which are *de facto* exempted from credit control;
quarterly growth rate, expressed in annual terms, of bank credits — that
is, total of controlled credits and exempted credits;
rate of unpaids, i.e. the ratio:

$$\frac{\text{total of cheques and bills unpaid}}{\text{total cheques presented in the clearing house}}$$

Starting with an analysis of the different elementary data, a scale
going from 0 to 4 has been devised to express the degree of constraint

exercised by credit control:

0 to 1 : none, or almost none
1 to 2 : little
2 to 3 : average
3 to 4 : severe
4 to 5 : more severe.

Relative figures for each datum have been calculated on a three-monthly basis. In the choice of weighting used to obtain a synthetic figure, an attempt has been made, using a method derived from the work of Julius Shishkin, to give a similar weight to each of various data:

Difference between actual balances and authorised balances	11.60%	
Exemption premium	11.60%	35%
Loans in foreign currencies to residents	11.60%	
Opinions of bank branches	15.0%	
'Bite' of credit control on banks	50.0%	
Growth of total bank credits	20.0%	
Rate of unpaids	15.0%	
Industrial cash balances	15.0%	30%
'Bite' of credit control on users of credit	50.0%	

SYNTHETIC INDICATOR DESIGNED TO SHOW THE 'BITE' OF MONETARY POLICY AND THE TREND OF THE TRANSACTION VELOCITY

M1 (seasonally adjusted quarterly averages)

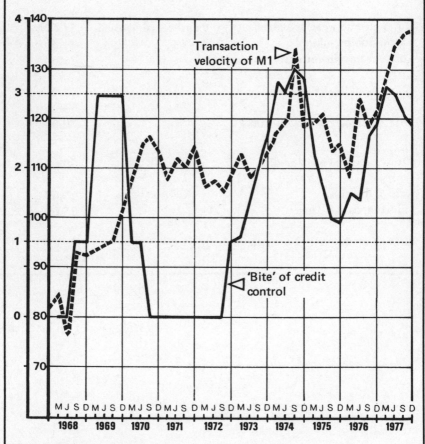

Source: Banque de France

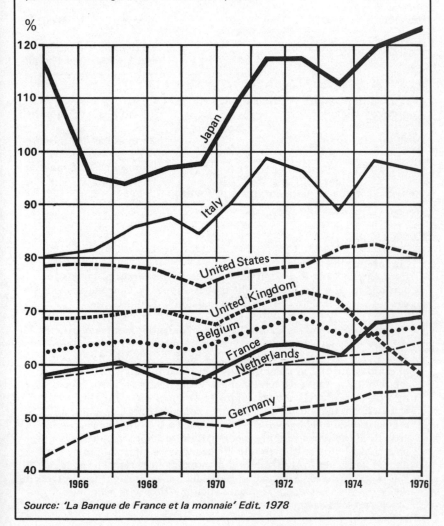

LIQUIDITY TRENDS IN VARIOUS COUNTRIES

Ratio = $\dfrac{\text{Cash and savings liquidities at year-end}}{\text{Gross national expenditure}}$

(arithmetical averages at end of month or quarter)

%

Japan

Italy

United States

United Kingdom

Belgium

France

Netherlands

Germany

Source: 'La Banque de France et la monnaie' Edit. 1978

Average periods during which certain categories of liquid or short-term financial assets are held

	1976	1977
Demand deposits of non-financial companies and individuals in banks	10 days	8 days
Deposits of non-financial companies	$6\frac{1}{2}$	5 days
Individuals' deposits	$34\frac{1}{2}$	31 days
Passbook deposits in banks	10 months and 1 week	9 months and 1 week
Passbook deposits in savings banks (passbook A and B in the Caisse Nationale and ordinary banks)	24 months	23 months
Passbook B	25 months	17 months
Passbook A	25 months	24 months

Source: Research Department, Bank of France.

PAGE 137

(1) Intermediate targets

Fred Aftalion and R. Portait have looked at the choice of targets to be adopted for the regulation of the money supply, a choice which varies according as the objective is in the long, medium or short term.

The preceding remarks lead us to choose a regular, moderate growth of the money supply as the final target of medium-term monetary policy — which implies control of M1 or M2 — and the maintenance of a moderate and, if possible, constant inflation rate. . . In studying medium-term policy we have compared the relative performance of interest rates and the money supply in terms of different objectives. It was shown that the interest rate does not constitute a desirable or even a practicable final target in the long term; on the other hand, regular growth of the money supply is compatible with all the objectives we have looked at. The growth rate of the money supply should be the annual target. As for the question of deciding between M1 and M2 this should be clear from empirical studies: as is apparent from preceding analyses, the most stable aggregate in connection with economic objectives such as prices and levels of activity ought to be chosen as a target.

It is true that the rule to follow in the choice of targets is the one that produces the best monetary effect as regards economic activity and the price level. But can we rely on a purely pragmatic correlation in order to give the preference to one indicator rather than another? The relationships between money, considered as an instrument, on the one hand, and economic activity and prices, on the other, are so variable and depend on so many different factors that it is doubtful whether simple pragmatism will be enough to perceive stable relationships, much less make it possible to predict a reliable response to a given monetary stimulus. Before choosing between the indicators, we ought to be sure of their exact meaning.

The monetary effect on activity and prices is a function of transactions. M1 includes monetary units that have the transaction function. M2 includes, and indeed confuses, units that have the transaction function with those that do not, which does not mean that one must necessarily rely on M1, because it may happen that it is better to follow M2 in order to achieve a certain aim or even use other indicators. What it does mean is that first of all we must define and understand what each individual aggregate means.

PAGE 137

(2) Monetary regulation in Germany
German monetary policy under examination, quoted from *Die Welt*, 22 February 1978.

Only two months have gone by since the Bundesbank fixed its targets for the growth of the primary money supply (M0, which includes central bank assets held by commercial banks) for the year 1978. As from today it is beyond doubt that this figure will be somewhat higher than the 8 per cent which the guardians of our money accepted as the rate that was most compatible with the objective of strong growth in real terms plus a high level of employment and a diminution of inflationary pressures. In fact, between November 1977 and January 1978, M0 increased at an annual rate of 15.5 per cent!

Because of the confused state of our economic situation, the authorities at the Bundesbank not only tolerated this rapid expansion but even favoured it by intervening on the exchange markets.

These foreign exchange market interventions were forced on the Bundesbank by the decline of the dollar, which, had they not intervened, would have caused an excessive appreciation of the mark. It is not fair to hold the German authorities responsible for this. It is rather the system that is at fault, that and the absence of a genuine extranational currency which would take the place of national currencies in international trade.

If the Bundesbank wishes to respect the bases of its monetary policy, such as it was defined in December, it ought to act now. It ought to apply the brakes to the growth of monetary liquidities and stop buying dollars to support the rate. . .

For reasons of short-term economic policy, such a change of direction is inconceivable. The result is that the Bundesbank is obliged to abandon its monetary targets, the credibility of which had in any case been jeopardised in December.

This abandonment by the Bundesbank of its targets leads one to wonder about the theoretical foundations of its monetary policy, the centre of which has been occupied for four years now by the growth of the quantity of central bank money as an objective in itself and an indicator of the growth of the overall money supply. . . The quantity of central bank money tends to increase when companies, tired of investing, start to accumulate excess liquid reserves. The expansion of the money supply can thus easily be distorted. Nothing, however, justifies the fear that it might be inflationary. . . But we should not hold against the Bundesbank the fact that it is gradually abandoning its quasi-monetarist policies with regard to credit in order to come back to its former doctrines.

Apropos the monetary ideas of the Swiss authorities, there follows an extract from an article that appeared in the *Neue Zürcher Zeitung*, 3 February, 1978:

In 1975 the central bank undertook to control the money supply formally by fixing a growth rate for M1, which thus became the intermediate target. As long as the different aggregates, M1 M2, M3 etc., change in parallel, the question of choosing one rather than another is a purely theoretical matter. Examination of the statistics nevertheless shows that the three monetary aggregates in fact do not vary homothetically and have been diverging for some time, which raises genuine problems of interpretation. Generally speaking, it can be seen that the relation between the money supply and the GNP is closer as the definition of the aggregate is broader. In other words, it is M3 that has the closest relation with the GNP. Consequently, the central bank ought to take M3 as the intermediate objective of its monetary policy. To that one can retort that according to the most recent developments in monetary theory it is the price level and not the GNP in value terms which needs to be taken as the final objective of monetary policy. From this point of view, M1 is a better medium-term objective than M3.

The choice of a medium-term target depends on the extent to which it can be controlled by the central bank. It would indeed appear that regulation of M1 is likely to be the most efficient means of control for the central bank.

PAGE 138

(1) American uncertainties

The following are excerpts from remarks made by Mr. Philip E. Coldwell, Member of the Board of Governors of the US Federal Reserve System, at

the 26th Annual UCLA Business Forecasting Conference in Los Angeles
on 8 December 1977.

Fundamentally the debate about the appropriate guides to the formulation and execution of monetary policy has centred upon the use of
monetary aggregates as a proxy for the supply of credit, or alternatively
interest rates as a reflection of the demand for credit. Events of recent
months have accentuated the debate as the monetary aggregates rose
sharply and adherents to these measures clamoured for a tighter policy.
At the same time, those favouring an interest rate approach began a
more insistent campaign for policy attention. With the monetary
aggregates expanding at rates considered potentially more inflationary
and short-term interest rates advancing as the Federal Reserve sought to
contain the money-supply growth, the elements of controntation have
become more pronounced. On the one hand, monetarists insist that the
central bank constrain money-supply growth and some even suggest:
a retrenchment to offset what they consider excessive growth over the
past nine months. On the other hand, the interest rate advocates say
that further increases in such rates to curtail money-supply growth will
jeopardise the economic expansion.

In our Federal Open Market Committee meetings, we are provided
with a staff forecast of the near-term expected rate of growth in
monetary aggregates and the impact of such growth on the economy.
Similarly, we are given the expected level of interest rates from the
forecast of the economy and the monetary aggregate assumptions. The
Committee is given a choice of several different paths of monetary
growth and several choices concerning the interest rate constraints
within which policy is to be implemented. If the Federal Reserve were
following a strict monetarist approach it would have no interest rate
constraints and would set its monetary aggregate guides for the long-
run expected needs of the economy. If the Federal Reserve were
following a strict interest rate approach, it would have no monetary
aggregate guides. Obviously, we are using both, to the considerable
unhappiness of both groups of advocates. Our policy development has
stressed aggregates at some meetings but interest rates at others.

The time frame for the monetarist is usually 18−24 months before
the full impact of money-supply changes is complete. In a policy
sense, therefore, the monetarist wants a money-supply growth objective
oriented to the one to two year future and since forecasts of economic
conditions for such a long-term span are extraordinarily difficult, he
suggests provision of money supplies at a steady non-inflationary long-term
rate. The interest rate advocate looks at the economy in a somewhat
shorter time frame of three to twelve months. To him monetary policy
should be tied to the relatively immediate prospects for the economy, and
policy would mean stimulus by lowering interest rates when the forecast
future is uncertain or when the economy is failing to achieve its full
potential without overt inflationary pressures.

A further difference appears to be in the causal relationships
between excess capacity, money supply and real growth, especially

when an economy is faced with unacceptably high levels of unemployment and inflation. The monetarist stresses the impact of inflation upon the economy and ultimately upon job-creating opportunities. Therefore, advocates of the monetary aggregates approach favour a long-range gradual reduction of inflation by curtailing money-supply growth. Such a programme is expected to lay the foundation for improved economic gains and reduced unemployment in the future. In contrast, those favouring a shorter time frame and an interest rate approach believe that appropriate monetary and fiscal stimulus, creating prompt job openings, will raise economic activity and the resulting increases in the supplies of goods and services will not aggravate price pressures and may, over time, reduce such pressures.

Finally, the two approaches are differentiated by certainty of data. The monetary aggregates are subject to very large swings in projections and great uncertainty of relevance in the short-term. With the problems of incomplete and untimely reporting, of shifts in definition of transaction balances and of the unknowns in velocity, the monetary aggregates have proved to be a highly unreliable and inadequate guide to short or intermediate-term policy formulation. Despite extensive analytical and computerised efforts, there have been very large unexplained shifts in the rates of growth of the aggregates. These have caused increased caution in the use of the aggregates and a widened band of tolerance for changes between meetings of the FOMC.

In contrast, there is a certainty to the interest rates of the moment and a certainty of Committee control over the short-term rate for inter-bank borrowing. These, coupled with the natural bias of policy-makers toward factual analysis and the uncertainties of the aggregates, have led to greater reliance upon the Federal funds rate as a constraint on policy reaction to changes in aggregate growth rates.

The monetarists are likely to say that this focus of the Committee away from reliance upon the aggregates has resulted in the Committee accepting higher rates of aggregate growth but unrealistically low levels on interest rates. On the other hand, the money market advocates are likely to be unhappy because of the rise in short-term rates.

In point of fact, the Committee has temporised on both approaches, and probably for the best. Policy is not made in a vacuum of theory but must respond to a host of pressures, including, recently, the impact of the uncertainty in energy and tax legislation, the high level of trade deficits, the decline in the exchange rate of the dollar and the public perception of a marked slowing of the economy. It would be a very pleasant life to make policy in an ivory tower devoid of these day-to-day and month-to-month pressures but this is not the life of a central banker. He must blend a healthy respect for the theoretical structure of policy formulation with both the immediacy of political and social pressures and the business, market and consumer perceptions.

As noted above, one of the principal problems in using the monetary aggregates as guides to policy is their volatile nature and their unpredictability over the near-term policy period. To remedy these difficulties, I have a number of suggestions:

(1) We need to clarify the nature of the aggregates and define them so that sudden moves or shifts can be identified and corrected. (2) Another change of some value might be to focus policy attention on the quarterly data with two-thirds weight on known figures. (3) Similarly, the Federal Reserve might widen the band of interest rate and aggregate guides, thus reducing the degree of desk intervention in the market and further de-emphasising the weekly data. (4) Finally, to reduce market sensitivity to weekly aggregates and lift the horizons of decision-makers, we shall consider the elimination of weekly calculations and publish adjusted data only on a monthly and quarterly basis. These proposed changes are refinements of the present system and do not change the fundamental focus of policy guides. However, they could be helpful in reducing 'street noise' and statistical aberrations which interfere at present with both policy formulation and the public's perception of policy intent.

PAGE 138

(2) A few words on the traditional economic theory of interest rates

There are numerous consistent reasons for believing that the rate of return on invested capital is generally nil if the capital gains or losses incurred by the claims that constitute the investment are left out of account. This admission goes well beyond the recent realisation by many small investors that interest rates on savings are negative in times of accelerating inflation. During recent years at least, this has become a permanent feature of western economies, of which the least that one can say is that it is totally alien to traditional or even modern theories with regard to the rate of interest.
Alain Cotta.

Keynesianism establishes a relationship between 'liquidity preference' and the cost of borrowing. It imagines investment as the result of a choice, depending on the cost of money, between productive plant (and the profit it may produce) and consumption goods. If one looks at the graphs set out by Alain Cotta in his book, one cannot help wondering what is left of this Keynesian theory. Apart from their purchases of property, which cannot be considered plant, householders who save make no investment choices. They are happy to save as and when they can.

The true private sector investor is in fact the industrialist. The first responsibility of a company director is to plan the future of his company. This is a reflection of his expectations, his imagination, his calculations and his decisions. When he thinks about the future, he thinks in real terms. The provisional budget forecast which he draws up for himself, if not for his shareholders, is calculated in real terms because he cannot calculate in any other way. Sales, salaries and other costs more or less follow the inflation rate. The only factor in his calculations which he cannot anticipate is interest rates in real terms. The result is that, today even more than yesterday, company directors have become gamblers, no different from those who dabble in football pools. This remark reminds one of Alain Cotta:

> In its early phase, capitalism was tied to the constraints of existing
> savings, which were themselves tied to the constraints of issue of
> money. As soon as its development made it possible, the banking
> system simultaneously demonstrated:
> the existence of a new economic agent, the banker;
> the growing liberation of companies with regard to existing savings;
> the growing liberation of the banker from central bank money — firstly
> from metal money and then from debt money

PAGE 145

(1) The powers of monetary creation of the banking system

Money is not neutral; the way it is created, the way it circulates and the
uses to which it is put have decisive effects on the economy. It is understandable that at a time when it is generally recognised that the state has
the right and the duty to direct the economy — and this is true everywhere,
even in those countries where classical liberalism is strongest — it should
also wish to control the money supply, the circulation of money and, in
consequence, the banking system.

It is the obvious difficulty of achieving this control that leads certain,
by no means faint-hearted liberals, such as Maurice Allais, to suggest that
the banking system should be deprived of its money-creating powers by
the imposition of obligatory 100 per cent reserve requirements. But it
is by no means certain that the State would make better use of these
powers if they were all concentrated in its hands. What is certain is that
there is a crying need for better understanding of the mechanism of the
banking system because it is too often confused with the mechanism of
money. Modern banking systems have developed enormously, but they
still remain little understood:

> Like all revolutions, the revolution of the banking system may be
> admired or deplored. . . It depends on one's view of it. But what one
> can't do is ignore it. And yet not one American in a thousand has the
> slightest idea of it. It is hard to see how we can ever reach sensible
> policies on a key sector of the economy such as the banking system as
> long as there is not a large proportion of the population that under-
> stands it. . .

The author of this book illustrates his point even better by relating
this little anecdote, which was passed on to him by the chairman of one
of the big American banks:

> We wanted to show our appreciation to one of our directors who had
> completed fifty years' service in the bank. Everyone stopped working
> and we had a little party in the banking hall, after which we all shook
> hands with him and offered him our presents. At the end of the

ceremony I took the microphone and said 'And now, old chap, you who are on the verge of retirement, you who have spent fifty years in banking and seen everything, tell us what is the most important and most radical change that you have seen in the profession over the last fifty years?' He thought for a moment and then got up and took the microphone and replied: 'Air-conditioning'.
Martin Mayer, *The bankers*, W. H. Allen, London).

PAGE 160

(1) Last words on the multiplier

If we go back to Chapter 7 of Part 1, 'Banks and non-banks', we can get a better idea of the true significance of the mistake of confusing units of money that have the payment function with those that do not. If we then examine the famous 'multiplier' in all its aspects, as Professor Guitton advises us to do, we shall perceive the consequences of this mistake.

Let us take the example we have already used once of a deposit at a bank which is lent, redeposited, re-lent, redeposited and so on. In other words, there is a series of 'deposits' arising from 'loans' which 'create' further 'deposits'.

Let us now suppose, for the sake of clarity and simplicity, that payments and deposits are effected in gold coins only. By replacing claims, which clearly constitute debts for the institutions on which they are drawn, by gold coins we shall eliminate the risk of confusing creditors and debtors.

Our gold coin, therefore, starts to circulate from bank to bank. It is deposited at bank A, which lends it to a customer. This customer uses it to pay X. X deposits the coin at bank B, which lends it to Y, who deposits it at bank C. Finally, it is lent by C to another customer, who pays Z with it.

At each transaction the current account of a depositor has been credited, which creates a demand, or current account, deposit which the customer is at liberty to draw on whenever he likes. To simplify our example further, let us suppose that each bank has given its customers a booklet of transfer orders and that each transfer order is carried out directly by moving gold coins.

Now let us eliminate A, B and C. The first borrower pays X directly, X pays Y directly and Y pays Z directly. In this case, the coin has effected three payments just as it did previously when it passed through A, B and C. Supposing the authorities decide to calculate the size of the money supply: how should they go about this? If they add to the credit balance at bank C the gold coin which has been put back into circulation, the result will be that the statistics will register two units of money. But in fact it is only the coin that has circulated and effected the payments, in the first case (by passing through A, B and C) as in the second (when it did not pass through A, B and C). The 'monetary effect' in both cases is identical. If they were to record two units of money instead of one, in the first case, the statisticians' calculations would be 100 per cent out. If the gold coin is replaced by a bank-note it makes no difference; adding total current account credit balances to the total of bank-notes in circulation still produces an erroneous money supply figure.

Money only has an effect on the economy when it is in circulation. Those units of money with the full payment function are hidden in M1, which, as we saw in the chapter on the Clearing House, is the total of claims on the banks with the payment function plus central bank assets which also have the payment function at the end of the clearing process.

'Quasi-money', or near-money', does not have this property. M2 should therefore not be substituted for M1.

PAGE 161

(1) The velocity of money: another fallacy

It is well known that the transaction velocity is the number of transactions effected on average during one year by a unit of M1 money. Income velocity, on the other hand, is the ratio of gross domestic expenditure to the M1, M2 or M3 money stock.

We have also seen that the Bank of France considers that the transaction velocity is the more satisfying because it gives rapid results, whereas the income velocity raises for the moment practical difficulties, particularly because of the need to make assessments of the short-term economic situation during the year. We could also add that the transaction velocity reflects all exchanges of goods or services, whereas the income velocity, strictly speaking, only reflects final exchanges for purposes of conversion of production into consumption or investment.

Nevertheless, certain experts from the Fed. still prefer M2 to M1 on the grounds that the income velocity of M2 is stabler than that of M1. This is a very curious reason for preferring M2 to M1. What would we think of a driver who preferred to rely on his oil-pressure gauge rather than his speedometer on the pretext that the oil-pressure gauge needle was steadier than the speedometer needle?

If we consider *all* bank deposits to be 'money' or if we take the so-called 'liquidity quotient' as criterion for deciding what is money and what is not, there is indeed no reason why we should not prefer M2 to M1. But in that case, logic rules out the use of the transaction velocity as a test. This indicator cannot be applied to M2 because the quasi-money included in M2 cannot be used to effect a transaction.

PAGE 164

(1) Cash deposits and savings deposits

In his book, *L'impôt sur le capital et la réforme monétaire* from which we have already quoted, Maurice Allais writes: 'It is impossible to establish a strict line of demarcation between those time deposits that may be considered the equivalent of cash and those that must be regarded as savings, at least initially.'

The central theme of Maurice Allais's view of inflation is the *ex nihilo* creation of money by banks — which is why he calls them 'forgers'. He produces a vehement, well argued attack on the seigniorage which accompanies the creation of a new unit of money. The notion of seigniorage, or *reduction* as we have called it, can only reinforce the special role given to M1 and the exclusion of payment money from near-money, M' (=M2−M1) even when M' is reduced by a third.

If we suppose a coefficient of two thirds for the effective monetarisation of near-money liquidities, we are led to an estimation of M' for the money supply, equal to the sum of the M1 money supply in the strict sense (monetary liquidities) and two thirds of M2−M1, or the amount of near-money liquidities) . . .

It is not unreasonable to estimate that two thirds of bank time deposits are considered by their holders as equivalent to cash. They correspond approximately to all the time deposits which have a maturity of less than three months.

It seems distinctly risky to base one's calculations on what holders of monetary assets consider cash and what they consider savings. Units of M' (near-money), even when they are short-term; effect no reduction for the simple reason that reduction, rightly understood, is the corollary of the use of a new unit of money by its first holder and affects other holders of money to the extent that the new unit changes hands, a process in which the constituents of M', since they are not transferable, are not involved.

As for the maturity of three months mentioned by Maurice Allais, however short it may appear, it is not a decisive criterion. The units of M' remain passive during this period, whereas those active units that remained within M1 are likely, on average, to have taken part in ten transactions.

PAGE 164

'Propensities' and 'preferences'

To base the classification of a unit of money on the 'propensities' of its holder seems as risky to me as to base it on the category of institution on which it is a claim, on its description or on its maturity.

On the other hand, there is no doubt that money may pass instantaneously from a savings account to a current account; this depends on the holder. It is just as certain that a unit of money which has the payment function and is not used for a transaction has an effect, or more exactly, an absence of effect, on transactions which is identical to that of a unit of what we may call 'savings money'. From this point of view, they are both inert. All these factors — ease of mobilisation, identity or not of effect between a unit of payment money that remains unused and a savings unit, dependence on the decisions of the holder — explain why people have concentrated on the holder's intentions in order to classify and differentiate the roles of money. This unfortunately has not led to greater clarity in monetary analysis.

A payment unit that is unused is, like a savings unit, immobile. A man who is merely asleep is also immobile, as is a dead man, but there is a difference between them. How can we establish this necessary distinction, without relying on 'propensities', 'desires' and 'intentions'?

For the payment unit to regain its mobility, all it needs to do is to 'wake up', because it is directly transferable as it is. This is not true of the unit of savings money. The institution where the saver has his account must substitute for the claim that the saver holds another transferable claim which has the payment function. It is this act of substitution, which the banking institution carries out, that makes all the difference. If the institution is a non-monetary intermediary it will transfer a pre-existing unit of payment; if it is a monetary intermediary it will create a claim on itself which is intrinsically transferable and acceptable to another bank.

This operation is clearly defined and easily discernible. It substitutes for a unit that cannot be directly used for a transaction one that can. It is on this basis that we should classify units of money. A transferable claim is a payment unit; a non-transferable claim is a savings unit. The indicators should register the two without mixing them up and − if it is necessary to make forecasts − take account of the velocity of circulation and the nature of the uses to which the money is put (see Chapter 5).

PAGE 165

(1) The Swiss negative interest rate

The decline of the dollar in the early months of 1978 and the subsequent rush into hard currencies, most notably the Deutschemark and the Swiss franc, was naturally a cause of concern for the monetary authorities in Frankfurt and Zürich. Their response was to adopt defensive measures, of which the most vigorous was probably that of the Swiss, who imposed a negative interest rate equal to 40 per cent a year on non-resident deposits in excess of 5 million francs. At the same time, the Kredietbank in Luxembourg merely announced that it was obliged to eliminate the ½ per cent interest it paid to depositors in Swiss francs.

One might be tempted to conclude that this shows that the Eurobanks are indeed able to create Swiss francs independently of the Swiss banking system and that the restrictive measures adopted by the Swiss authorities leave them unscathed. But by interpreting the events in this way, one would once again be wrong.

The deposits in Swiss francs at the Kredietbank are not Swiss francs but merely deposits *denominated in Swiss francs*. They are credits to the accounts of depositors, corresponding to sums they have paid in and which have been re-lent by the bank. These francs are no longer held by the original depositor or by the bank; they have been transferred to a borrower, who has probably used them to make a purchase in Switzerland and thus pay a Swiss resident, which means that the 40 per cent negative interest rate affects neither the bank nor its customer.

Nevertheless, there remain two deposits denominated in Swiss francs,

Euro-Swiss francs, namely the original credit to the account of the depositor and the Kredietbank's claim on its borrower. Should the depositor decide to withdraw his asset, in order to pay a Swiss exporter for example, the Kredietbank will have to obtain the necessary Swiss francs by borrowing. It cannot, as it would in its own national banking system, simply give its depositor a claim on itself. It must obtain Swiss francs in the form of a claim on a bank domiciled in Switzerland. It is most probable that it would do that by borrowing.

The restrictive measures adopted by the Swiss authorites have, in fact, a triple effect. Firstly, they discourage speculation aiming at a revaluation of its currency; secondly, they favour outflows of capital, and thirdly, they encourage exports and thus correct the handicap which the rise of their currency on the markets imposes on their export industries. This example shows once again how appearances can be deceptive and how a wrong interpretation of the Euromarket mechanism may lead to erroneous conclusions. It also shows the consequences of a confusion between payment money and simple claims.

PAGE 166

(1) The search for the monetary effect
The formula also ought to help to solve a problem which remains without an answer, namely the problem of the integration of non-monetary intermediaries into the regulatory mechanisms.

At the beginning of the sixties, the Radcliffe Report and the studies of Gurley and Shaw in England drew attention to the fact that non-monetary intermediaries such as Savings and Loan Associations and Building Societies could get round monetary restrictions applied by the central bank to the growth of the money supply in order to control inflation. In fact, the interest rate rises that generally accompany these restrictive measures may encourage the Savings Associations to bid for more deposits, which would mean that they would have more lendable funds, demand for which would be all the greater as borrowers would be getting little from the banks. This, in turn, means they would be prepared to pay high interest rates, thanks to the anticipation of higher inflation which an inflationary atmosphere encourages.

These non-monetary institutions are in addition induced to modify the composition of their reserves by replacing government paper, with intentionally staggered maturities, by easily negotiable paper, which acts in the same direction. It is probable that this monetary effect of the savings institutions plays a bigger role in the Anglo-Saxon countries than in France because of the importance these institutions have in those countries and because of their greater independence of the authorities. But one comment is called for apropos of this effect produced by savings, namely that it is not obvious that this 'investment surplus' should have an inflationary effect through the creation of money *ex nihilo*. I must admit that I cannot see how, as people maintain, savings deposits in a non-monetary institution can set off an inflationary spiral through an 'excess of investment' of *ex ante* savings. Such would certainly be the effect in the case of a monetary intermediary, because it would set off a multiplier, but there is no multiplier in the case of a non-monetary intermediary. Indeed, it seems to me that one of the merits of this search for a new indicator is that it shows the real mechanism of the inflationary effect generated by increased savings, both in the case of monetary intermediaries and in the case of non-monetary intermediaries.

This mechanism, which even the measurement of circulation velocity does not reveal, is for the same number of transactions the growth of conversions of production into consumption (or investment) consequent on increased activity on the part of savings institutions, whether monetary or not. This is the mechanism that the search for a new indicator reveals.

PAGE 188

(1) The lessons of John Law's System

An odd person, this John Law. At one and the same time a theoretician and a man of action (even, and above all, a man of *actions*, as the French call shares, in Law's case, the shares of the *Compagnie des Indes*), a Scotchman and yet a great spendthrift, a serious and somewhat melancholic man in a century of frivolity and wit, a gentleman amongst scoundrels, the defender of a flag that was not his own and as fascinating a man as his latest biographer, Edgar Faure, who brings him to life so well in his book, *La banqueroute de John Law*.

The interest of this book lies not just in the fact that it gives us some insight into a famous episode in monetary history which is well known but very much misunderstood, but also in the fact that it reveals two people to us, John Law and Edgar Faure. Through his opinions and judgments, the criticisms he makes of Law and the praise he gives him, the author, a former finance minister, tells us what he thinks about money, inflation, the role of the central bank, monetary regulation and many other extremely topical matters.

The opinions which an author expresses concerning his heroes are often more revealing than any amount of memoirs and autobiographies. A historian is less diffident and makes less of an effort to speak for posterity or to persuade his readers. Detailed criticisms, admirably documented and very laudable attempts to clear up obscurities, points of view expressed by the author without any shifts or subterfuges, are all things which are infinitely richer in what they can teach us than mere memoirs, which are often only examples of special pleading. Before our eyes, we see a scene unfold in which the actors are ministers, dukes, bourgeois and lackeys, all bent on speculation and conspiracy, whilst at the same time we witness, in miniature, one of the most extraordinary exercises of monetary manipulation that has ever been seen, by that Houdini of the bank-note, John Law.

Two hundred and fifty years later, and after many other monetary experiences, one is still staggered at the contemplation of this succession of revaluations, devaluations and withdrawals from circulation. Decrees, edicts, plans, programmes, explanations and prohibitions succeed one another, leap over each other in a ballet that becomes faster and faster — this is the image used by Edgar Faure — like the finale of *La Vie Parisienne*, which leaves the spectator dazzled and almost as exhausted as the dancers on the stage. Once the tumult has died down and the calm that is necessary for reflection has been restored, we can, perhaps, attempt to draw some conclusions from this first unrestrained experiment with bank-notes, conclusions that may be useful at a moment in economic history when monetarism seems everywhere triumphant.

In order to understand and appreciate Law's achievement, we should first of all remember how, in France, the currency was manipulated under the *ancien régime* by the monarch for his own profit, and occasionally for that of the economy, as part of his royal prerogative and monopoly of the minting of money. It was not so much, as is often believed, by clipping coins or by otherwise debasing their value. Such measures are necessarily limited; one cannot go on for ever diminishing the diameter and the thickness of coins or diluting the precious metal with copper or lead (the practice was in any case the exact reverse under Louis XV). The technique was different and infinitely more efficient. It was based on the strict separation of specie, — gold *Louis d'or* or silver *écu* — and their value expressed in terms of units of account, the so-called *livre tournois* or 'tournois pound'. Contracts, payments, loans, repayments and, in general, all transactions, were expressed in pounds; but the face value of the *Louis d'or* or the *écu* was not marked on the coins, which only bore the royal effigy. The value of the coin in pounds was fixed by royal decree and frequently modified, up or down. If the modification was in an upward direction it corresponded to what we call today a 'devaluation'; if, on the other hand, it was in a downward direction it corresponded to what we call a 'revaluation'.

In less than five years, from 1716 to 1720, the gold value of the pound varied, in both directions, in proportions of 1 to 4 and 4 to 1: even today we have not managed to exceed such wide swings. It was only after Law and the failure of his system that the face value was stamped on coins and that the pound, rechristened the franc, came to be identified with a certain weight of gold or silver. This identification of the abstract unit of account with its vehicle in an immutable relationship was destined to last for two hundred years.

The abstract nature of the pound as unit of account and the modification of its value in terms of gold made it possible to diminish the public debt. By increasing the value of the *Louis d'or* in terms of pounds, the state was able to eliminate part of its obligations, which remained expressed in terms of pounds. But this trick did not merely have the great advantage of easing the state's debt burden and thereby every other debtor's burden — and we shall see later that this favouring of debtors is, in Edgar Faure's eyes, one of the principal merits of Law's system — but it had an even more important merit, that of remedying to some extent the chronic shortage of specie which inhibited economic development from the Middle Ages to recent times, with the exception of that brief

period following the discovery of America and the return from the New
World of the Spanish galleons.

John Law turned this dichotomy between the unit of account and coins
to his own advantage as no one had ever done before. At the end of Louis
XIV's long reign, the 20 pound *Louis* had been reduced to 14 by the
controller of the finances, Desmarets, who had presided over a deflation
of unprecedented proportions, the result of which had been to give France
a strong currency and a depressed economy. Three years after the death
of the Sun King, on 1 April 1718, the *Louis* came back to 20 pounds.
Simultaneously, all coins in circulation were declared no longer legal
tender and withdrawn from circulation, and a new *Louis* was issued. This
was known as the *chevalier*, because a knight's cross was stamped on one
of its faces. The *chevalier* was worth 36 pounds, but it was slightly heavier
than the old *Louis* (25 to the mark, i.e. 244 grammes of gold, instead of
30 to the mark). In comparison with what it had been worth in gold at the
death of Louis XIV, the pound had thus been devalued by more than
50 per cent. But at the same time, the *écu* note made its first appearance,
soon to be replaced by the first pound note — one of the most important
moments in the history of money.

For the first time, the pound, hitherto an abstract unit of account, with
no existence on any coin, started to take concrete shape; simultaneously
the notion of money as a simple claim made its first appearance in history
and gave industry and commerce the means of prodigious expansion. The
note payable to bearer was the instrument of the manipulations of the
great monetary conjurer, soaring upwards as the *Louis* went down from
36 to 35 pounds, then 34, then 32 and then, on 1 January 1720, to 31.
Once paper had been thus revalued in terms of gold, which had the effect
of attracting specie to the coffers of the Bank of France, on 5 May the
flow of funds changed direction. The *Louis* went up to 48 pounds and,
at the same time, the people were forbidden to hold specie. 'Stair (a
contemporary of John Law) took great pleasure in saying that Law had
managed to demonstrate the transsubstantiation of specie into paper
and to establish the Inquisition in a country which had never accepted it.
Even religious communities and parish priests were not spared, and the
practice of dununciation of neighbours reached odious proportions.
Nevertheless', Edgar Faure adds, 'only a few decrees imposing confiscations
are extant. . .'

By the middle of 1720, the bank-note, alone, like the star of the *corps
de ballet*, held the centre of the stage, whilst the other participants relaxed
in the wings awaiting their moment to return to take part in another equally
well choreographed ensemble. The 1000 pound note gradually began to
contract and fell to 500 in December. Then, by government decree, the
Louis came back to 48 pounds, then 36, after which it shot up to 49
again.

On 1 July 1721 the restrictive measures were abolished and the circulation
of specie was re-established. From this moment, things began to move at
an ever dizzier rate. The Treasury needed to cope with its debt maturities,
and for this it needed specie. Overnight, by virtue of the decree of 30 July,
the *Louis* went up to 72 pounds, but no sooner had the metal flowed into

the coffers of the Bank of France, than it began to flow out again. On 15 September the *Louis* was back at 36 pounds, after which it fell to the value that it was subsequently to keep for two centuries, namely 20 pounds.

In order to simplify things, I have spoken only of the merry-go-round of *Louis d'or, écus* and notes. But on a different part of the stage and at the same time, a different ballet was being danced: that of the shares of the *Compagnie des Indes*, which was intimately bound up with the money. Space precludes a detailed account of the affairs of this company but what we can note here is that the first shares were issued at 500 pounds and that Law supported the price at 10,000 pounds for a short period, by getting the Bank of France to buy them. In order to do this, he clandestinely created almost a thousand million pounds of paper money (not quite a half of the entire money supply) which give rise to a public enquiry that was suddenly and inexplicably interrupted:

> It was now clear to everyone that Law had illicitly issued more than a thousand million pounds in notes. For this he could have been subject to criminal proceedings, as was remarked during the course of the *Conseil de Régence* of 26 January; the Regent implicitly protected Law by maintaining him in his official post. No one seemed shocked or even surprised by this.

What happy days those were, when scandals could be quietly ignored and the whole business closed by a bonfire. This is what happened during what was called at the time the *brûlement*, when several loads of shares and notes were burnt wholesale in a large iron cage under the gaze of the crowds, relieved at the end of an experiment in which one does not know what to admire most, the skill of the great manipulator himself, the loyalty of the Regent head of the government in keeping Law at his post as 'controller of finances', or the patience of the French public.

So here we are at the end of this astonishing spectacle and at the beginning of the most interesting part of the story, namely the critical analysis which Edgar Faure gives of Law's monetary innovations, in the field of theory as well as practice. John Law was, in fact, not just a great manipulator, but also a great theoretician (he published a book called *Money and Trade*). He was two hundred years ahead of his time in perceiving the importance of something that was unknown then but which is nowadays universally recognised, namely the notion of money as a simple claim on an institution. But, whereas in practice he went to the extreme, in theory he did not follow his ideas to their logical conclusion and did not construct a solid body of doctrine, which could have been extremely useful. On the contrary, after a few steps in the right direction we see him lose sight of his main objective and set off down various cul-de-sacs.

Throughout his book, Edgar Faure follows his hero step by step, approving of some things, disapproving of others, distributing praise and blame, and by no means the least interesting aspect of this book is the fact that we can accompany in it these two personages, both trying to find

their way throught the maze of monetary theory. In the field of theory –
and it is from this point of view that we are looking at things now – the
curtain really goes up on 4 December 1718. There were, at that time, *écu*,
notes in circulation, that is to say, notes which could be exchanged for a
sum in silver *écus* corresponding to the face value printed on them, whether
10,000, 1000, 100 or 10. This was an anticipation of something which
could be called the 'silver standard', according to which notes and silver
écus circulated in parallel, interchangeable according to certain invariable
ratios, payments in gold being reserved for sums in excess of 600 pounds.

On 4 December 1728, the pound note appeared. The abstract unit of
account then took on a concrete from, independently of gold. The note
bore, to be sure, the information that it could be exchanged on demand,
into precious metal, but without specifying, unlike the *écu*, the amount of
precious metal. The pound no longer had specie as its vehicle; instead it
had become a claim on an institution, with an indeterminate exchange
value and maturity. Furthermore, it had the wonderful power of passing
from hand to hand, promoting trade and the conversion of finished goods
into consumption, the fundamental aspects of the economy.

4 December 1718 is a famous date in monetary history. It was the
beginning of a development in the understanding of money which is not
yet at an end. Edgar Faure has no doubt on the matter:

> Here we pause for a moment, because it seems impossible to us not to
> mention the enormous misapprehensions of certain authors, by no
> means the least distinguished, with regard to this system and in
> particular the decree of 22 April which is its principal feature. Not only
> have these authors not understood the stroke of genius in the strategy
> Law was pursuing at this time. . . but they have also thought that,
> for reasons either of constraint or pure weakness, Law had betrayed his
> own convictions. . . by freeing the paper pound from the consequence
> of the revaluation of specie. . . The creation of the tournois pound, its
> rise, its victorious struggle – at the beginning at least – with gold, all
> this is the work of a revolutionary economist, bent on the creation of a
> money freed from the shackles of myth and capable of reflecting and
> stimulating the progress of the real national wealth, production and
> labour . . .

A less perspicacious author than Edgar Faure would not have missed
this opportunity of pointing out the irony of the situation and would not
have failed to see in the creation of the pound note the beginning of a
gigantic tax on established fortunes, instead of seeing in it the start of a
monetary revolution. But John Law, after having opened the doors to this
revolution, side-tracked and deflected it in the direction of 'backed'
money and convertibility. After this stroke of genius, he got bogged
down in subsidiary matters and failed to perceive the real nature of money
and the real nature of the commodity guarantee. He yielded to the
temptations of a concept to which, two centuries later, many well-
meaning people still cling tenaciously: the concept of money as representative of a commodity. Instead of concerning himself with the business of

procuring for the economy the money it needed in the quantity it needed, and creating the mechanism most likely to keep the money supply below the optimum quantity ceiling, Law took refuge in another concept, that of 'backing' and covertibility, and made a vital mistake in the field of theory which naturally led him, in the field of practice, to a catastrophe. He could not conceive of paper money in terms other than those of its backing.

Just as interesting, since the author is a politician and an economist, are the opinions that Edgar Faure expresses on the galloping inflation set off by John Law's system, which caused the cost of living to double in less than three years. Instead of indulging in the usual lamentations on inflation, Edgar Faure has the courage to speak approvingly of the benefits it had on an economy that had been reduced to a condition almost of *rigor mortis* by seventy-two years of the reign of the Sun King:

> Christopher Columbus set off to look for the Indies and discovered America instead. Law had set off with the intention of abolishing commodity money, i.e. gold, and substituting for it the bank-note. He didn't succeed, but he did manage to blow the cobwebs off the French economy and free it of debts accumulated over several generations. . . The standard of living increased, consumption grew and people were better fed. . . The consumption of meat almost doubled and that of wine increased by a third. . .

To be sure, the system of Law acted as a catalyst: it woke up a lethargic society and set a nation of peasants and land-owners off in pursuit of commerce, industry, navigation and the New World. One might wish that Edgar Faure had gone further and had let us know his opinions on the less favourable aspects of inflation: its instability and the difficulty of bringing it under control again once it has got out of hand, without causing a recession. It is also a pity that Edgar Faure ignores completely the disastrous consequences of the 'System', that is, the influence it had on monetary opinions and the political decisions that emanated from them. The repercussions of Law's ideas were felt for a very long time afterwards. He ensured the arrival of gold-backed money; he confirmed in the minds of everyone, high and low, theoreticians and practical people, faith in a money with an intrinsic value. He anchored in people's minds distrust in mere debt money and, as a corollary, encouraged people in their refusal to organise a rationally designed and controlled monetary system.

The failure of the most famous auriphobe of all time ensured the triumph of the auriphiles for centuries, in both theory and practice. The only thing the public learnt from Law's experiments was the risk of an uncontrolled issue of bank-notes by the government and the dire need to prevent it. It did not take note of the advantages for the economy of debt money; it did not understand that the economy could only grow once it had been freed from the straitjacket in which it was kept by the lack of specie. Even worse, after Law there no longer existed that very useful device that was the separation of coins and the unit of account; the two were henceforth indissolubly linked by the stamping of value in pounds on the coins.

Not only did people not understand, but they actually denied the brilliant invention — to use Edgar Faure's term — of debt money, liberated from any connection with metal coins and what in Edgar Faure's eyes constitutes the weak point of the system was erected into an article of faith, namely the idea of commodity backing, and its corollary, convertibility (since, in the absence of convertibility, there is no point in having a commodity backing), a backing which was successively gold, a piece of merchandise, in the case of discounting, and then a claim on a borrower or counterparty. This is why it is surprising that Edgar Faure, who saw straight away the originality of the system as well as its weakness — the reliance on a backing — did not take advantage of this occasion in order to show what awful distortions followed, in both monetary theory and monetary practice. The collapse of the System and, 75 years later, the *débâcle* of the *assignats*, turned the French away from abstract debt money. Whereas England financed its wars against Napoleon with paper money, France was reduced to pillaging the gold of its conquered peoples. Long after the fall of the Empire, the notes of the Bank of France, as big as pocket handkerchiefs, were only rarely used, whilst the faith in gold continued right up to the present day.

In 1963, General de Gaulle declared:

We consider it vital that international trade should be reestablished, as was the case in happier days, on an undisputed monetary basis, something that does not bear allegiance to any one country. What basis should we choose? We really cannot see that there can be any other criterion for a standard of value than gold, which does not change its nature and which can be converted as one pleases into ingots, bars and coins. . .

In May 1973, the Committee of Twenty of the IMF put to the vote the principles that ought to be used for the reconstruction of the international monetary system. Only France and South Africa voted for a return to the gold standard.

It is only since 1975 and the arrival in power at the very top of politicians who are also economists, that the French government has ceased to profess its faith in the resurrection of a dead monetary system. The System of John Law and the echo that its failure set off from generation to generation are not without their influence on the tardiness with which facts have finally been admitted.

Part Three

Composite currency units, their future and their shortcomings: the Eurostable

1 The implications of present-day monetary disorders

It often happens in human affairs that a process of change is set off under our noses but without our being aware of it; that institutions, organisations and ways of thinking are modified; that our physical and spiritual environment is disturbed by events of which we are aware only superficially, without perceiving their real meaning.

At all times, men have tried to adapt existing, time-honoured systems to changing circumstances and new conditions. As often as not, such adaptations, when they occur, are the result of a strictly *ad hoc* approach. They proceed in fits and starts and are rarely determined by conscious, deliberate decisions, based on a careful analysis of the past with a view to predicting the future. Nevertheless, this process of gradual adaptation is a good example of a tendency which it is worthwhile to attempt to analyse: the monetary disorders of the modern world and the attempts that have been made to remedy them will serve as illustrations.

The abandonment of the gold standard after nearly sixty years of protracted death throes; the inconvertibility of the dollar; the dethronement of the American currency from its role as queen of the world monetary system; exchange market upheavals and the prolonged absence of a genuine standard of value independent of time and place; a snake in a tunnel which has become the very symbol of broken-backed policies; plans and promises of monetary union lacking any realism and therefore still-born: such is the scene that presents itself to the present day observer. At the same time, monetary relations between states are expanding rapidly, the role of the IMF is growing, the financial flows in the Euromarkets are increasing in importance, petrodollars are being recycled in ever greater quantities and the creation of the SDR and, with it, other units of account and currency cocktails, prefigures the emergence of separate monetary zones.

If we step back a little to get this confused scene into perspective, we can see, beyond the failures and uncertainties, a deeper trend and a fast emerging need: the need for a new international payment unit devoid of links to any one nation, stable in terms of its purchasing power, independent of the exchange markets and price levels and, above all, an instrument that will not be the privileged tool of a national government for the management of its domestic economy.

The attempts that have been made to devise such units of account in terms of baskets of national currencies are, from this point of view, very instructive: they prove the existence of this need. That they have all failed should not be a matter of surprise to us. A radically different departure from what our habits of thought have led us to expect, and from what the past has bequeathed us, will only succeed gradually, after many unsuccessful experiments. Something of this will be set out in Chapter 2, which discusses the views on this subject of two Princeton economists.

The reasons why the basket-formula currencies have failed are manifold.

Firstly, they were conceived as composite currencies with all the weaknesses of the national currencies that make up the baskets, instead of being created, as they could have been, with a property that national currencies have not got and cannot have, namely a stable value in terms of purchasing power, protected against exchange rate and price variations, thereby constituting that standard of reference which the monetary system of today, alone among systems of measurement, lacks.

Secondly, they were confined to the role of units of account, instead of being payment units, whereas only a unit that has the payment function can be called a currency.

Thirdly, they were expected to compete, internally, with national currencies, instead of being limited to external exchanges.

Finally, instead of being tried and tested in the Euromarkets, they were created on the premiss that governments would undertake certain initiatives which in reality they are incapable of taking. Only in this way could lessons have been learnt which would have helped the authorities to innovate. This is the aim with which the project to launch an extra-territorial payment unit with constant purchasing power, called the Eurostable, has been conceived.

2 The International Monetary Fund and its Special Drawing Right

In Ponca City, in the middle-west of the USA, there is a statue in the main square representing a woman, a 'pioneer woman', holding a child by the hand. Her eyes fixed on a distant horizon, she is taking her child towards a better tomorrow, turning her back on a world in which she no longer has any faith.

The Managing Director of the IMF would do well to have a replica of that statue erected at the entrance to the headquarters of his organisation, on the banks of the Potomac. It would be the perfect symbol of the IMF, leading its little SDR in search of new horizons, towards a new monetary system. This is the way I like to think about the IMF and the SDR; as a courageous and important initiative in a direction which is still uncertain, and full of pitfalls that ought to be better recognised from the start.

This is not the general opinion, however. Some people, such as the late Jacques Rueff, have called the SDR 'a nullity dressed up as money', whilst others have called it an 'instrument of US imperialism'. Michel Debré sees in the SDR the primary cause of world inflation and in the IMF a threat to national independence. In Parliament, whilst the subject of the increase of France's IMF quota (that is, the obligation to provide its own currency in return for which it may obtain credit itself) was being discussed, right-wingers and left-wingers were united in suspicion and hostility. As for the pundits and professional commentators, all, with the honourable exception of Pascal Salin, whether radio, television or newspaper journalists, were hard put to explain events to the public.

On 3 March 1978, the second amendment to the statutes of the IMF took effect.[1] Simultaneously, the official demise of the gold standard was notified to the world. The 133 member states of the IMF are henceforward committed not to define the value of their currencies in terms of precious metals, and to abolish the use of gold as a money and a standard

of value. At the same time, a new international monetary unit, defined
as equivalent to a 'basket' of 16 national currencies and promoted to the
unexpected role of monetary standard in place of gold and the dollar, saw
the light of day. A revolution was thereby accomplished: for the first
time in monetary history, an attempt was made to create a currency.
which no longer claimed to represent gold and which at the same time
was no longer the national currency of any privileged country.

The demonetisation of gold only amounts to official recognition of a
fait accompli; it marks the end of a long agony. As for the dollar,
experience has shown that it is unjust and dangerous to concede to any
single state a world-wide privilege of issue and thereby to put the
international monetary system at the mercy of the ups and downs of
the domestic economic policy of a national government. Commodity-
backed money is dead; long live abstract composite money! Its first
steps are sure to be clumsy and uncertain; it represents a great hope but
it also involves considerable risk of failure. The future of this bold
venture and the eventual reform of the international monetary system
depend on the way the notion of a composite currency is understood
and applied in practice, on the way its defects, such as its instability of
value, may be corrected, and on the way its various properties, such as
its neutrality and its freedom from the law of the market, are put to
use. The real originality of the International Monetary Fund's initiative
is not to be found in the increase in members' quotas, nor in the
modification of the process by which the Fund intervenes and provides
assistance to member States, nor even in the legitimisation of floating
exchange rates or the increase in SDR allocations. The real originality
lies in this attempt to define a new international monetary standard in the
form of a composite monetary unit which will take the place of gold.

The first thing to say – and this is necessary for the clarity of the
argument – is that it is a pity that this new unit has not been given a
more suitable name, peculiar to it. Strictly speaking, the SDR is only a
transfer mechanism and a means of guaranteeing certain credit operations.
Giving the same name to the mechanism and the standard of value makes
it difficult not to confuse the two things.

The IMF has three roles. It is:

a powerful financial intermediary, a taker of deposits and a distributor
of loans;
the inventor of a transfer mechanism (the SDR) and a reducer of risks;
the inventor of a new standard of value (the SDR).

Of these three rôles, the first is, nowadays, the most important and the most useful, but it lacks any conceptual originality. The second is newer; but it is in the third role, that of creator of a new monetary standard, that the IMF points towards the future and at the same time invites criticism and comments.

The IMF is responsible for managing the 'international monetary system'. Its primary responsibility is to supply the world's needs in international liquidity; in other words, its job is to supply the currencies needed by a country whose balance of payments is in deficit. Within a State, the central bank and the commercial banks distribute payment instruments which for the most part are created by them; the IMF, on the other hand, as a non-monetary financial intermediary, only re-lends what it borrows and creates no payment instruments *ex nihilo*. This is the role of the quota which every member state must pay as a kind of entry fee, 75 per cent in its own currency and 25 per cent in other convertible currencies (before the amendment to the statutes this part was supposed to be paid in gold). Since the amendment, the IMF has increased its holdings to 39,000 million SDRs, or about 45,000 million dollars. Participation in the IMF and payment of its quota give a country the right to draw the foreign currency it may need in the future, against a further payment in its own currency. At the end of a certain period, which is not supposed to exceed five years, the IMF is reimbursed and gives back to the State in question the sum in its own currency which it had deposited, corrected, if necessary, to allow for exchange rate changes. What the IMF provides is thus not really a loan but a line of credit extended in the form of a swap. Such credits are limited to 200 per cent of the country's quota and are divided into tranches, accompanied by progressively severer economic measures which the borrowing country must agree to adopt in order to right its balance of payments.

Apart from this system of collection and redistribution of funds, the IMF has created another: the Special Drawing Right (SDR) system. Though it was created in 1969, the SDR has so far been little used. The basic idea behind it is the fact that, as far as international trade is concerned, the deficit of one country necessarily has a counterpart in the surplus of another. In order to guarantee the liquidity of the international monetary system, all that is needed is that a surplus country should lend to a deficit country. But if such agreements are left to the initiatives of the countries involved, they are not easy to arrange, partly because the connection between one country's deficit and another's surplus is not obvious, and partly because of the difficulty of guaranteeing the loans. The consequence is that the authorities of each country are obliged to accumulate intervention currencies, usually dollars, in order to protect their own currency.

By giving each state a 'drawing right' on an unspecified surplus country, the IMF makes it less necessary for each country to accumulate foreign currencies, which means that there is less competition for dollars amongst the central banks. This drawing right[2] takes concrete form in issues which are distributed amongst the member countries on an optional basis. In order to make use of its drawing right, a member country may make direct arrangements with another country to exchange drawing rights for currency. If such a direct agreement cannot be made, the country in question asks the IMF to designate a country, which is then obliged to provide convertible currencies in exchange for SDRs. A complex system of rules sets out the limits of the obligations incumbent on the surplus country (the total of currency it can be asked to provide may not exceed twice its quota). These rules also set out the repayment terms (limited to 30 per cent of the SDRs that have been used). In its monthly bulletin, the IMF says that the transformation of the SDR into the principal reserve asset of the world monetary system must take place gradually; the 9300 million SDRs in circulation only constitute a small proportion of total assets in gold and currencies, the total of which exceeds 180,000 million SDRs.

From the point of view of pure monetary theory, the SDR cannot be considered a currency created *ex nihilo*. When Italy uses its SDRs in order to receive dollars from Germany, there is no creation of new money, but simply a transfer of funds. On the other hand, it may be argued that the SDR encourages laxity, but this is true of any credit system. The truth is that the golden rule of a system intended to steer a middle course between inflation and deflation must be on the one hand to develop transfer mechanisms and on the other to set up strict domestic controls. It is pointless to try to create an international monetary system without at the same time drawing up efficient means of domestic monetary regulation. The two things go hand in hand. To encourage this is part of the IMF's task. The measures it proposes in the field of exchange rates are based on the notion that the essential aim of the international monetary system is to furnish the framework within which exchanges of goods, services and capital among nations will be facilitated and healthy economic growth will be encouraged. Another important aim is 'to ensure that the basic conditions deemed necessary for economic and financial stability should be maintained. . . In particular each member will attempt . . . . so to arrange its economic and financial policy that reasonable price stability results . . . '. This is not just wishful thinking: all over the world the stern demands of the IMF are resented by debtor countries, in some cases with a distinct degree of bitterness.

A fundamental feature of the SDR system is the definition of a new standard of value. I have already remarked on the anomaly of using the same term to describe a loan mechanism and a standard of value. Keynes did not make the same mistake when he devised his own system of issue of a new monetary unit, to which he gave the name of *Bancor*. A monetary unit and the claim denominated in this unit are not the same thing. There is, on the one hand, the pound and on the other a £10 note. The first is a unit of measurement whilst the second is a claim denominated in this same unit. The dollar and the pound are reference units for purposes of exchange, as the gram and the metre are reference units for weights and measures. In the process of monetary analysis we must treat separately the problems of creation and circulation of monetary claims and those concerning the reference unit in which these claims are denominated.

As a standard of value – and from now on it is from this point of view that we shall look at it – the SDR has serious deficiencies. At a time when gold has been abolished as a standard and no national currency is allowed to replace it, it is indispensable that the new standard that is to take its place should be rationally defined. The IMF cannot function without an extranational monetary standard. The essence of its function demands that it should have at its disposal a common denominator with which to link the currencies of the 133 member states. Otherwise, how would it be possible to compare, add together, lend and reimburse the Korean *won*, the Gambian *dalasie*, the Ghanaian *cedi*, the Guatemalan *quetzal*, the Guinean *syli*, the *ekuele* of Equatorial Guinea, the Panamanian *balboa* and the Malawian *kwacha*?

A point of reference which is both stable and recognised by everyone is all the more necessary as IMF operations involve transactions between sovereign states, which is why, before the last amendment to the statutes, allusions to the gold value of currencies occurred frequently in the proceedings of the Fund, in conformity with Article Four of the statutes, which stated that the gold value of the Funds assets would be constant and unchanging, in spite of parity changes or effective exchange rate changes in the currency of any member State. This strict rule meant that in the case of a permanent or even a temporary devaluation of its currency, a country had to make supplementary payments to the Fund in its own currency in order to maintain the gold value of its quota. At the same time, borrowers were obliged to make compensatory payments in order to take account of the same variations.

Gold was thus the common denominator, even if it was no longer the effective medium of exchange. This latter role devolved onto the dollar. As long as the American currency was convertible into gold, it was able to fulfil this double role of reference unit and instrument of exchange and intervention. When the SDR was created in 1969, it was defined simultaneously in terms of gold and the dollar: an SDR was worth 0.888671 grams of gold, which was the official gold value of one dollar. The abolition of the convertibility of the dollar into gold, the rapid rise of the market price of the metal, the depreciation of the dollar, the breaking of all links between currencies and fixed parities, all these factors turned the Bretton Woods system upside down, not only in practice but also in theory, and the result was an astonishing hotch-potch, in which gold valued at a quarter of its market price, the dollar, the SDR based on gold and the SDR based on a basket of currencies were all mixed up together.

The second amendment, which has been in force since 31 March 1978, at least has the merit of clarifying a confused situation which defied logic and even analysis. From now on, gold is quite simply stripped of any monetary role. The amendment says that 'currencies will not have any parities, unless the Fund decides . . . that parities shall be expressed in terms of SDRs or any other common denominator that the Fund may prescribe. This common denominator may not be gold or a national currency. . . . The definition of the Special Drawing Right in terms of gold is abolished. . .'

Here we have the crux of the matter, the absolutely historic transition from a metal standard to an abstract standard, from reference to a product to reference to a composite currency. Here, at the same time, we see the very concept of money setting off once again on yet another storm-tossed voyage towards who knows what distant shore. The IMF has stated that in future the method of evaluation of the SDR will be decided by the Fund itself with a majority of 85 per cent of the votes cast. Given the central role played by the SDR in the IMF's operations, any change in the method of calculation of the value of the SDR will of course presuppose a detailed examination of the problem and will require very strong grounds for such a move. The moment has therefore come to consider the origin and the characteristics of what we shall henceforth designate by the abbreviation ACU (Artificial Currency Unit), as well as the unique opportunities that such a concept makes possible.

A new monetary standard of value can only be defined by its equivalence to something else. Failing a commodity to which it could be tied, its value must be measured by what it can buy in goods and services. Such an equivalence in terms of goods and services would be variable and would tend to diminish under the effect of inflation. What the new unit will buy and what will consequently serve as the basis of its definition is to be found within the borders of states and is ultimately paid for in the national currency of these states, which naturally leads us to define the unit in terms of these national currencies, since it is by means of them that its purchasing power will be measured.

The new monetary unit will therefore be composed by putting a certain quantity of currency A (pounds, for example) a certain quantity of currency B (marks for example) and a certain quantity of currency C, etc. into a 'basket'. The value of the unit will then be measured by what this quantity of currency A will buy in country A, to which we must add what the quantity of currency B will buy in country B etc. If we convert these currencies A, B, C etc. into a currency X, the value in terms of goods and services thus produced will be measured by what the sum of X will buy in country X.

In addition, A, B and C each have a certain weight in this composite unit. This weight is calculated by converting A, B and C into a third currency X and then comparing each sum in the X that results to X expressed in terms of the ACU. The quantities of A, B and C are calculated at the starting date, so as to respect the weighting coefficients chosen on the basis of certain criteria (in the case of the SDR, shares in world trade) of the reference countries. Once these quantities have been chosen, the ACU is defined; its conversion rate into a currency Y can be calculated each day using the cross exchange rates.

From time to time, the composition of the ACU will be modified. For example, on 1 July 1978 the 1974 SDR was modified; the Danish crown, with a weighting of 1.5 per cent and the South African rand, with a weighting of 1 per cent, were eliminated, whilst the Iranian rial and the Saudi Arabian rial were introduced, with a respective weighting of 2 per cent and 3 per cent. At the same time, the pound sterling went down from 9 per cent to 7.5 per cent, whilst the dollar, the French franc and the Deutschemark remained unchanged at 33 per cent, 7.5 per cent and 12.5 per cent. The ACU, such as it has been described, which is the way the SDR is defined, consists of a number of units of national currencies which remain fixed for a relatively long period. These quantities are the only fixed elements in the unit. All the others, such as the conversion rate of the ACU into foreign currencies, the weight of these currencies in the ACU etc., vary from day to day, since they depend on external factors, namely the exchange rates of the various currencies in the market. An analysis of the basic formulae by which an ACU is defined (see page 278)(1) shows that the ACU has three defects which prevent it from being a real monetary standard. The first is the variation of the weight of each component currency as the exchange rates vary, which causes the relative positions of each of the currencies to change. Suppose, for example, that there is a currency A which is included in the ACU with an initial weight of 10 per cent. Let us further suppose that its exchange rate *vis-à-vis* the average of the other currencies rises by 18 per cent. This means that the conversion rate $t_{A/ACU}$ will also rise by 18 per cent; the weight of A in the ACU will therefore pass from 10 per cent to 11.8 per cent. It is of course comforting that the weight that increases should be the weight of the currency that is strongest on the exchange markets, but the weight of a component currency should not be determined by this parameter only.

A second, more serious defect, is the fact that it is impossible to use the SDR as a standard to define the component currencies. The subconscious need to tie currencies to something is so strong that the habit of defining them in terms of a weight of gold was kept for a long time, even though it no longer had any sense in terms of the market value of gold, and was, *a fortiori*, pointless, seeing that most currencies were no longer exchangeable into gold. But the theoretical connection between a currency and a weight of gold or a quantity of another currency at least had the merit of being independent of variations in the value of third currencies. Such is not the case with the SDR. The basic formula that defines the ACU shows that a money can only be tied to the SDR in an unvarying relationship if the sixteen component currencies are interconnected by fixed exchange rates; if only one of the sixteen starts to float, the conversion rates of the fifteen others will also start to vary in terms of SDR.

Here is an illustration. Peter measures the height of his ceiling: it is three metres. Some distance away, Robert enlarges his house. Peter measures his ceiling again and is surprised to see that it now measures only 2.7 metres. Soon John's house catches fire; immediately, to Peter's great astonishment, his ceiling increases in height to 3.25 metres. Such are the unexpected gyrations of a standard which is made up of the very things it is supposed to measure. Under the gold standard, or in a fixed exchange rate system, one could for example say that a franc was worth 1.777 grams of gold, or 20 cents. Whatever happened to the Deutschemark or the florin, the franc would still be defined by these 1.777 grams of gold and these 20 cents. 'Tying' the franc to the SDR as it was once tied to gold or the dollar would presuppose an immutable equivalence, if not for ever, then at least for some time. Let us suppose that a franc equals

0.15 SDR. How could this *continue* to be true, given that the Iranian rial or any other of the sixteen component currencies, by declining in value, would cause the franc to be worth more than 0.15 SDR, or perhaps less? A government is free to defend its currency against speculation but it cannot defend it against mathematics, and the independence of the component currencies *vis-à-vis* the SDR is a mathematical fact.

The *Journal de Genève* wrote, on 20 April 1978:

> The facts show that we are living in limbo. People take pleasure in the most flagrant contradictions and nonsenses. . . If SDRs are supposed to be exchangeable for currencies, they must be defined by something. Originally they were defined in terms of gold. Since 31 July 1974, this has ceased to be the case, and instead they are supposed to be defined in terms of a basket of currencies. Central banks want a reserve currency which will be neither gold nor the dollar. Very good, but this something still has to be found; there is no point in putting hot air into one's reserves.
>
> Here people bring in the definition of the SDR in terms of a cocktail of currencies. Appearances have been saved at the price of a contravention of the rules of logic. . . There is a big temptation to define national currencies in terms of SDRs. In that case, the absurdity would be complete. The value of the international reserve asset would be defined by the value of the currencies in the cocktail and their value would be defined by it, which is equivalent to defining the thing one is measuring by what one is measuring with.
>
> What is now called for is a new examination of the nature of money. . . To eliminate any form of backing from a currency is to open the doors to each and every form of excess. . .

The third defect of the SDR, as it is conceived at present, is its instability of value, an instability which should not be confused with the logical inconsistency outlined above. An ACU, like any currency, makes it possible to compare currencies amongst themselves, at a given moment, but it cannot be used to compare currencies over time, which is the very purpose of a standard of reference. The standard metre, made of platinum, which is kept in Paris at the Conservatory (formerly it was in Berlin) was not considered absolutely safe from the ravages of time. For this reason it has been defined in terms of light waves. The gram, the second, the lux and the watt are similarly precisely defined. They are the same whether in China or on the Niger and they are the same now as they were twenty years ago: in 100 years' time they will still not have

The creation of an international currency unit confined exclusively to exchanges between states is one of the major tasks of our time. Since innovation can no longer be avoided in this field, we ought to take advantage of this fact in order to restore to the concept of money those essential properties that are so sadly lacking in most currencies today, namely the ability to act as:

standard of measurement
store of value
reliable medium of exchange.

A composite currency such as the SDR, which consists of national currencies in invariable proportions, is affected by all the weaknesses of the national currencies and even by certain others peculiar to it. A healthy currency cannot be created by putting a lot of sick currencies together in a basket, even if some are less sick than others.

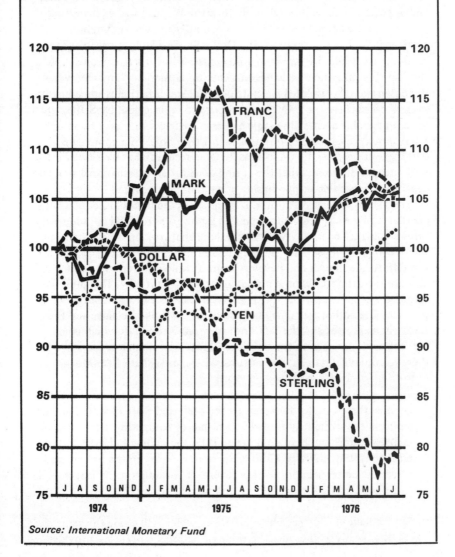

VARIATIONS IN THE CONVERSION RATES INTO SDRs OF FIVE MAJOR CURRENCIES BETWEEN 1974 AND 1977

1 Jan 1974 = 100

Source: *International Monetary Fund*

changed. A unit of money is also a measure — a measure of purchasing power. By defining currencies in terms of a weight of gold, man had a reference instrument which was independent of time and place; if they are tied to a freely floating SDR, any objective value in time is lost.

Gold clauses have been abolished and the standard of value is now the SDR. But its value, by definition, is only that of the currencies that make it up, all of which are depreciating. When the dollar was the key currency and appeared invulnerable, when the Bretton Woods fixed exchange rate system was considered impregnable, when inflation was only nibbling away at the value of currencies, the IMF still considered it necessary to reinforce its system by means of gold clauses. How, then, can one explain the fact that just when exchange markets are lapsing into anarchy, when the dollar has been toppled from its pedestal and inflation is spreading its ravages everywhere the IMF should choose to replace gold by SDRs, which are as vulnerable and as unreliable as the currencies that make them up? What should be called into question is not the choice of a composite currency unit as basis for an international currency; what we *should* call into question is the fact that the crying need for an extranational standard capable of preserving its purchasing power has been ignored.

The IMF is a great institution. It symbolises the hopes of peoples who are divided by everything, but who still aspire to peace, and consequently some semblance of unity. No one will deny that free and active trade and the opening of frontiers are the very conditions of unity, and it is up to the IMF to watch over and develop them. It follows, therefore, that it is also up to the IMF to choose a solid and reliable currency. The gold standard system is unviable for theoretical reasons and abolished in practice. The authorities sit by helplessly, as the dollar declines and the Deutschemark rises and the IMF tries to promote an SDR which is defenceless in the face of the attacks of those who oppose it for theoretical, political or private reasons. Thus, Mr William Rees-Mogg, Editor of *The Times*, wrote on 21 April 1978:

> Gold is, therefore, for two reasons the preferred store of value; the net addition to its quantity is lower than that of competing industries; an increase in the supply of gold depends on the mining industry and not on the printing industry. Gold is the better money in the present and offers the better security for the future. If Washington challenges gold to a knockout fight there is only one possible victor.

But we have already seen how inflation, which will erode the value of the SDR as surely as it erodes the value of national currencies, provides the die-hards of the gold standard with arguments which impress public opinion, in much the same way as the objections to the effect that the USA is 'tying the new unit to the dollar' also impress public opinion.

The general public understands little of contemporary monetary problems and nothing of the SDR. Leaders, political or otherwise, do not understand much more; but some of them have no hesitation in using whatever arguments are at hand for the purpose of bolstering their own economic, monetary or political prejudices. *The Times* has no trouble in showing that the SDR, if it were to be pitted against gold, would stand no chance of winning the contest; on the other hand, it makes no attempt to show how the gold standard could in fact be restored. In the same way, the *Journal de Genève* has no difficulty in proving to its readers that nothing can take the place of a backed money, but it makes no attempt to see whether it would be possible to find a backing or a commodity guarantee into which the currency could actually be rendered freely convertible, since without convertibility a backed money is pointless.

The alternative to a composite currency of the sort we have described is a merchandise standard. But a merchandise standard only fulfils its function of solidly fixing the value of a monetary claim on two conditions: firstly, that it is, in fact, possible to convert this monetary claim into a given weight of goods, and secondly, that this merchandise should itself be in some fixed value relationship with goods and services offered on the markets, which will not be affected by circumstances. No commodity can fulfil these conditions, which explains why a currency basket is preferred.

But such a new standard of value will only unite public opinion and will only obtain acceptability in competition with national currencies if it has an exceptional property. The answer to the criticisms which are likely to be levelled at the SDR must be to put to good use the special properties of an extranational payment unit used exclusively in financial exchanges between states, namely the quality of being stable in terms of purchasing power.

In any case, the use of the SDR as a reserve currency by central banks is bound to increase in time, if only because the temptation to distribute to the poorer member states what is in effect an interest-free loan, or even an outright gift if repayment obligations are abolished, will be hard to resist. But, of course, the SDR is more than this — it is also the embryo of a payment currency which will probably be used increasingly by central banks before it passes into general use in the international markets. This is not likely to happen overnight; it will probably be held up by clashes of interest and even more by ignorance and incomprehension. The inherent weaknesses of any composite currency whose composition is fixed will not help either.

The ECU, or European Currency Unit, is the most recent arrival on the scene and it, too, has been conceived in terms of a fixed basket of currencies in immutable proportions. No matter how well-intentioned the heads of government who have promoted it may be, one cannot help wondering whether the ECU has any greater chance of success than the SDR. This question cannot really be answered without some knowledge of the theoretical foundations of composite currencies, which will be found in the Supplementary Note (1) on page 282.

NOTES

[1] The extracts from official IMF publications quoted in this chapter are taken from press releases dealing with the latest amendments to the statutes, and from the 19 December 1977 and 10 April 1978 numbers of the IMF's official bulletin.

[2] The present tendency is for the IMF itself to collect the funds and then distribute them to the deficit countries in return for SDRs.

3 An American view of composite currency units

The deeper significance of the disorders of the international monetary
system and the potential implications of the rise of composite currency
units were realised some time ago by Professor Machlup of Princeton
University and set out in the following terms in an article published in
Euromoney in November 1973:

> There may, in fact, emerge a private counterpart to the official SDR,
> perhaps in the form of a Euro-SDR in which commercial banks may
> grant loans and accept deposits. If this should happen, we would be
> on the way toward a world currency, not created by governments
> and central banks but rather self-grown in response to private demand.
>   It would be possible to devise techniques of stabilizing the commodity
> value of the SDR. This is only a slightly more complicated task as it
> calls for superimposing a price index of internationally traded
> commodities on the par value index or exchange rate index of
> national currencies. What is important in the creation of an SDR of
> stable value in terms of a group of currencies is that the exchange risk
> in holding it is smaller than that in holding national currencies.
>   The new feature of stability in terms of an index of the exchange
> values of currencies will appeal not only to monetary authorities, for
> whom SDRs will be the principal reserve asset. It would have great
> appeal also to private transactors—importers, exporters, traders.
>   Private use of a composite monetary unit may be confined to
> contracts, such as bonds issued in Eurco, or may go beyond that to
> more widely conceived monetary functions.
>   Now, if increasing numbers of private transactors use SDRs for
> invoicing, they will want to use them also for lending and borrowing,
> first in international business transactions, later perhaps also in those
> national transactions that are closely linked with foreign trade and
> finance. As a result, there will develop a demand for loans
> denominated in SDRs and for deposit balances denominated in

SDRs (or whatever its new name may be). If banks meet this demand and grant loans and accept deposits denominated in SDRs, a beginning is made toward SDRs as a private transaction money.

Privately held SDRs would be deposit claims against commercial banks, usable for anything that another private party is willing to sell for this 'money'. The banks' assets balancing their SDR deposit liabilities would be neither SDR claims against central banks (because the latter have no SDR liabilities) nor any specified reserves (unless reserve requirements for SDR deposits are established), but simply loans and securities denominated in SDRs (or in currencies that are constituents of the SDR).

Needless to say, the SDR obligations of commercial banks would be honoured by these banks legally through payment of the currencies 'contained' in the SDR: in practice, however, more often through transfers to other commercial banks, domestic or foreign, of balances denominated in SDRs or in any national currency in amounts equivalent to the transaction values of the currencies composing the SDR.

The same considerations which have led some experts to suggest that the official SDR with the feature of value maintenance would be so desirable a reserve asset that the interest rate it carried could be very low, or even zero, may point to the possibility that the interest rates in the private SDR market would be much lower than in most other Eurocurrency markets.

The most significant implication of the development hastily sketched in these statements is that a good valuation method for the official SDR (appropriately renamed) might work as a stimulus for the emergence of an international transactions currency. This world money would not be created and imposed 'from above', by any law or edict, or by any action of an official agency, national or international, but would be 'self-grown' on the soil of free enterprise in response to private demand.

Joseph Aschheim and Yoon Shik Park continue thus:[1]

Amid the turmoil and upheaval of the current international monetary system, a series of eventful developments are underway involving the emergence of new artificial (or composite) currency units. The number of such units is growing constantly as a reflection of mounting discontent with the practice of using one or another national currency as the major unit of account in international transactions, either official or private.

Because the values of such key national currencies as the US dollar and the British pound have been highly unstable since the emergence of floating exchange rates, there have been growing efforts to create substitute, so-called 'artificial' currency units for use in international accounting and international settlements. Some of the efforts have been official, others unofficial . . .

A prominent example of such an ACU is the Special Drawing Right (SDR) of the international Monetary Fund, but other ACUs have been assuming a vital role in international finance, even though they have been less publicized or hardly recognised. . . At its present stage of development, an ACU's main function is as a *numéraire*, or unit of account, in international transactions. As such, an ACU is simply a yardstick to measure the value of a transaction, with the aim of keeping that value as stable as possible. Therefore, most ACUs are not full-fledged money, being used neither as a medium of exchange nor as a means of payment. Even though the value of a payment obligation is expressed in an ACU, the actual payment is generally made in one of the national currencies.

It should be noted, however, that there is nothing inherent in the concept of an ACU to limit its role to that of a *numeraire*. The main arguments of this essay are developed with an eye to the potential, as well as the likelihood, of ACUs playing an increasingly important role as full-fledged international money . . .

When an official institution creates an official ACU, it may borrow the idea from a private ACU, as in the case of the IMF's 'new' SDR, which is patterned after the currency-basket, or currency-cocktail, concept of the Eurco (a private ACU). . .

Private ACUs are used primarily to denominate bond issues. Actual payments for bonds by purchasers, as well as service payments by borrowers (interest and principal), are all carried out in a major national currency. The role of a private ACU is thus confined to that of a unit of account whose sole function is to determine payment obligations in terms of a national currency, while keeping the face value of the bond as stable as possible.

It would be feasible, however, for a private ACU to serve also as a medium of exchange, if a banking institution accepted demand deposits denominated in the ACU from private parties and cleared transactions through book-entry transfers . . .

The essential difference between national currencies and ACUs is that the former developed in a domestic context as essentially national means of payment, while the latter have been created exclusively in the context of international transactions, initially as units of account but with the potential of being developed to a limited extent into international means of payment . . .

The development of an ACU as a means of payment in international transactions may ensue from the bank deposits denominated in that ACU. To take the SDR for illustration, suppose that investors seek to keep some of their liquid financial assets denominated in SDRs in order to reduce the exposure to foreign-exchange risk inherent in a national currency.

We can more easily understand Aschheim and Park's ideas by taking an example. Let us imagine a transaction in which the price is expressed in SDRs. The buyer pays for his purchase in dollars, at the rate calculated for that day by the IMF. If an SDR is worth 2 dollars and the man's debt is 100 SDRs, he will pay 200 dollars. The dollar has functioned as payment unit and vehicle, whereas the SDR has only functioned as a unit of account. Let us now suppose that the purchaser gives his supplier a piece of paper signed by the cashier of a bank on which is written 'I promise to pay the bearer 100 SDRs'.

If the purchaser's bank transfers this claim denominated in SDRs to the seller's bank and if the latter keeps his asset donominated in SDRs, the SDR unit of account has functioned as a payment unit.

In other words, there is a transformation from the role of unit of account to that of transaction unit when the payment is carried out by means of a transfer of a claim on an institution denominated in that unit of account and entered thus to the credit of a current account and on condition that the unit remains so denominated for a certain time without being converted into another currency.[2](1)

The growing internationalization of economic institutions in many countries makes it imperative to adopt a multicurrency concept for those institutions' global operations. Assets and liabilities of multinational corporations or international banks can no longer be denominated in a single optimum currency. Increasingly, international transactions, either financial or commercial, will be executed in the ACU most functionally suitable for that transaction. Multinational institutions have discovered that the use of a key national currency is patently inadequate for their international operations, which require new types of global currencies. Mundell observes that there is an inherent tendency for a common international money to develop based on economies of scale in the production of information. The emergence of ACUs can be viewed as a practical response to this new institutional demand for a dual currency sytem, where national currencies are used mostly in intra-country transactions, while ACUs are used for international transactions.

Aschheim and Park indicate their preference for an ACU limited to external transactions, national currencies being reserved for trade within the states in question. In this way, the well-known defects of a national currency used as dominant currency for international trade would be eliminated, as would also the use of such a currency for central bank interventions in the foreign exchange markets. But they could have gone further and shown that an ACU limited to external trade and excluded from internal transactions may thereby acquire a unique and highly desirable property which men have long sought after, namely a stable value, i.e. a purchasing power independent of exchange rates and price levels, because the value of money can only be expressed in terms of what it will purchase. An ACU confined to external trade could therefore have this constant purchasing power and so constitute that fixed standard of measure which is so patently lacking in modern monetary systems.

The rise and proliferation of artificial currency units that we have reviewed in these pages illustrate the pervasiveness, spontaneity, and diversity of the recourse to the formation of functional currency areas. In a fundamental sense, the reference to 'artificiality' in ACUs is a misnomer: the voluntary, profit-oriented cooperation that characterizes the establishment of private ACUs may just as readily be regarded as a 'natural' outgrowth of international monetary practice. In any event, the development of both official and private ACUs indicates that compulsory (i.e. intergovernmental) as well as voluntary (i.e. private) cooperative ventures may further propagate the ACU phenomenon. Whether this phenomenon represents 'the wave of the future' in international monetary economies we do not hazard to predict. Suffice it to note that the duration of the regime of floating exchange rates among national currencies, the development and use of ACUs is likely to continue . . .

What, then, is the lesson of ACUs for the pursuit of international monetary reform? Perhaps much of the current agenda for monetary reform is cast within too narrow a framework; the reform debate tends to focus on such traditional topics as demonetisation of gold, restoration of the fixed-rate system and convertibility of currencies. The emergence and prospective wider use of ACUs may make the future monetary system more pluralistic. Accordingly, concern about a new monetary system can no longer be confined to the issues that arise in the context of national currencies alone.

The agenda for monetary reform must be broadened to consider the new issues raised by the emergence of ACUs. The versatile response of official and private institutions to international monetary instability has led to the creation of various ACUs, with complex implications for the international monetary systems.

It will be quite a challenge for economists to fathom these new monetary developments and innovations so as to make possible a viable reform of the international monetary system. . . .

NOTES

[1] Extracts from *Essays in International Finance*, No. 114, April 1976, published by Princeton University.

[2] I am afraid that purist theoreticians may find this definition somewhat simplistic. They are bound to mention Don Patinkin and his attempts to incorporate within the same concept the functions of payment unit, medium of exchange and store of value, each one of these roles having, moreover, a different degree of intensity according to its duration, whether a week or a month.

In practice, however, we must come back to definitions that are closer to reality, without necessarily taking issue with Don Patinkin. More exactly, we must explain and justify the ellipsis of comparing a unit of account to a payment unit. The proof of this will be found on page 285.

4 An extranational payment unit with constant purchasing power: the Eurostable

The modern world lacks any kind of reliable international currency. There is no currency capable of correctly carrying out the role of international *numéraire* – that of medium of exchange and reserve and intervention instrument for central banks. Alone among systems of measurement, modern monetary systems are devoid of a genuine standard of value against which the value of goods and services can be compared in space and time.

For thousands of years, these functions, which are so important for the health of the world economy, were fulfilled by gold. Over the last hundred years, the task devolved first on to sterling and then the US dollar. The system got weaker and then finally disappeared for good on 15 August 1971 when, on President Nixon's orders, the American Treasury rescinded its obligation to convert into gold on demand dollars presented to it by foreign central banks.

It happens not infrequently that in industry, in the field of technology and in fact in almost all human activities, a particular process, a particular mode of manufacture, a product or a system become obsolete. When this happens they must be discarded and replaced by new techniques and systems, requiring imagination and research. This is what is known as innovation; it is what lies at the heart of the fantastic pace of change that is so characteristic of the era we live in. The need for innovation is nowhere more urgent than in the monetary field. The very term 'non-system', given to what is left of the international monetary system, is a desperate appeal for something new to replace what no longer works or has disappeared.

All this is well known. What is less well known is the fact that governments and political institutions face many obstacles in their efforts at innovation. The truth is that they are, by their very nature, ill-equipped to invent, to test and to correct — the essential features of innovation. It would be unfair, therefore, to hold this against them. Their true roles and responsibilities lie elsewhere. The very process of innovation implies experiments, changes of direction, alacrity of reaction, flexibility in execution, above all the right to make a mistake, something that political institutions trapped in the strait-jacket of rules and regulations that they must be the first to respect, hesitate to claim.

This is why most monetary and financial techniques have been the invention of the private sector. The examples are innumerable, but let us just mention bank-notes, bank-money, the money market, the Euromarket, commercial paper, Fed. Funds, swaps, credit cards and the forward market. It follows that it is the job of the private sector, and, more particularly, the international banking sector, to experiment where the urgency is greatest, where the deficiencies of the system are the most obvious and likely to have the most serious consequences. Once their experiments have been completed they must offer the results to the international authorities, which will then be able to make use of them and carry out the necessary reforms in full knowledge of what they are doing and with a reasonable chance of success.[1] (1)

The Eurostable derives directly from the ideas that inspired the Special Drawing Right and is intended to correct the deficiencies which have paralysed this instrument's development. An instrument designed to act as a store of value and a standard of reference over time cannot be said to be fulfilling its role if its purchasing power varies unpredictably, most often downwards. The purchasing power of the French franc, for example, has fallen as much during the past sixty years as throughout the whole of the preceding sixteen centuries: *The Economist* has similarly shown that at an annual inflation rate of 25 per cent a house bought for £15,000 will be worth £2500 million in seventy-five years' time.

New units of account conceived in the form of baskets of currencies, and irrevocable in their composition, offer no guarantee of stability. They are evidence of progress in monetary thinking; they constitute a step forward towards the creation of an international currency *ex nihilo*; but they alone will not cure our ills. There is no hope that a healthy currency will result from putting a collection of sick currencies in a basket, even if some are less sick than others. Everywhere, these days, is felt the lack of an international means of payment which would eliminate from business dealings the elements of risk, chance and the possibility of inequitable gains or losses; a currency is needed that would offer protection against *uncertainty* to both debtors and creditors, producers and consumers, buyers and sellers, and which would provide a solution to the worrying problem of recycling of international capital and the stabilisation of international liquidities.

This is the aim of the Eurostable experiment proposed in this book, in which a group of Eurobanks would be brought together in a consortium called 'The International Eurostable Consortium'. Only a preliminary experiment of this sort has any chance of overcoming the problems raised by a project which differs so radically from traditional ideas, for the truth is that there has never been an international currency which was exclusively extranational and did not circulate within national borders, just as there has never been a currency which maintained its purchasing power.

The Eurostable project was first presented to the world in a paper read before the *Société d'Economie Politique*[2] on 12 June 1974. Its characteristics are the following.

(i) It will be a payment unit and not merely a unit of account. A payment unit is accepted directly in transactions and transferred, deposited and lent *as such*. A unit of account is nothing but a convenient yardstick for the calculation of a payment that is carried out in national currency. A payment unit may always serve as a unit of account, but the opposite is not true: Metro tickets, kilowatts and many other things have been and still are used as units of account, but they are not transferred, deposited or lent.

(ii) The Eurostable is solely extraterritorial and will be used only for international transactions — payments by a resident of one country to a resident of another. Thus it circulates in that no man's (or rather, no government's) land which is the province of the Eurocurrencies. It does not circulate within any country, i.e. it is not used for transactions between residents.

(iii) Lastly, the Eurostable has constant purchasing power. But because of the fact that it is an extraterritorial currency, the definition of this constant purchasing power is special and different from what it would be if the Eurostable were a national currency. The Eurostable is a composite currency equivalent to an aggregate of given quantities of several reference currencies, the initial amount of each such reference currency being modified each day in line with the cost·of living index of the country of issue of the currency. The conversion rate of the Eurostable into a third currency is calculated each day by means of a formula that incorporates two sets of parameters: the median cross exchange rates, as they are determined by the market, and the

consumer price indices in the countries of the reference currencies, as
they are calculated by the national statistical services.

Before going any further, let us look more closely at this notion of
constant purchasing power. It is unusual because it is not possible for any
national currency to be equipped with such a property. Only a stateless
currency circulating within a real or imaginary monetary no man's land can
have it. The purchasing power of a monetary unit is defined by what the
unit will purchase. But what a currency will buy can only be discovered
inside states and is expressed in the national currencies of these states.
Between the frontiers there are no buyers or sellers; in order to find any
we have to cross territorial boundaries and go inside. The Eurostable must
therefore be defined in terms of national currencies and what they will
buy. Here is an example.

Let us suppose that the Eurostable is defined in terms of three
currencies, the mark, the franc and sterling. On the first day, the
composition of the Eutostable basket is as follows: DM 4 + £1 + FF 8.
That means that on the first day the bearer of one Eurostable can buy in
Germany a certain quantity of goods and services corresponding to what
the statistical services define as the purchasing power of DM 4; in Britain
he can buy a basket corresponding to £1; and in France he can buy a
basket corresponding to FF 8. Together these baskets constitute the
international basket which the Eurostable will buy: this is the Eurostable's
international purchasing power. If the bearer wishes to convert his asset
into a single currency, francs for example, and if the exchange rate is 1
mark for FF 2 and £1 for DM 8 he will receive FF 32 instead of DM 4 +
£1 + FF 8.

After a certain time, a year, for example, the price indices have moved
by 5 per cent in Germany, 15 per cent in Britain and 10 per cent in France.
The holder of Eurostable, by exchanging one Eurostable for the reference
currencies, will receive 4 x 1.05 = DM 4.2, plus £1.15, plus 8 x 1.10 =
FF 8.80. He will be able to buy with the different currencies exactly the
same basket in each currency as he could have bought a year before. If, as
is likely, he prefers to convert his Eurostable into one single currency,
francs, for example, he will receive at the current rate a certain sum in
francs which will most probably be different from the thirty-two he would
have received before. This obviously depends on exchange rate movements.

It can thus be seen that the daily conversion rate of the Eurostable into
a given currency is a function of the price indices in the reference
currencies (calculated by extrapolation from the last known figure for the
price indices, taking account of the number of days that have elapsed) and

the exchange rates of the reference currencies into the chosen vehicle-currency. This conversion can be calculated by means of a formula, the proof of which can be found on page 287.[3]

The essential features of the Eurostable must be maintained, for the following reasons.

Constant purchasing power will give the new payment unit the prestige necessary to make it desirable. It will thus fill a void that constitutes one of the most serious handicaps of our monetary system: the absence of a reference unit against which values can be compared independently of time and place.[4] (1) In this way the Eurostable will have a characteristic that no other currency possesses and which even gold has not got. This is the only way one can hope to compete with well established national currencies.

The Eurostable is confined exclusively to the Eurocurrency market, for various reasons, of which the most important is the simple fact that no government will accept a parallel currency in direct competition with its own on its own territory. The main drawback of most past projects in this field, and the reason why they failed, was their chimerical nature. The most recent example was the Werner Plan, which announced that a single common currency would replace all the national currencies in the member states of the EEC by the year 1980.

A fundamental rule to abide by when marketing a new product is to start in a 'soft' sector, not in one that is jealously defended by national authorities who are also direct competitors. Pragmatism and a sense of realism ought to warn us not to encroach on the sovereign rights of national governments. But pragmatism is not the only reason for confining the Eurostable to the sphere of the Euromarkets; the other reason is that this is the only way to maintain the Eurostable's constant purchasing power.

An extraterritorial unit of payment can retain its purchasing power because: (i) it is free from the strains and stresses of every kind, political, social, economic and fiscal, to which a national currency is subject; (ii) (and this is the most important feature) it is not subject to the law of the market, since it is not used either for initial payments to producers (or sellers), or for ultimate payments to final users or consumers but only for intermediate transactions. The first and final payments are always carried out in national currencies. The Eurostable is thus insulated from national currencies by what may be called 'monetary locks', namely the offices in which the Eurostable is converted, according to the formula, into national currencies.

Having thus defined the Eurostable, we must now develop a mechanism which would make it possible for a group of Eurobanks, grouped together in a Eurostable consortium, to create the unit and circulate it amongst themselves as a payment unit and not simply as a unit of account. The Eurostable will not, in fact, cross that magic boundary that separates the unit of account from the unit of payment unless and until a customer of a member bank of the consortium agrees to be paid in Eurostable by another agent, who is a customer of the same bank or of another bank, and he agrees to keep his asset, at least for a while, denominated in Eurostable.

Such is, in fact, the nature of a claim on an institution – in the case of the Eurostable, the bank that created it – with the payment function. The way such a system would operate raises certain banking problems, which have gradually been overcome after consultations with various experts from various countries and many simulations. An example of one of these simulations will be found later in this chapter.

A complete account of how this banking mechanism works would be out of place here; its main features, however, are as follows:

Each member bank is responsible for its own operations in Eurostable as part of the obligations that bind it to the other member banks of the consortium. From time to time, a member bank will create, in agreement with the other banks, a certain number of Eurostable by simultaneous entry on the asset and liability side of its balance sheet. This represents an obligation with regard to the other members, and at the same time a claim on them. The 'liquid' Eurostable thus created are lent, transferred by depositors and redeposited at the same bank or at another member bank. Deposits may be withdrawn or converted into currency at 24 hours notice at the daily conversion rate. The peculiarity of the system – and its originality – is that it provides substitutes for the instruments and techniques, such as the clearing house and central bank, peculiar to a national banking system, but which cannot be reproduced in a purely international system. After a certain quantity of Eurostable have been created by mutual agreement among the banks, each bank operates as a non-monetary intermediary, i.e. it does not transfer any claims on itself, as a bank in a national banking system would, but only such available Eurostable liquidities as it may have. In this way, no member bank can be committed beyond the amounts it had agreed on.

In present conditions, most experts consider that the Eurostable could be lent at an annual interest rate of 2 per cent. In reality, of course, these rates would have to be adjusted in line with the competitive margins of the Eurocurrency market.

This project requires no investment and does not imply any serious risks for those who take part in it. Nevertheless, it ought to be tried out in the beginning on a very small scale and with the greatest prudence.[5] It would provide governments with useful information for the generalisation within a given monetary zone of the use of a unit of payment peculiar to the zone. Such a unit could also be later transformed into a fully-fledged currency with the following characteristics.

It will be a standard by means of which values can be measured and compared independently of time and place, thus constituting an instrument for gauging and comparing. Amongst all systems of measurement, our monetary system is the only one not to have a permanent stable standard of value.

It will challenge the dollar and the mark in their all too exclusive role in the field of international trade, and thus help to eliminate the grave danger that, in spite of the efforts by the German government to prevent it, the mark will become the European currency *par excellence*.

It will give new life to that great project of a genuine union of European nations, conscious of their common interest and their common heritage.

It will give the authorities a better control of Euromarket operations, since the Eurostable will circulate among a small number of banks directly under their supervision, whereas ordinary Eurocurrencies move rapidly between banks all over the world and sometimes even fail to appear in the statistics.

It will help to stabilise international capital flows by fixing floating assets, thus providing a corrective to the disorders caused by masses of funds moving from one place to the other, deserting weak currencies and besieging strong ones.

It will constitute a useful tool for central banks, being a unit with no nationality, which would not suffer from the defects of a national currency when used by them as an instrument of intervention and reserve.

The way the Eurostable would function in practice can best be illustrated by means of a game similar to the 'Lotto-money' and 'Lotto-clearing' games. The object of the game is to stimulate the operation of the Eurostable Consortium. It derives directly from the various experiments using models which were carried out during the development of the mechanism.

The Eurostable is so defined that a given quantity of the unit will
purchase an international basket of goods and services which remains
constant and which is itself composed of a number of constant
national baskets of goods and services.

This is one of the remarkable characteristics of a purely international
monetary unit reserved exclusively for transactions between states, such
as are carried out at present in Eurocurrencies, namely that it can be
equipped with constant purchasing power. This also means that such a
unit is capable of fulfilling the three roles traditionally expected of money,
namely act as a standard of measurement, a store of value and a reliable
medium of exchange.

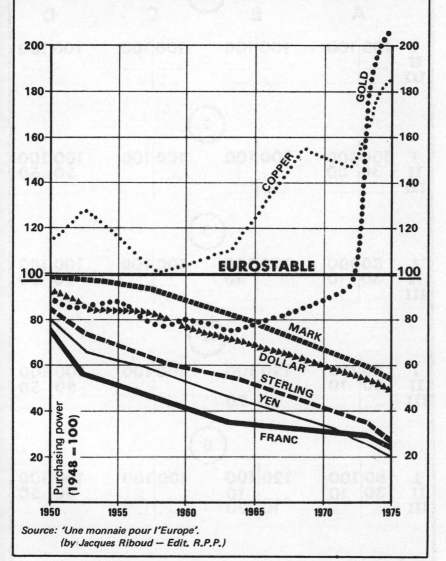

COMPARATIVE PURCHASING POWER

Trends in the purchasing power of copper, gold, major national currencies and the Eurostable, between 1950 and 1975.

EUROSTABLE

GOLD

COPPER

MARK

DOLLAR

STERLING

YEN

FRANC

Purchasing power (1948 = 100)

Source: 'Une monnaie pour l'Europe'.
(by Jacques Riboud — Edit. R.P.P.)

Balance sheets (I)

	A		B		C		D	

① A   B   C   D

	A		B		C		D	
I	100	100	100	100	100	100	100	100
II	....	....	....	....	....	....	....	....
III	....	....	....	....	....	....	....	....

②

	A		B		C		D	
I	100	100	100	100	100	100	100	100
II	30	30	....	....	....	....	50	50
III	....	....	....	....	....	....	....	....

③

	A		B		C		D	
I	80	100	120	100	100	100	100	100
II	30	10	....	20	....	....	50	50
III	....	....	....	....	....	....	....	....

④

	A		B		C		D	
I	80	100	120	100	100	100	100	100
II	30	10	....	....	....	....	50	50
III	....	....	....	20	....	....	....	....

⑤

	A		B		C		D	
I	80	100	120	100	100	100	100	100
II	30	10	....	10	....	....	50	50
III	....	....	10	20	....	....	....	....

Balance sheets (II)

(6)

	A		B		C		D	
I	80	100	120	100	100	100	100	100
II	30	10	.....	10	.....	.....	50	.....
III	.....	.....	10	20	.....	.....	.....	50

(7)

	A		B		C		D	
I	80	100	120	100	100	100	100	100
II	.....	10	.....	10	.....	.....	50	.....
III	30	.....	10	20	.....	.....	.....	50

(8)

	A		B		C		D	
I	110	100	120	100	100	100	70	100
II	.....	10	.....	10	.....	.....	50	.....
III	30	30	10	20	.....	.....	30	50

(9)

	A		B		C		D	
I	110	100	120	100	75	100	95	100
II	.....	10	.....	10	25	.....	50	25
III	30	30	10	20	.....	.....	30	50

(10)

	A		B		C		D	
I	100	100	100	100	100	100	100	100
II	.....	10	15	10	10	.....	50	25
III	40	30	15	20	.....	10	30	55

The member banks of the consortium are, let us suppose, four in number, A, B, C and D, domiciled, as is usually the case with Eurobanks, in different countries. The players, who represent bankers from the different banks, are grouped around the manager of the consortium and exchange messages which, in reality, would be transmitted by telephone or telex between the head office of the consortium and the head offices of the banks. Balance sheet movements representing the Eurostable operations are written up on a blackboard as the game proceeds.

On line one, on the assets side, are the Eurostable liquidities (claims on the other banks) and on the liabilities side are the bank's obligations towards the other banks from the creation of Eurostable by the bank. On line two, there are claims on third parties and liabilities towards third parties and other members of the consortium other than those that were contracted at the moment the Eurostable were first created. Finally, on line three, there are currency assets and liabilities, represented in terms of Eurostable, in order to simplify the accounting, and without any adjustments for fluctuating exchange rates.

The simple transactions which the participants carry out during the course of the game are those that Eurobankers are carrying out every day and they take account of the special rules devised in order to obviate the need for a central bank and a clearing house in the Eurostable system.

The rules involve a compulsory 100 per cent reserve ratio and the elimination of any Eurostable exchange risk. They can be reduced to the following:

Assets (2) $\leqslant$ liabilities (1) (excluding interbank loans)

Assets (1) + (2) $\geqslant$ liabilities (1) + (2)

Here is an example of a simple series of transactions (ES = Eurostable):

1 — Unanimous decision to create 100 freely available ES by each member bank of the consortium.
2 — Granting of a credit of 30 ES by Bank A to its customer X and 50 ES by Bank D to Y.
3 — X pays 20 ES to his supplier X', who deposits the money at Bank B. Y sells his asset to Y' who deposits the money with D.
4 — X' converts his 20 ES into dollars at the daily rate.
5 — Sale by B to a customer, Z, of 10 ES against dollars.
6 — Y' converts his deposit at D into dollars.

7 — *X'* repays his loan to *A*.

8 — *A* buys 30 ES from *D*, in accordance with one of the rules of the consortium, which says that ES assets must be at least equal to liabilities.

9 — Loan of 25 ES by Bank *C* to Bank *D*, in order to supply a loan which *D* wishes to make.

10 — Winding up of the consortium. Each bank reconstitutes its assets in available ES (line 1) by buying or selling ES against other claims or currency.

Once the rules have been established and the elementary operations explained, the game proceeds thus: during each round a roulette wheel with three colours indicates three figures which stand for amounts of loans, payment orders and requests for conversion into currency. Another roulette wheel, with two colours, indicates inter-bank interest rates and the spread for loans to customers. A set of dice indicate the banks in question, bearing in mind that a bank may refuse a request for a loan but not a transfer order or a request for conversion into currency. Interest is paid at the moment the loans are repaid; at the end of the game the consortium is wound up and each bank has to re-establish equilibrium between its assets and its liabilities in available Eurostable (line 1). Sales of available Eurostable against claims, liabilities or currency attract a premium according to a pre-arranged system. The winner is the player who has received the most in interest.

The game shows how the Eurostable adapts the mechanism of the Euromarket to its own uses and supplements it so as to correct the absence of central bank and clearing house. It may be enlarged to simulate the use of the Eurostable by a corporate body, the European Community for example, which would then operate like a central bank. In this case the Eurostable would not be created by the members but by the community body. They would be used by the central banks for their reciprocal financial transactions, their interventions in the exchange markets, etc. The game thus shows how an international payment unit could be successfully substituted for national currencies in financial relations between countries. But what has been outlined above is only a game. Useful information, such as may help to contribute to the development of tomorrow's Monetary Mechanisms, will only be obtained on condition that we try first of all to understand the monetary mechanisms of today.

NOTES

[1] Since the collapse of the Bretton Woods agreement, proposals for the reform of the world monetary system have succeeded each other thick and fast. Everybody, economists, politicians, thinkers and visionaries, has at some time tried his hand at it. These projects have been, in the main, highly intelligent. What they have in common is that they all presuppose a common political will on the part of governments which are in fact separated by their habits of thought, their ideas of what constitutes the interest of their country and the wishes of their voters. See also the first note on page 287 for further remarks on this subject.

[2] The upshot of this paper, read to the *Société d'Economie Politique*, was the publication by the 'Editions de la RPP' of a book called *Une monnaie pour l'Europe: l'Eurostable*.

[3] For the conversion formula of the Eurostable into third currencies see page 287, second note.

[4] In his book *A la recherche du temps économique* (Published by Fayard), Henri Guitton writes:

> One might wonder whether this ideal of indefinite flexibility does not cause the concept of money to disappear altogether. Such a world would be one in which exchanges would be perpetually adjusting to each other, a kind of indexation extended to embrace trade as well. The discipline of gold was awkward for people and stifled enterprise. The total absence of any discipline, which is intended to make progress easier, may, on the other hand, be another sort of constraint. How can one keep accurate accounts, how can one make plans without any reliable standard?

[5] The restrictive nature of the proposed system, in which the banks operate as non-monetary intermediaries, is increased by imposing on each bank of the consortium a loan ceiling of twice the total amount of ES which it creates in concert with the other member banks. One could go further still and demand a 100 per cent cover, that is, oblige a member bank to keep available each deposit that it receives. In this case, a member bank can only lend the ES that it creates or which it borrows from other member banks. This is the rule observed in the Lotto-Eurostable game (see Chapter 5).

5 Thirty questions on the Eurostable

Question – The Eurostable is an extranational unit of payment. Does that mean that it has constant purchasing power in any particular country?

Answer – No, because that would presuppose exactly parallel movements in exchange rates and price indices within the countries of the component currencies, which is very unlikely. The purchasing power of a national currency is defined in terms of the sum of units of that currency necessary to buy a specific 'basket' of goods and services in the country of the currency. The purchasing power of the Eurostable is defined in terms of an international basket of goods and services, which is nothing more than the aggregate of the different baskets corresponding to the countries of the component currencies.

If the purchasing power of the Eurostable were to remain stable in any particular country it would have to be defined exclusively in terms of the currency of that country, which would deprive it of its international character. Differences between the relative variations in exchange rates and price indices diminish after a certain time, but they do exist. This is something well known to economists: they call it Purchasing Power Parity (PPP).

Q – Rather than take a group of national baskets, the composition of each of which is fixed by the national authorities in each country, would it not be preferable to devise a special international basket?

A – No, because it would give rise to interminable arguments about the composition of the basket: the Danes would insist on including beer, whereas the Italians would prefer wine. It is easier to adopt the baskets and statistics which are already in use in the country of origin of each component currency.

Q – It is well known that the price indices are open to serious criticisms. Does that not create problems, given that the conversion rate of the Eurostable into currencies depends on the national price indices, as they are calculated in the countries of origin of the component currencies?

A – Everything is under attack these days, not just price indices. In fact, the margin of error in the indices is very small compared with the accumulating depreciation of money. The concept of 'inflation' is by now well established in the popular imagination. The term is used every day without anybody noticing that what they call the inflation rate is nothing more than the consumer price index.

Jacqueline Fourastié has looked into the question of the accuracy of the indices and has worked out the margin of error present in the figures published by national statistical services (see her book *Les Formules d'indice de prix à la consommation*, Armand Colin). For example, she has compared the prices of various baskets (*A, B, C*) over more than a hundred years (from the beginning of 1840), varying the composition of the individual baskets in the following ways:

The first (basket *A*) corresponds to the average consumption patterns of a family in 1952. The variations in the prices of commodities that disappear as one goes back in time, either because they were not in common use or had not been invented, were calculated by taking the analogy of those commodities that were most similar to them and which were in use at that time. The second basket (*B*) was obtained by removing the commodities that did not exist in 1880, and the third basket (*C*) was obtained by removing all the commodities that did not exist in 1840. Given an identical total cost of each basket in 1952, fixed at 100,000, the prices for each basket in 1880 were 762, 727 and 753 respectively and in 1840 they were 621, 611 and 611.

Thus it can be seen that the divergences between the costs of the baskets, whose contents have been so arbitrarily modified, are very small, which has led certain experts to recommend choosing much simpler baskets (whereas it is usually the composition of the baskets rather than the price surveys that is criticised).

If we wish to solve contemporary problems we must make use of the techniques of the present day: that is one of the rules of progress. The problems that arise from the attempt to create a stable monetary standard of reference can and must be solved by making use of recent advances in statistical methods, which have been tested and have become established practice.

Q – Which are the currencies that make up the Eurostable and what weightings do they have?

A – The original plan was to use the component currencies of the new European Unit of Account, as defined by the EEC. But Mr Jean Denizet of the Banque de Paris et des Pays Bas has pointed out that a purely European formula might not be attractive enough for depositors such as the Arab oil producers, who are accustomed to dealing in dollars. A formula incorporating the dollar with a weighting of 30 per cent and the EUA currencies for the remaining 70 per cent has therefore been envisaged; but the final choice must be left up to the member banks of the consortium.

Q — It is sometimes claimed that the conversion formula is a complication, as is the need to calculate the daily conversion rates. Is this so?

A — There are two sorts of parameter in the formula that gives the conversion rate of the Eurostable into currencies. There are the price indices and the rates of exchange *vis-à-vis* a vehicular currency, usually the dollar. The calculation is very easy. It takes about twenty seconds on the kind of pocket calculator commonly on sale in shops. These 'posted prices' would then be communicated to the member banks by telex. Such calculations are made every day by the IMF and other bodies in order to work out the daily conversion rate of the SDR and the EUA into currencies.

Q — How does the Eurostable compare with the various composite currency units (Artificial Currency Units, or ACUs) which have appeared over the last ten years, such as the Eurco, the SDR, etc?

A — The Eurostable is different, first of all because it is a payment unit and not just a unit of account, as all these units are. Secondly, it has constant purchasing power, which is not the case with any of the other units.

Q — The notion of constant purchasing power is sometimes criticised on the grounds that it makes a currency too 'hard', a certain depreciation being necessary in order to favour the borrower and induce him to borrow. Why not introduce into the formula a certain moderating coefficient?

A — Constant purchasing power is essential and must be kept for two reasons.
(i) Such constant purchasing power does not mean that a currency is impossibly hard, because it gives the borrower the benefit of increased productivity. A really hard unit would be one which was defined in terms of a constant number of hours of work. A Eurostable defined with constant purchasing power will depreciate in terms of hours of work at the same rate as productivity increases (on average, 2 per cent a year).
(ii) If one introduced into the formula a moderating factor which deprived the Eurostable of some of its constant purchasing power, the 'quality image' of the unit would deteriorate. But this image is necessary if it is to succeed in rivalling the dollar and the mark.

A payment unit that is immune to the universal disease of inflation will be very attractive and will have in that feature one of its strongest selling points. It would be a mistake to remove this advantage in favour of something which would put it at the mercy of manipulation by governments.

Q – How does the Eurostable compare with the Europa?[1]

A – A unit with constant purchasing power called the Europa was presented to the world by nine economists in November 1975, that is to say, more than a year and a half after the Eurostable was presented to the *Société d'Economie Politique* in Paris. It is conceived as a real circulating medium of exchange, intended to be used inside existing states.

The Eurostable has no such ambitions; it is simply intended to be an extraterritorial Eurocurrency; that is, one that circulates outside, not inside, the frontiers of countries.

There is no fundamental opposition between the Eurostable and the Europa. The Eurostable experiment ought to be useful for the eventual promotion of the Europa; it was indeed specifically conceived to be capable of being launched without the aid of national governments, which it is pointless to depend on in present circumstances.

Q – The Eurostable is fundamentally extranational, that is, without nationality, which is its most original feature. Why should it be confined to Europe?

A – The prefix 'Euro' by no means signifies that the Eurostable is purely European. The territory of the Eurostable is the Euromarket. It so happens that the European Community is studying the creation of a specifically European currency. The Eurostable is offered as an experiment from which useful lessons may be learnt that will help in the setting up of a a common European medium of exchange, but it could be used just as well in any other monetary zone.

Q – What is the role of the Consortium management and how is it combined with that of the member banks?

A – Each member bank is responsible for its own operations, for the creation of Eurostable and for loans, etc. The Consortium itself has no banking function. Its management's only role is to coordinate, collect statistics and promote the idea. Each day the Consortium will calculate the conversion rates of the Eurostable into currencies and communicate them to the member banks. In brief, it will advertise the Eurostable and attempt to promote the use of it.

Q – What are the rules governing the formation of Eurostable?

A – The Regulations of the Eurostable system stipulate that from time to time a given quantity of 'liquid' Eurostable will be created. The amount decided upon is distributed equally amongst the member banks. Each one registers the quota assigned to it simultaneously as an asset and as a liability in its balance sheet. The liquid Eurostable thus created represent a claim on the entirety of the member banks and constitute at the same time a liability with regard to them.

Q — Is this *ex nihilo* creation of Eurostable in conformity with established banking practice?

A — It is nothing other than a direct adaptation to the special conditions of the Eurodollar system of the usual mechanism by which banks in a national banking system create money. In order to open a credit in favour of X, bank A enters a claim on itself on the liability side of its balance sheet and simultaneously enters a corresponding liability towards its customer. Subsequently, the borrower makes a payment and gives an order to this effect to bank A, or, alternatively, draws a cheque, which X's creditor, Y, then pays into his account with bank B. On the liability side of B's balance sheet, a liability towards Y takes the place of A's liability towards X. X's claim on A and subsequently on B has effected the payment.

The Eurostable system does nothing other than adapt the fundamental principle of money as a claim on an institution, the institutions being the member banks of the consortium, instead of, as is the case in a national banking system, the bank that receives the deposit.

Q — Liquid Eurostable represent a liability on the part of the bank that created them towards the others. They also represent a claim for the same amount on these other members, which means that the other banks will have to distribute amongst themselves and enter off balance sheet the liquid Eurostable created by one of them. What is the reason for this procedure?

A — This is so because of the need to satisfy several different requirements: the need to create a fully operational banking system and its most characteristic feature, the transfer or conversion into currency of an asset; and, at the same time, precisely circumscribe the risks and responsibilities of each member bank in a system which, unlike a national banking system, has no central bank and no clearing mechanism. The very mechanism of creation of Eurostable is so designed that the responsibility of a member bank of the consortium arising from the creation of a certain quantity of Eurostable by another member bank does not exceed the amount that the bank accepted in full knowledge of what it was doing. The liquid Eurostable thus created are lent, transferred, deposited, re-lent, redeposited etc., each bank acting as a non-monetary intermediary with regard to these Eurostable, which means that the bank that receives the transfer order effectively transfers freely available Eurostable.

Q — Why this emphasis on confining the banks that create the Eurostable to the role of non-monetary financial intermediaries?

A — Operations carried out by a non-monetary intermediary make for much stricter discipline and control than is the case with monetary intermediary, since the payment money in circulation is never other than what has been consciously and deliberately issued by the central bank. There is no addition of simultaneously created money through the banking system.

In a national banking system, the creation of new money by the commercial banks is superimposed on the creation of money by the central bank and any bank can make itself the debtor of any other bank without the latter's agreement.

This is of no importance in a national banking system because at the end of each day the balances are cleared; but this is not possible in the case of the Eurostable system, because there is neither central bank nor clearing house. The available Eurostable are created with the agreement of all the member banks. Loans are made by a member to the extent of the Eurostable it has created. Payments are made in 'available' — i.e. 'liquid' — Eurostable. For this reason, no clearing process is necessary. No bank may become debtor or creditor of another bank without the latter's previous agreement. Liabilities of a bank towards other banks are limited to the total liabilities it accepted when the Eurostable were created.

Q — Eurostable-denominated liabilities constitute a debt for the bank that creates them. Does that not involve an exchange risk which banks would not be willing to accept?

A — One of the rules of the Consortium is that banks must always have on the asset side of their balance sheet a quantity of Eurostable, i.e. of indexed money, greater than their Eurostable liabilities. This is the reason why the Eurostable can only be introduced into circulation by means of a credit. A Eurostable borrower pays his supplier, who then has the option of converting the amount he has received into currency. The Eurostable which the bank thus receives can then be replaced in the market in exchange for currency, without disturbing the indexed part of the bank's balance sheet.

Q — Once the Eurostable has been introduced into circulation by crediting an account, the borrower pays his creditor, who deposits the payment at a member bank of the Consortium. Is it not probable that this same creditor will immediately convert into currency, which will thus remove the Eurostable from circulation?

A — This is quite possible, as long as the Eurostable is not well known and well established. But it is not important, since the Eurostable, once it has been converted, can easily be sold again, instead of being re-lent, thereby causing an influx of currency proportionate to the outflow at the moment of conversion. The whole project rests on a probability and a hypothesis, namely that there will always be a market for a liquid unit of payment which is protected against inflation.

That said, it is obviously up to the member banks of the consortium to develop and advertise the merits of the Eurostable market. In order to achieve this, they will keep themselves informed regarding the Eurostable payments that their clients intend to make and they will attempt to persuade the recipient of a Eurostable payment of the importance of keeping his asset denominated in Eurostable.

Q – How does the Eurostable system procure its reserves?

A – Here again there is a transfer of banking techniques in use in national banking systems to the Eurostable system. A member bank of the consortium needs to be able either to carry out a transfer of Eurostable in response to a transfer order or convert into currency a quantity of Eurostable presented to it by a holder of Eurostable. In order to comply with these requests, the bank needs to have enough available Eurostable in order to carry out the transfer or have enough currency to effect the conversion. The problem here is no different from the problem that a bank in a national banking system has to face. In order to effect a transfer or pay a cheque presented to it it needs adequate liquid or semi-liquid reserves. In the same way, a member bank of the Consortium needs to have available Eurostable or adequate currency reserves. As regards the Eurostable, the compulsory 100 per cent reserve requirement means there will always be enough liquid Eurostable. As far as the question of currency reserves is concerned, they will be replenished after the bank has made conversion payments, by placing the Eurostable thus acquired back in the market. What is more, Eurostable operations will only be a fraction of the bank's total activities in foreign currencies. It will calculate the value of its Eurostable position in the same way as it calculates its foreign exchange position, by converting into a common denominator, and it will take the same care to balance its liabilities with its assets.

Q – All the evidence suggests, then, that the Eurostable will be very much in demand. Is there not a risk that the member banks will be tempted to indulge in excessive creation of Eurostable?

A – The mechanism by which Eurostable are created is more restrictive than the mechanism by which money is created in a national banking system. In fact the member banks are obliged to act in concert with each other. Each Eurostable created represents a claim on the aggregate of banks as well as a liability, not only for the bank that creates the Eurostable but for all the other banks as well. This collective responsibility is likely to have a strongly moderating influence on the banks. In any case, the quantity of Eurostable in the market is likely to be very small when compared with the uncontrolled growth of Eurocurrency liabilities (40,000 million dollars in 1975).

Q — The success of the Eurostable project presupposes the existence of a real two-way market, that is, not just depositors, but borrowers as well. It is easy to see that depositors would not be hard to find, but can the same be said of borrowers? Inflation makes it possible for a borrower to borrow at negative interest rates. Will a money which is to be lent at a real positive interest rate be able to compete in such a market?

A — In principle, Eurostable operations are most likely to be short-term bank loans. Borrowers on the Euromarket only manage to get away with negative interest rates in exceptional market conditions, and generally only in the case of weak currencies. Eurocurrencies are strong currencies for the simple reason that Euromarket banks only lend what they receive in deposits and these deposits are in strong currencies. In real terms, the interest earned on the Euromarkets is about 2 per cent, which is the reason why the interest rate initially suggested for the Eurostable was 2 per cent though the rate can always be revised.

What we must take into consideration here is the motivation which would be appealed to in order to interest people in the Eurostable. The main selling point is the elimination of the element of uncertainty which results from unpredictable exchange market movements and from equally unpredictable movements in the price index. The idea of a constant purchasing power currency lent at very low real rates of interest will be welcome, even if people know that this constant purchasing power is only true on an international basis and not necessarily true inside each member state. The difference between that and real constant purchasing power is very small and, indeed, negligible in comparison with the security which the Eurostable would give.

In addition, we must take into consideration the obstacles which the strong currency countries put in the way of deposits by non-residents, a factor which is vary favourable to the Eurostable. The Swiss authorities, for example, have imposed negative interest rates of 40 per cent on non-resident deposits, whilst the German monetary authorities impose a reserve ratio of 100 per cent on Eurobanks domiciled within the Federal Republic. Restrictive measures of this kind make Eurocurrency business very expensive and are likely to curb the growth of the market.

Q — It still remains true that the depositor can convert his asset when-ever he likes into currency, whereas the claim which the bank has on its asset side may have a longer maturity. Does that not expose the bank to special risks?

A — This question goes to the very heart of the principles on which the banking business operates. From this point of view there is no difference between a bank operating in national currencies, one operating in Euro-curencies and one operating in Eurostable. A bank always immobilises one part of its assets and takes a chance that the difference between deposits and withdrawals will be less than its liquid reserves.

There is a greater chance that this will be the case with the Eurostable than with a national currency for several reasons:

There are no obligatory reserve requirements with the Eurostable. Deposits in Eurostable should be more stable precisely because of the protection against monetary erosion which the Eurostable enjoys and from which depositors benefit.
The bank can be sure that there will always be a seller's market for the Eurostable, which means that it will be able to place back in the market any Eurostable that are converted.

This is the reason why banking experts have considered that reserve ratios in liquid currency or semi-liquid currency assets are likely to be smaller for the Eurostable than for Eurocurrencies or national currencies.

Q — Is there not a risk that there may be too strong a demand for Eurostable and that, supply being strictly limited, there may develop a parallel market with different conversion rates from those calculated by the Consortium, reflecting the excessive demand?

A — Any effect exercised by the forces of supply and demand in the market on the 'price' of the Eurostable can only be in one direction, that is to say, sending it to a premium, since if there was a risk of its being driven down to a discount, the holder of Eurostable assets could exercise his option of conversion into currency. The possibility that the Eurostable might trade at a premium in the market is one that cannot be ignored; but it is unlikely that the premium would be very great.

Nevertheless, this eventuality must be taken into account, and so one of the rules of the system is that member banks have the option of obligatory repayment of Eurostable deposits in currency. This is the exact counterpart of the depositor's right to convert on demand into currency. It is not likely to happen often, but it would help to prevent the emergence of a parallel market and, in addition, help to obviate another risk which cannot be completely eliminated: the risk that a repayment of a Eurostable loan in currency might upset a bank's balance sheet and cause the total Eurostable assets to fall below the total of Eurostable liabilities — in other words, create an exchange risk.

As a general rule, the bank will use the currency obtained at the moment of repayment to purchase Eurostable made available in another bank by a depositor's exercising his right to conversion. But provision should be made for the situation where there are not enough available Eurostable. In such an exceptional case, the bank has the option of putting its balance sheet straight by repaying its Eurostable liabilities in currency.

Q — In a national banking system a bank may appeal to the central bank to solve its liquidity problems. As the Eurostable is an extranational currency, a bank dealing in Eurostable has no lender of last resort.

A — The question has already been dealt with as regards Eurocurrencies in general. Banks operating in Eurocurrencies also have no obvious lender of last resort. The tacit rule is that the central bank of the country of origin of the bank in trouble acts as lender of last resort, whatever the currency that has caused the trouble. There is no reason why the situation should be any different in the case of the Eurostable, which is nothing more than an aggregate of national currencies.

Risk is inherent in the nature of banking. Apart from currency speculation, the main risks are of two kinds: illiquidity and the default of a borrower. The rules of the Eurostable system and the universally recognised existence of a strong demand for Eurostable practically eliminate the risk of illiquidity. As for the risk of a default, it is no different in the case of the Eurostable from what it is in the case of any currency.

Q — The Eurostable is a monetary instrument created *ex nihilo*. Is not such a method of monetary creation inflationary?

A — Inflation is a complex phenomenon, the causes of which are manifold and certainly not all monetary. It occurs within the frontiers of a state and the vehicle by which it spreads is the national currency. It is only by observing the requisite discipline and by controlling the creation and velocity of money that national authorities can control inflation within a state. The Eurostable is a neutral currency which would not circulate within a state but only within that specialised area that lies between the 'locks' that the exchange offices constitute. In the purely monetary field, the chaos on the exchange markets and its inflationary consequences are caused to a great extent by the use by central banks of national currencies as reserve and intervention currencies, and also by the massive flows of international capital in search of protection from monetary depreciation.

The Eurostable eliminates these defects and has, in addition, two other special advantages. The first is that the creation of the Eurostable will be under the surveillance of the authorities and will be more efficiently regulated than is the case with the Euromarkets, which are supplied freely and with no chance of control by the banking systems of the strong currency countries. The second advantage is that once the Eurostable has been created, lent, deposited, re-lent, etc., the member banks are limited in their activities to acting as non-monetary intermediaries. A member bank, therefore, does not superimpose its own monetary creation on that of the central bank in the form of a claim on itself, as is the case in a national banking system. The depositor abandons the right to goods and services that his asset represents. The intermediary (i.e. the member bank of the Consortium) transfers this right to the borrower, who uses it in the place of the depositor.

All these considerations mean that not only will the Eurostable not contribute to inflation but it will even help to limit it.

Q – What will be the attitude of the national authorities with regard to this enterprise? Will they accept this encroachment on their traditional domain of issuer of money?

A – In reality, the lion's share of creation of new money belongs nowadays to the national banking systems and not to the central banks. It is also a fact that the central banks have some difficulty in disciplining the banking system in this respect. Such a discipline will be much easier to impose in the case of the Eurostable system because of the very nature of the mechanism whereby the Eurostable is created.

Moreover, there is theoretically no obligation to obtain the agreement of the central bank in order to operate in the Euromarket; extraterritorial operations are carried out outside the jurisdiction of the national monetary authorities. In practice, of course, it is obvious that the agreement of the authorities must be obtained in order to launch the Eurostable. But there is no reason to suppose that they would be hostile towards an experiment which they cannot perform themselves and which follows the political line laid down by the various national governments.

Q – Should we not expect opposition from the strong currency countries to a project which is intended to compete with their own currencies and thereby deprive them of the well-known advantages of seigniorage?

A – The monetary authorities of such countries have long recognised the inconveniences of having their currency used as a medium of exchange for international transactions. Robert Triffin explains (in *Les Annales*

d'Economie Politique, vol. 23) why the American authorities would
prefer to withdraw the dollar from international use:

> The first and most obvious reason is that the creation of world reserve
> money must be determined in harmony with the needs of the world
> economy and not by the more or less unforeseeable fluctuations of the
> balance of payments of one country.
>
> The second reason is the exorbitant privilege that such a system
> confers on the reserve money countries: the opportunity to finance their
> deficits through foreign central banks' printing presses. The United
> States, which obtained its independence two hundred years ago, is the
> first to accept the refusal of foreign countries to finance at the price of
> their own internal inflation deficits caused by policies or mistakes of
> policy in which they have no say and with which they may even be in
> total disagreement.
>
> The third reason is that the United States also considers that its
> privilege constitutes an intolerable responsibility for its internal
> economy. The financing of its deficits by foreign countries paralyses
> the adjustment mechanisms of the balance of payments and, in
> particular, hampers the exchange rate adjustments which disparities in
> price and cost changes impose from time to time on all countries. This
> asymmetry inevitably leads, sooner or later, to a gradual revaluation of
> the dominant money, diminishes the competitivity of American
> producers on world markets, as also on the home market, causes losses
> to industry and aggravates unemployment.
>
> In the absence of the necessary exchange rate adjustments, companies
> and unions exercise almost irresistible pressures on the government and
> on Congress. This is why both official and American academic circles
> nowadays recommend not only a widening of exchange rate fluctuation
> margins but also more rapid and more frequent readjustments, even a
> system of sliding or floating rates.

The German authorities, whose currency nowadays rivals the dollar
as an international currency, are of the same opinion, for the same reasons
of domestic politics, to which must be added others, of relevance to their
foreign policy. The Germans know that the preponderance of their currency
in Europe, foretaste of an unacceptable economic domination, would
destroy the European Economic Community and exacerbate their exposed
geographical position. Time and again the German Finance Minister and
the governor of the Bundesbank have repeated that it is anathema for them
to see the mark become an international reserve currency. This, moreover,

is why they attempt to discourage, through penal interest rates, deposits in marks by non-residents.

These countries should therefore look with favour upon an initiative designed to remedy the inconveniences, which are now universally recognised, of the use of a national currency for international transactions.

Q – What about the objection of a famous monetarist, who has been awarded the Nobel Prize, and who is moreover favourably inclined towards the Eurostable, that, since men have never used an invented money before, it is doubtful that they will use this one?

A – The world has been transformed because men began to use things, objects and systems they had never used before. Why should there not be such a thing as an invented money, in view of the fact that there are invented modes of transport and invented information media? If there is one area of enquiry where the need for innovation is pressing it is the field of money. It is probably precisely because this field has remained untouched by change throughout history that the defects of the world monetary system from which we are all suffering have arisen.

Q – Could the Eurostable be used in the forward markets?

A – There is no reason why not. The Eurostable is an extranational payment instrument which circulates within the Eurocurrency zone. Like any Eurocurrency it may be bought and sold forward.

At the same time, however, the restricted nature of the Eurostable market, especially at the beginning, should be recognised. The result of that is that forward purchase orders will come down in practice to an attempt on the part of borrowers of Eurostable to obtain cover before a repayment of a loan, whereas the majority of forward purchase orders in the Eurocurrency market are motived either by the payments that, for example, importers have to make, or by pure speculation.

In order to understand how the forward market mechanisms, such as they exist in the currency markets, could be transferred to the Eurostable system, we must first of all remember how the forward market in currencies works. An importer gives a purchase order for X dollars to bank A, the maturity being 3 months. The bank quotes a forward rate for the dollar. The operation will be completed at maturity, i.e. in three months' time. At maturity, the importer will be credited with X dollars, which he will pay to his supplier in the United States. His sterling account at bank A will then be simultaneously debited by the amount agreed on three months before. The operation will then be completed.

When it receives the purchase order, A, assuming it has not got any corresponding sell orders, will cover itself by buying the dollars which it will need in three months' time. It then places the dollars it has just bought in the money market at a maturity of three months.

The cost of the operation, apart from the brokerage fees, is calculated by working out the difference between the interest paid on the dollars and the interest arising from the sterling which the bank has 'borrowed' from its reserves in order to buy the dollars. This operation may be adapted to the Eurostable system. A member bank of the Consortium which receives a forward purchase order turns to the other member banks and obtains from one of them the Eurostable it needs. Because the Eurostable market is likely to be a small one at the beginning, the bank does not try to place its Eurostable. The discount which it will charge to its customer will only take account of the interest on the sum in currency which it will have paid out in order to obtain the liquid Eurostable.

Q – Would it be possible to tie a national currency to the Eurostable, just as national currencies used to be tied to gold; in other words, would it be possible to define the value of a national currency in terms of Eurostable?

A – It would be possible, but it would require a certain discipline. The exchange rates of the currencies defined in this way would no longer be free *vis-à-vis* other currencies. They would be a function of the price indices. As for arbitrage possibilities, they would require certain calculations using these very indices.

Q – What are the obstacles to the realisation of the project?

A – The same ones that innovation always has to overcome. A new idea always comes up against routine, accepted ideas, the fear of change. But the Eurostable adds to that another problem which is peculiar to it, namely the fact that it depends on certain basic monetary ideas which differ from the conventional wisdom.

The conventional wisdom still regards money as representative of a commodity, defined by the security that guarantees it. Modern notions of money are quite different. Money is seen as an arbitrary claim on an institution, created *ex-nihilo*, without any natural connection with a commodity or a security and with an exchange value that is independent of any form of backing..[2]

Q – Once the main lessons have been drawn from this experiment, how will the experience be passed on to international institutions?

A – The defects of a national currency in the role of international currency are no longer doubted. The need for a real international currency is growing. The danger represented by a mass of floating capital is quite plain, just as is the need to 'fix' this capital by correcting its principal cause of instability, namely uncertainty over exchange rates and price levels. This development means that the creation of a stable international currency is inevitable, and must happen sooner or later. But having recognised this principle, one is bound to admit that the creation of a mechanism suitable to create it and make it work can only cause disagreements that are likely to delay decisions for a long time. (1)

This is where the experiment of the Eurostable will be very useful, It will give people a ready working system, easier to adapt than the creation *ex nihilo* of an entirely new mechanism. Even if politicians were able to agree, they would be paralysed by the memory of doubtful promises, the failure of which has demonstrated the chimerical nature of proclamations belied by events and then discredited.

This is why an experiment that is not under the direct control of politicians has more chance than any other of making some progress towards so ardently desired an objective.

NOTES

[1] The Europa was proposed in November 1975 in the so-called *All Saints Day Manifesto* published by *The Economist* and signed by nine economists: G. Basevi (Italy), M. Fratianni (Belgium), H. Giersch (Germany), P. Korteweg (Holland), D. O'Mahony (Ireland), M. Parkin (England), T. Peeters (Belgium), P. Salin (France) and N. Thygesen (Denmark).

[2] Robert Mundell points out the financial advantages that the European Community could derive from the issue of its own currency (the ECU):

> The ECU could be put directly into circulation for the payment of Community administrative expenses, for regional development, for European universities, for control of the environment or for any other purpose of general interest. . . The currency would thus be introduced into current payments and the quantity would grow in line with European growth and would represent a substantial source of seigniorage and purchasing power for the European institutions . . .

> Directorate General for Economic and Financial Affairs of the Commission of the European Communities, Brussels, October 1973.

SUPPLEMENTARY NOTES

PAGE 236

(1) Composite currency units: the basic conversion equations

One reason why composite currencies are still sometimes
misunderstood is that the concept of a composite currency and the way
it works can only be properly grasped with the aid of certain formulae
and algebraic relations which frighten most readers off. Let us therefore
try another approach.

Let us imagine that the two sides of a set of scales are evenly balanced
by, on the one hand, a composite unit (an ACU) and, on the other, an
aggregate of FF1, £0.11 and DM0.8. This means that one ACU has the
same value as the total of the sums in francs, pounds and marks placed
on the other side of the scales. In other words, one ACU can buy an
international basket of goods and services composed of what FF1 will
buy in France, what £0.11 will buy in Britain and what DM0.8 will buy
in Germany, or, if one prefers to buy the whole of one's basket in a
third country (in Italy for example), what the sum in lire obtained by
converting at the going exchange rate FF1, £0.11 etc. will buy.

An ACU so defined is a heterogenous aggregate. If we want to
calculate the relative weights, or weighting coefficients, of each of the
component currencies within the ACU, they must all be expressed in
terms of a common denominator, that is, they must be converted into
the same vehicular currency, e.g. the dollar (the result is the same
whatever the currency chosen, since we are talking of relative positions).

If FF1 = \$0.2,
£1   = \$2
and DM1 = \$0.4,
the resulting value of the ACU in terms of the dollar will be obtained by
converting into dollars the sums in francs, pounds and marks thus:

$$1 \times 0.2 + 0.11 \times 2 + 0.8 \times 0.4 = 0.20 + 0.22 + 0.32 = \$0.74$$

The conversion rate of one dollar into one ACU is therefore 0.74
($t_{\text{ACU/D}} = 0.74$).

The weighting coefficients in the ACU are, therefore, respectively,

for the franc $\dfrac{0.20}{0.74} = 0.27$

for the pound, $\dfrac{0.22}{0.74} = 0.30$

for the mark, $\dfrac{0.32}{0.74} = 0.43$

$0.27 + 0.30 + 0.43 = 1.$

The conversion rate of the ACU into a third currency, X, can be obtained by starting with $t_{\text{ACU}/D} = 0.74$ and multiplying by the exchange rate of D (= dollar) into currency X (the result is the same whatever the vehicular currency used in place of the dollar):

for the franc: $t_{\text{ACU}/F} = 0.74 \times \dfrac{1}{0.2} = 3.70$

for the pound: $t_{\text{ACU}/\pounds} = 0.74 \times \dfrac{1}{2} = 0.37$

for the mark: $t_{\text{ACU}/DM} = 0.74 \times \dfrac{1}{0.4} = 1.85$

The relations between an ACU and its component national currencies are thus established. We shall be able to use them in order to solve the problems posed by the creation of a new composite currency unit. These problems are the following.

Firstly, how to create an ACU in which the national currencies are included on day 1 in a particular relationship to each other, i.e. with weighting coefficients chosen by virtue of certain criteria such as shares in world trade (one of the criteria chosen in the case of the SDR).

The second concerns the value of the unit. This is what is called the 'choice of scale' and is what results when the basket is made up of FF1, £0.11 and DM0.4 instead of, for example, FF2, £0.22 and DM0.8. Starting from these data in terms of the market exchange rates of the currencies *vis-à-vis* a vehicular currency such as the dollar, we can calculate the quantities of the national currencies to be included in the ACU on day 1. In the case of the SDR, these quantities remain fixed until the SDR is redefined.

An examination of the above operations shows that for each national currency included in the ACU there is only one quantity of that currency which satisfies the conditions mentioned above. In fact, if an ACU is composed of n currencies, the variables — i.e. the number of units of each currency — number n in all, whereas the relationships between the respective weights and the original value chosen for the ACU (the choice of scale) constitute $n - 1 + 1 = n$ equations.

The calculation of the sums of each component currency on day 1 is thus as follows.

Let A and B be the component national currencies and u_A, u_B the sums of units of A and B entering into the composition of the ACU on day 1.

$t_{\text{ACU}/A}$, $t_{\text{ACU}/B}$ etc. are the conversion rates (1 ACU = $t_{\text{ACU}/A} \times A$) of the ACU into A, B etc.

$t_{\text{ACU}/D}$ is the conversion rate of the ACU into a currency D, which is known on day 1.

P_A, P_B are the weighting coefficients of A and B (also known on day 1).

To express the value of the ACU in terms of the sum of its components is to say

$$1 \text{ ACU} = 1 = u_A t_{A/\text{ACU}} + u_B t_{B/\text{ACU}} \text{ etc. (Formula (a))}$$

The weights of each component of an ACU (weighting coefficient) are:

$$P_A = u_A \times t_{A/\text{ACU}} = u_A \times t_{A/D} \times t_{D/\text{ACU}}$$

In practice, the calculations involve an intermediary currency, which may be any currency, but which is most usually the dollar. Formula (a) is written as follows in terms of the dollar.

$$t_{\text{ACU}/D} = u_A t_{A/D} + u_B t_{B/D} + \text{etc.}$$

$t_{A/D}$ and $t_{B/D}$ are given by the exchange markets, whilst $t_{\text{ACU}/D}$ is given by the choice of scale (0.74 in the example given above). The other data are the ratios between the weights of the component currencies:

$$P_A = u_A t_{A/D} \times t_{D/\text{ACU}}, \quad P_B = u_B t_{B/D} \times t_{D/\text{ACU}}, \quad \text{etc.}$$

($P_A + P_B$ etc. = 1). The sums u_A, u_B etc. are thus determined, as are $t_{A/\text{ACU}}$, $t_{B/\text{ACU}}$ etc.

The sums u_A, u_B etc. will, therefore, remain fixed for some time (perhaps several years) but the conversion rates of the ACU into a given currency, as well as the weights of the component currencies, which depend on the market exchange rates, will vary from day to day in a flexible exchange rate system.

Example: the exchange rate of the franc into dollars moves from 0.2 on day 1 to 0.25 on day *D*, whilst the pound goes from 2 to 2.22 and the mark from 0.4 to 0.55.

$$t_{\text{ACU}/D} = u_A t_{A/D} + u_B t_{B/D} + u_C t_{C/D}$$

is then written

$$t_{\text{ACU}/D} = 1 \times 0.25 + 0.11 \times 2.20 + 0.8 \times 0.55 = 0.932.$$

Therefore $t_{\text{ACU}/D}$ increases from 0.74 on day 1 to 0.932 on day *D*. The conversion rates of the ACU into *A* (francs), *B* (pounds) and *C* (marks) become 3.72 (3.70), 0.42 (0.37), 1.69 (1.85), whereas their weights change to 0.27 (0.27), 0.26 (0.30) and 0.47 (0.43).

Adjustment

The weight of each currency, just like its conversion rate into the ACU, varies as a function of the exchange rates of the currencies among themselves on the market. The basic data, in terms of which the weights (weighting coefficients) have themselves been chosen, vary also (GNP, exports etc.). Finally, it may be desirable, at a later date, to include in the composition of the ACU certain national currencies which were not there at the beginning, or, alternatively, remove some that were. This is why from time to time it is necessary to make an adjustment to the basic ACU formula (in principle, every five years, in the case of the SDR). This adjustment is made for each currency X, by calculating the sum u'_X in X such that on the chosen day, the new weighting coefficient P'_X may replace the weight calculated according to the old formula, whilst at the same time the exchange rate of X into the ACU remains unchanged.

All that needs to be done, therefore, is to calculate on day D the effective weight of X before the change, i.e. $u_X t'_{X/ACU}$ and, using the rule of three, determine the new total, u_X, of the sum in X.

Example: On day D, the dollar is introduced into the basket with a weight of 50 per cent, without modifying the relations prevailing between the original currencies. Let us come back to our pair of scales. The composition of the basket into which the currencies are put may be changed, but the arm of the scales must remain in equilibrium. This means that the value of the ACU on day D must remain the same expressed in dollars, for example: 0.932 (expressed in ACU its value is 1).

The sum in dollars to be put into the basket with a weighting of 50 per cent will be

$$0.5 \times 0.932 = \$0.466.$$

The new weights of the other currencies are those that are calculated on day D with the original composition multiplied by 0.5 in order to make place for the dollar, i.e. 0.135 for the franc, 0.130 for the pound, 0.235 for the mark. The number of units of money in the ACU then becomes:

$$u'_F = \frac{1 \times 0.135}{0.27} = FF0.50$$

$$u'_£ = \frac{0.11 \times 0.130}{0.260} = £0.055$$

$$u'_{DM} = \frac{0.8 \times 0.235}{0.4} = DM0.40$$

The value of the ACU on day D expressed in any currency remains the same, but eventually it will differ, i.e. it will not be what it would have been if the weights had remained unchanged.

These formulae demonstrate certain special features of an ACU, such as it has been defined here, i.e. made up of component currencies with quantities which remain fixed for a long period. The consequences of such a definition are:

The conversion rate of a component currency into the ACU is a function of the exchange rates, amongst themselves, of the other component currencies. It is sufficient that one of them should float, that is, that its exchange rate should vary *vis-à-vis* the others, for all

the others to do the same *vis-à-vis* the ACU, even if they are in a
fixed exchange rate system amongst themselves.
The value of the ACU in terms of purchasing power is that of the
weighted average of the monetary units that make it up.

These two peculiarities make the ACU unsuitable as a standard of
value. They can be corrected by modifying the definition of the ACU.
This idea is developed later on in the section of the book that deals with
the Eurostable.

PAGE 242

(1) The theoretical foundations of composite currency units

The relationship between a composite currency unit and the national
currencies that compose it or third currencies external to it can be
expressed by saying that one unit of the composite currency is equal to
the sum of the units making it up (e.g. national currencies A, B and C).

If $t_{A/CU}$ is the conversion rate of A into CU (CU = composite currency
unit) and if u_A is the amount of currency A in the 'basket', the value of
this amount in terms of CU is $u_A t_{A/CU}$.

The total amount of the component currencies expressed in terms of
CU is equal to I, i.e.

$$I = u_A t_{A/CU} + u_B t_{B/CU} \text{ etc.}$$

If we wish to work out the conversion rate of the CU into a currency X
($t_{CU/X}$), all we need to do is replace $t_{A/CU}$ and $t_{B/CU}$ by their equivalents
expressed in terms of X:

$$t_{A/CU} = t_{A/X} t_{X/CU}.$$

From this we can say

$$I = t_{X/CU}(u_A t_{A/X} + u_B t_{B/X} + \text{etc.})$$

or

$$t_{CU/X} = u_A t_{A/X} + u_B t_{B/X} \text{ etc.}$$

With the aid of this basic formula we shall be able to analyse the properties
of a composite currency unit made up of invariable quantities of
component currencies.

The functions required of any currency may be divided into five
categories. The first three are those that have been known since the time
of Aristotle — universal standard of measurement, store of value and
medium of exchange. In addition to these, there are two new ones,
peculiar to our times, namely that of reference unit (that is, unit in terms
of which other currencies may be defined) and intervention instrument.
The question is: how well equipped is a composite currency unit such as

the ECU, which consists of invariable quantities of national currencies, to fulfil these roles?

A standard of measurement must be capable of comparing the values of different goods and services, not just at one given moment but over a period of time. If this is to be the case, the unit must have stable value. The value of a currency is defined in terms of what it will buy, so a currency that is to function as a standard of measurement must have stable purchasing power, which was more or less the case with gold and the dollar during the period when they were used as international standards of measurement.

The second function, that of store of value, obviously also presupposes stability of value. But this is not the case with a composite currency whose purchasing power is only the average of the purchasing powers of the component currencies, almost of all of which are declining in purchasing power. The ECU has only one strong currency, the mark, in its composition; thirty-three per cent of the SDR is dollars.

The third property, namely medium of exchange, means that a claim denominated in the currency must be directly exchangeable for a supply of goods or services. If a claim denominated in ECU is handed in payment to a creditor, the ECU can only be said to have payment power if the new holder of the claim keeps it denominated exactly as it was when he received it, without converting it. If he does convert it, the real payment will have been carried out by the currency he converts it into; in that case the ECU will have acted merely as a unit of account.

What decides whether a given monetary unit ceases to be a unit of account and becomes a payment unit, is the lapse of time during which the holder of the claim denominated in the unit keeps it so denominated without converting it. This, in turn, depends on the extent to which the currency unit inspires confidence in the holder of the claim. Clearly, the stabler the value of the unit the greater will be the holder's confidence.

In order to clarify this, let us take an example. Let us suppose that our composite currency is composed of three national currencies, *A*, *B* and *C*. The creation of a currency on the basis of this basket definition depends on the creation of a claim on an institution denominated in this same composite unit. This claim is subsequently transferred; it can be said to effect a payment on two conditions, first that the institution to which the claim is transferred accepts it, that is, accepts a liability denominated in this unit, and secondly, that the new holder of the claim also agrees not to convert the claim into one of the underlying currencies or into a third currency. Of course, we could imagine an inconvertible composite currency, just as the dollar is inconvertible into gold or the rouble is inconvertible into other currencies. But in the case of a new currency, such a property must be rejected because it would paralyse the development of the currency from the start.

We can therefore only imagine the ECU, for example, becoming a commonly used currency for international transactions (apart from purely politically inspired and motivated dealings between central banks) if the ECU inspires confidence, or, in other words, if the ECU is a good reserve currency and if it appears less vulnerable than other currencies.

But a composite currency based on a fixed basket of national currencies, though it may be better than its weakest component currency, is certain to be weaker than its strongest component. It is, therefore, hard to see how the ECU could come to be preferred to national currencies that are stronger than it and which have, in addition, the inestimable advantage of being well established.

The fourth property required of our new currency is that of being a standard of reference, an anchor to which other currencies could be tied or 'pegged'. For a long time, currencies continued to be defined in terms of a weight of gold, even when they were no longer convertible into gold: subsequently, they were defined in terms of dollars. Could they be defined in terms of ECUs? The formula at the beginning of this note shows that the conversion rate of a composite currency in terms of a third currency, X, depends on the exchange rate of its individual component currencies *vis-à-vis* X. It would be pointless to peg A and B to the ECU in a fixed relationship because this same relationship would also depend on C.

The use of a composite currency as reference unit is only valid for the purpose of providing an approximate indication — not an exact measurement. This, moreover, is exactly what the thirty-two states which decided to 'define' their currencies in terms of a basket of currencies from 1 June 1978 onwards meant by so doing. (Another sixty-three, on the other hand, opted for defining their currencies in terms of a single currency.) The loose relationship between a composite currency and a national currency is of little consequence in a system of floating exchange rates or even in a system of limited fluctuation bands. It is quite another matter when there is a fixed exchange rate *régime* of the sort that used to exist prior to 1971.

The fifth function of the composite currency is that of exchange vehicle and intervention instrument. A vehicular currency functions in the foreign exchange markets in a similar way to a national currency in domestic markets where goods and services are exchanged: that is, it acts as common denominator. A foreign exchange system requires such a vehicle by means of which exchange operations may be carried out.

Let us suppose that currency A is worth two dollars and currency B is worth one dollar. A direct exchange of A for B can be made at the rate of $2B = 1A$. The equilibrium of exchange rates between currencies is thus achieved by means of a third currency, which is usually the dollar. The internal consistency of the exchange system is guaranteed by the fact that the reciprocal exchange rates of any two currencies are equal to the ratio of their exchange rates *vis-à-vis* a third currency:

$$t_{A/B} = \frac{t_{A/X}}{t_{B/X}}.$$

This vital function of vehicle currency cannot be adequately performed by a composite currency such as the ECU.

Let us look, for example, at such a unit having three components, A, B and C. The value of A varies by two per cent with regards to B. B and C in turn, are related to each other by fixed exchange rates. If the system is to remain in equilibrium, A must also vary by two per cent *vis-à-vis* C. Equilibrium will be regained by means of X, which means that on the exchange markets the rate of exchange of A into X must gradually change until the difference is two per cent, whilst the exchange rates of B and C into X remain stable. This would be the case if X was a freely circulating national currency, but it will never be the case if X is a composite currency.

In fact, the relationship between the composite currency and A is as follows:

$$t_{CU/A} = u_A + u_B t_{B/A} + u_C t_{C/A}.$$

The relative variations of B and C *vis-à-vis* A are the same, i.e. two per cent. The relative variation of $t_{CU/A}$ is lower by $u_A/t_{CU/A}$ than two per cent (in relative value). In practice, X cannot be used as an arbitrage vehicle except in order to sell a currency (A for X) or buy another (B with X). In reality, the composite currency can only be used as an intervention instrument on condition that it is tied to a national currency which is in general use. In this case, the composite currency acts as a 'storeroom', from which the national currency that is really desired can be obtained. This function, like the four previous ones, presupposes one important quality: stable value.

If the composite currency is to have a chance of fulfilling these conditions, it must be equipped with constant purchasing power. It also needs to have these properties if it is to be able to attract depositors and borrowers. Such stability of value cannot be guaranteed by a composite currency defined in terms of a fixed basket of component currencies. This deficiency is likely to severely handicap such a currency and inhibit its development.

PAGE 246

(1) Units of account and units of payment

The dollar, the franc and the mark, *as such*, are always purely abstract units of account and nothing but units of account. They are reference units used to determine the value of claims, in the same way as the gram and the metre are used as references to determine the weight and the size of an object.

The franc, the mark and the SDR are thus not strictly currencies. What constitutes money is the *claim* denominated in one of these units, a claim, moreover, which has legal-tender power and can be freely transferred from one person to another or, more usually, from one bank account to another. This claim, in the form of a credit to a current account, is not a unit of account but a store of value and a payment instrument. It seems to me as pointless to dilate on the difference between a store of value and a payment instrument as to talk at length about the difference between a stationary vehicle and a vehicle which is in motion. A claim acts as a store of value for as long as it remains unused in the holder's account; it functions as a payment instrument when it passes from X's account to Y's account.

If we want to make perfectly plain the circumstances in which a claim exercises its transaction function, we must go back to the search for the final stage of the operation of exchange of a unit of money for a provision of goods or services. (Part 1, Chapters 4 and 5). Let us look at another example: X makes a payment to Y by means of a cheque drawn on A. In the end it is probably another claim, that of A on B, which will effect the payment (if A is a non-monetary intermediary it will be a claim on bank B, where A has funds). Using this example, we can establish whether or not a claim denominated in a certain unit of account, whether mark, dollar or SDR, is used for a payment. If this claim is transferred directly from X's to Y's account (at the same bank or at another), it can be said that it has exercised a payment function, allowing for the reserves expressed above and on condition that it remains the same claim and stays for a certain amount of time in Y's account without being converted into a unit of account other than the one it was denominated in at the moment of the transfer.

If, on the other hand, it is changed into another unit, the bank will have to obtain money denominated in this other unit. Suppose the claim is denominated in SDRs and credited to Y's account in SDRs, and suppose the new holder wishes to convert his asset immediately into dollars. In this case, the bank will have to obtain dollars from somewhere and it will be those dollars that effect the final payment. More exactly, one could say that the payment has been carried out by the SDR claim but only momentarily, until the dollar claim replaced it. The same would be true if the bank, whilst on the one hand accepting SDR-denominated liabilities, nevertheless carried out in dollars transfer orders expressed in SDRs.

But if the SDR claim remains as it is and if there is no final parallel transfer of another claim denominated in another unit of account than the SDR, then it is the SDR that has effected the payment and consequently functioned as payment instrument. From this it may be concluded that it is the final claim, transferred in a given unit of account, which its new holder chooses to keep as it is for a certain period of time, which effects the payment.

It is a convenient simplification, but it is also elliptical to speak of the SDR as a payment unit, as it is to speak of the Eurostable as a payment unit. What is meant is that the *claim* denominated in SDRs (or Eurostable) effects the payment when it is transferred exactly as it is from one account to another and kept so denominated by its new holder for a certain period of time. We shall see later, apropos of the Eurostable, the use that is made of this observation. The mechanism developed for the Eurostable has been conceived precisely in order that the final transfer of a claim arising from a payment by X to Y in Eurostable may be carried out by the bank in claims which are also denominated in Eurostable. It is only on this condition that the Eurostable can really be considered a payment unit.

PAGE 250

(1) The importance of not counting too much on political initiatives
In 1971, in his excellent book *Le système monétaire international – Aspect économique* (Published by Armand Colin), J. L'Huillier proposed 'A fixed exchange-rate system, in which gold played the role of universal standard and liquidity base, the dollar was the intervention currency on the exchange markets, whilst conditional IMF credits gave the system a certain flexibility by expanding and contracting as required'. Eight years later, gold has been abandoned everywhere as a means of payment, exchange rates are freely floating, the dollar has been dethroned and, as for the IMF, its conditional credits expand rather more than they contract.

The Werner Plan provides another example of a plan for monetary union announced amid much clamour but which aborted even before it got going (see the Marjolin Report for further details). On the other hand, a certain spontaneous development of the IMF is perceptible, the result of which will probably be the transformation of the Fund into a kind of world central bank. But this transformation will not be the result of conscious decisions on the part of governments but rather the result of the pressure of circumstances. The IMF will become the great distributor of credits and the principal means of recycling of oil dollars. Arab oil producers, in fact, prefer, like the Eurobanks, an international guarantee from the IMF, to simple promises from governments. The IMF, faced with the insolvency of certain of its debtors, will be forced to put into circulation claims on itself which states will use to finance their trade. An international currency will then be born.

But at the same time, the problem of how to define this currency will also arise, and people will recognise the infinitely greater weight it would have if it were equipped with an eminently desirable characteristic, namely constant purchasing power.

PAGE 253

(1) Conversion formula for the Eurostable
The formula with which the Eurostable may be converted into another currency is based on the fundamental property of the Eurostable, namely, its constant purchasing power. This property connects $t_{ES/D}$, the conversion rate of the Eurostable on day n into a currency D (which is what we want to calculate) to two groups of parameters – first, the exchange rates on day n between D and the reference currencies and secondly the consumer price indices on day n in the reference currency countries, which can be calculated by extrapolation from the most recent figures provided by the national statistical services.

Let u_A, u_B etc. be the number of units of the reference currencies included in the Eurostable basket on day 1 (in our previous example these were: four marks, one pound etc.).

Let $t_{A/D}$ be the middle exchange rate, on day n, of A into D ($1A = t_{A/D}$).

Let $t_{B/D}$ be the middle exchange rate of B into D, on n ($1B = t_{B/D}$).

Let i_A be the price index on day n in the country of reference currency A. It is equal to the index for the previous month extrapolated to allow for the number of days that have elapsed during the current month. Similarly, i_B is the price index in country of reference currency B.

The formula is then as follows:

$$t_{ES/D} = u_A i_A t_{A/D} + u_B i_B t_{B/D} + \ldots$$

It can be proved as follows. The quantity of units of currency A which were put into the basket on day 1 in order to represent a certain basket of goods and services was u_A, and in country B it was u_B. The quantity of units that must be in the basket on day n in order that the basket of goods and services represented by the first quantity may remain constant is $u_A i_A$. To say that the Eurostable has constant purchasing power is the same as saying that the sum of quantities of each national currency in the basket needed to purchase a constant basket remains unchanged after conversion into Eurostable.

This conversion of $u_A i_A$, $u_B i_B$ etc. into Eurostable can be made using the exchange rates $t_{A/ES}$, $t_{B/ES}$ etc. The monetary value in Eurostable of the number of units of A (i.e. $u_A i_A$) and B (i.e. $u_B i_B$) can be written as follows: $u_A i_A t_{A/ES}$, $u_B i_B t_{B/ES}$.

To say that the Eurostable has constant purchasing power is the same as saying that $u_A i_A t_{A/ES} + u_B i_B t_{B/ES} +$ etc. remains constant. If we take as our definition of the Eurostable a value such as 1, we get:

$$1 = u_A i_A t_{A/ES} + u_B i_B t_{B/ES} + \text{etc.}$$

Let us now replace t by its expression in terms of what we are trying to calculate ($t_{D/ES}$) and in terms of the exchange rates, which are known:

$$t_{A/ES} = t_{A/D} \times t_{D/ES}; t_{B/ES} = t_{B/D} \times t_{D/ES}; \text{etc.}$$

and then we get:

$$1 = u_A i_A t_{A/D} t_{D/ES} \text{ etc.}$$

which gives us:

$$t_{ES/D} = u_A i_A t_{A/D} + u_B i_B t_{B/D} \text{ etc.}$$

The conversion rate of the Eurostable into a currency D ($t_{ES/D}$) has thus been calculated. Each day the foreign exchange markets determine the exchange rates $t_{A/D}$, $t_{B/D}$ etc. The price indices can be found using the last published indices and extrapolating to cover the number of days that have elapsed in the current month, up to day n. Thus we have all the necessary parameters for the formula and with them the conversion rate of the Eurostable into currency D can be calculated.

If the holder of Eurostable wishes to convert his assets into reference currencies instead of into currency D, he will receive a number of units of A equal to $u_A i_A$, a number of units of B equal to $u_B i_B$ etc. which he will be able to use to purchase a basket of goods in country A and in country B etc., which will be exactly the same as he could have got when he first changed his currencies into Eurostable.

PAGE 277

(1) 'Pegging' currencies

The creation of a new international monetary system cannot fail to encounter certain problems, of which the hardest is that of finding a new standard of value to which currencies could be tied, just as they were previously tied to gold.

An analysis of composite currency units of the SDR type (see Chapter 2) shows that, except in a system of fixed exchange rates, it is not possible to define a currency in terms of its relationship to the SDR. If the exchange rate of only one of the sixteen currencies that make up the SDR varies, the values of all fifteen other currencies in terms of SDRs also change. This close interdependence is a feature of all composite currencies and inevitably implies a revision of the idea of a standard of value, which can no longer be treated analogously to a commodity standard. When a currency was defined in terms of a weight of precious metal this meant that the monetary unit could purchase the same amount of goods and services as the weight of precious metal, though this purchasing power still suffered some variation, both in the course of time and from country to country.

Another way of tackling this problem is to define the currency in terms of 'international purchasing power'. To tie a currency to the Eurostable in an immutable relationship would mean that the currency in question would be able to purchase an immutable quantity of goods and services. But the consequence of this would be that its value in terms of gold or other currencies could not be fixed. The interdependence between a composite currency and its components is inevitable. This, naturally, would not be likely to favour the choice of a composite unit as reference unit, unless the unit had a special quality that distinguished it from others: this could only be constant purchasing power.

Epilogue

The 'Lotto-clearing' game mentioned in Chapter 6 of Part 1 has already been tried out once in a practical simulation. Readers of this book will by now be well aware of the rules of this game and its aims, which are as follows.

The players, representing the member banks of the Clearing House, are grouped around a table. At the beginning of the game, tickets are distributed to them. Each ticket bears a number which indicates the total amount of the cheques drawn on other banks and deposited at the bank which the player represents; each player thus receives as many tickets as there are other banks present. The figures are written up on a blackboard, on which a clearing chart has been drawn, and the balances are worked out and written up in the appropriate column. These balances represent the amounts in central bank money which each player is to pay over or receive. The difference between the overall total and the sum of the transfers in central bank money represents the amount of payments carried out in claims on the banks, i.e. payment money created by the banks over and above the total of central bank money.

During the second stage of the game, the players no longer settle their payments by mutual clearing; instead, those who, previously, had to make payments in central bank money — that is, those who had negative final balances — are given a quantity of counters equivalent to the sum of these balances. These counters are transferred amongst the players in a series of rounds until all the payments have been made. The winner is the one who settles all his debts first.

During the third stage, non-member banks are gradually introduced into the game, which has an equivalent effect to that of a cash withdrawal by a depositor; and during the fourth stage, the exchanges of claims are deliberately delayed so as to simulate the sort of obstacles which a clearing system would encounter in the Euromarkets.

This game not only demonstrates the mechanism by which a national banking system creates money but also illustrates the various techniques of monetary regulation used by the monetary authorities, such as open-market dealings, rediscount rate manipulations and the imposition of compulsory reserve requirements. In addition, it shows exactly why the Euromarkets only create a tiny amount of payment money and gives us some idea of the likely effects that new banking techniques, which are only now being developed, such as the system of giro transfers, will have on banks' abilities to create money, and on the velocity of money.

Amongst the audience at the 'simulation', during which the Lotto-clearing game was tried out, were some university students. They appeared to be quite convinced by the demonstration, but the same could not be said of some of the distinguished monetary experts who were also present. In spite of the clarity of the demonstration, they remained firmly of the opinion that the clearing process only played a very minor role in the creation of bank money.

The lesson to be learnt from this experience is that people generally cling to what they already know and what they are familiar with. That is why this book will probably be criticised less for what is in it than for what is not in it. The truth is that the topics that are most usually the subject of passionate debate in monetary economics are ignored here: the question of the supply and demand for money, for example, is not even mentioned. The equations worked out by Fisher, Keynes, Hicks and others are also ignored. No attempt is made to take sides in the debate over floating and fixed exchange rates and the categorisation of cash balances — whether they are held for transactions, as a reserve, or as pure savings — is also absent from these pages. There is no ardent prayer for an attempt on the part of the American government to correct its balance of payments deficit, and there are only a few words, in small print in the Supplementary Notes, on those great matters, inflation and unemployment, that dominate the modern world and fill the pages of the newspapers and the shop-windows of the book-sellers. That so many important subjects should be left out will be the really disconcerting aspect of this book in the eyes of many people. And yet I persist in believing that before we get down to these things we ought to have a clearer idea of how the 'mechanics of money' works.

A unit of money is put into circulation. It starts to pass from one person to another and transactions, the essential features of the economy, result. When a certain number of transactions have taken place, the unit of money is destroyed. The creation of the unit of money, the transactions it takes part in and its eventual destruction, are all operations that conform to a certain pattern: in a word, a system of 'mechanics'. Like other branches of mechanics, such as the mechanics of fluids, or soil mechanics, this monetary mechanics attempts to analyse units of money according to their nature (whether or not they have the payment function), their states (whether held by individuals, companies or banks) and their effects on economic activity and prices in terms of time (the distribution of a new unit of money amongst the holders of money) and certain other factors (loans, savings and the uses to which money is put).

Having said that, however, we must be ready to admit that this system of mechanics is only one part of the story. Alongside it, and complementing it, is the whole panoply of the social sciences. Ultimately, the behaviour of money is the result of decisions, anticipations, and individual or collective reactions on the part of both the government and those they govern. All these things are external to the mechanics of money, but still take their effect through it. It therefore follows that if we want to understand money and predict how it will behave, we ought to understand the mechanics of money. But this is, alas, not the case. If it were, there would be some sort of consensus regarding the way this system of mechanics works, because if we can accept differences of opinion on matters that belong to the realm of psychology, factors, that is, that are inherently subjective, we must admit that in the case of something like a system of mechanics, differences and divergences are proof that something has not been correctly understood. The subject matter with which this book deals does not involve purely human factors such as psychological reactions, which is not to say that such things are unimportant but merely that they are not what this book sets out to investigate.

The controversy about the Euromarkets and whether or not they have the power to create new money is not a matter where it is appropriate to talk of 'preferences' and 'propensities', but rather one where we should examine the mechanics of the process. There ought to be a clear answer to the question: do the Eurobanks create new payment dollars, or do they not? If they do, should the M1 which the authorities attempt to measure in Washington include all the dollar deposits in the world-wide Eurodollar system? Until these questions are settled, one way or the other, there can be no hope of disciplining the Euromarkets; which does not mean that once these questions have been answered the serious problem of the unbridled growth of the Euromarkets will also be solved, but merely that it will be more likely to be solved if people have a clear understanding of what goes on in the Eurodollar system than if they do not.

If savings banks are allowed to distribute chequebooks to their customers, will the result be an acceleration of inflation because of an upsurge of *ex nihilo* creation of money? Before answering this question and worrying about the behaviour of the savings banks, we ought, above all, to have some clear notion of how the process of monetary creation might work in the case of savings banks. Nor can we hope to reconstruct the international monetary system or set up an efficient system of monetary regulation without a proper understanding of how money is created.

The various subjects this book looks at, such as the payment function of money, the way the clearing system works, the way a new unit of money is put into circulation and begins to effect its 'reduction' of the available resources of the community, and the critical examination of the concept of a composite currency based on a basket of national currencies, are all topics which, though the way they are treated seems to suggest that psychological factors are ignored, in fact merely anticipate this side of things. The psychological aspects of these matters can only be studied when the nature and functions of the instruments have been properly understood.

Monetary matters dominate the headlines of the newspapers nowadays as they can rarely have done before. But there is a big difference between what may be called the 'surface' of things — the well-publicised 'summits' of heads of state — and the background work of the various committees of experts, which take place well away from the public gaze. What happens on the surface is the subject of endless comments and discussions; what goes on 'underground', as it were, is something that the professional commentators and pundits usually prefer to ignore.

Thus it is that the celebrated sociologist, Raymond Aron, can say *'la monnaie, c'est trop compliquée* ('money is too complicated a matter'). I suppose that what puts him off the study of money is the bewildering profusion of theories and conjectures, many of them in contradiction with each other, and the repeated failures of monetary policy — the discouraging gap between promises and intentions and actual results.

All this is understandable, but it is not enough to justify the neglect with which important events in the world of money are generally greeted. Let me mention only one recent example in France. When Mr Raymond Barre came to power, the French government decided, for the first time in history, to establish a maximum rate of growth for the money supply. This was nothing less than a revolution in traditional habits of thought on political and economic matters; yet, with few exceptions, the Press ignored it. This is all the odder as it is now a well-established fact that the creation of new money tends to get out of hand if some kind of discipline is not imposed: the 'Barber boom' of 1972–3 is only the most recent example in England. Everyone knows that the old disciplines, such as balancing the budget, fixed exchange rates and gold cover have disappeared or are no longer abided by. Everyone knows, equally well, that something must be put in their place. What is more natural, then, in such circumstances, than to turn towards controlling the mass of the means of

payment? I have the feeling that the concept of money supply is easier
to explain to the general public than the GNP, and yet the GNP is
something that the television newscasters and commentators mention as if
it were a matter of course. In arguing thus, I do not mean to imply that
the definition of the monetary aggregates, the choice of growth rate for
the money supply and the application of such policies do not raise serious
problems. Of course they do; but the principles behind them are simple
and accessible to the general public.

It is hard to see why there should be such a deplorable absence of
information with regard to monetary matters, but the cause is probably
to be found in the fact that the opinion-formers are themselves sadly
divided: some, the rearguard, are still vainly struggling in a last-ditch
attempt to defend the gold standard, whilst the members of the vanguard,
though they have forged far ahead, are dispersed across the field and are
no longer even in agreement on the road to take. The rank-and-file of this
army — the general public — are lost somewhere between these two
groups, uncertain what to think, and ill-informed. Yet the reorganisation
of monetary matters concerns no group of people more nearly than the
members of the general public; it holds the key to the prosperity, and even,
perhaps, the future, of our civilisation.

It was ignorance of money and, more particularly, of the mechanics of
money, that during the thirties transformed what should only have been a
temporary crisis into a deep and lasting depression which plunged the world
first into mass unemployment and then into war. The prevailing ignorance
of money was backed up and its evil consequences magnified by an almost
obsessive fear of inflation, which was considered at the time to derive
exclusively from abuse of the 'printing-press'. One of the most distinguished
economists of the inter-war period, Charles Rist, even denied that bank
demand deposits were payment instruments! Indeed, it was not until
after the war that current account deposits came to be included in the
statistics of a brand-new monetary aggregate, called M1. But at the time
of the Great Depression, the only things that mattered were bank-notes
and their backing, whether gold, foreign currency or other claims. The use
of cheques was encouraged because it was considered 'anti-inflationary',
and the gold reserves were the subject of anxious scrutiny. When the
metallic backing of the currency began to move back towards a hundred
per cent, the result was general rejoicing.

The ignorance and the absurdity of the conventional wisdom of the
time may be said to have reached its zenith when a respected author,
Georges Lacou, could write in all seriousness: 'The aggravation of the
deficit of the balance of payments was the direct consequence of the

influx of gold. . . Nevertheless, we should be glad that this was so. . . It is better that a country should suffer in opulence than in poverty.' Later, when the crisis had become chronic, people realised that money had stopped circulating and that the economy was crippled. The result was a rapid change of tack: suddenly the existence of demand was 'discovered'. The theories of Jean-Baptiste Say became the villains of the piece and were soon swept from the stage of economic history by the resistless force of J. M. Keynes. One French Prime Minister even spoke of having bank-notes scattered across the country from aeroplanes in an effort to shake people out of their apathy and set something circulating in the place of the millions of francs of liquidity piled up in bank deposits that had become so many monetary 'traps'.

At the same time, the obsessive fear of inflation persisted tenaciously, though, throughout the thirties, prices fell continuously. Just as obstinate, too, was the way those in power clung to the grand principles of monetary orthodoxy, which sent the succession of governments that were such a typical feature of the period off on a hopeless chase after budgetary equilibrium. Heavier taxes, combined with a burden of debt service that was actually increasing in real terms, served both to destroy entrepreneurial initiative and to undermine the government's tax income.

Nowadays, we cannot imagine such gross errors ever being committed again, but we still do not know how to slow down price increases and at the same time stimulate the economy. Our priorities, meanwhile, have changed: now we are more afraid of deflation than of inflation and the grand principles of the Thirties have ceased to occupy government's attentions. The great progress that has been achieved has been this emancipation from the erroneous doctrines of the pre-war period which almost brought about the destruction of our civilisation. Nevertheless, doubts and uncertainties remain, as is evident from the many disagreements and divergences of opinion which monetary matters give rise to.

These uncertainties will never be cleared up and the divergences of opinion reconciled so long as we have not achieved better knowledge of the monetary mechanisms and the way they work. This is the aim of this book. Its conclusions are sometimes in disagreement with contemporary ideas — not the ideas of the leading figures of contemporary economic thought, but rather those that are still cherished by many members of the general public and even by some professionals. What follows is a list of the twenty-one points on which this book is in disagreement with these traditional conceptions.

1. It is a traditional belief that money 'represents a commodity', that is, that it is an emanation of its commodity backing, whether precious

metal, foreign currency, claim on the Treasury or the economy or whatever. On this basis, the whole edifice of credit, discounting and the creation of new money has traditionally been founded.

Nowadays, we know that this notion is erroneous and that it is pointless to search for a natural link between a unit of money and a commodity or good that is supposed to guarantee it. The backing, if there is any, only has the function of providing a surety for the lender and, perhaps, a degree of automaticity for the credit mechanisms and the process of monetary creation. No rational monetary system will be constructed until money is recognised for what it is, namely a simple claim on an institution, created arbitrarily and artificially, with the remarkable power of being exchangeable for a supply of goods and services, thereby assuring the money transfers and the conversion of produced goods into consumption or investment which are the foundation of a modern economy.

2. There is a growing and extremely widespread conviction that the criterion for defining the monetary function which a unit of money possesses is its 'liquidity quotient'.

This book considers that the 'liquidity quotient' is a very bad criterion. A piece of furniture has a higher liquidity quotient than a one-month bank deposit because it can be sold and its cash value realised within the space of a single day. Two-year bank deposits, on the other hand, which remain idle until maturity, are included in M2. At the same time, deposits in savings banks, which can be withdrawn at any moment, are excluded from the same definition of the money sypply. Such paradoxes do not, in fact, pass unnoticed, and worry the analysts, whence the tendency to broaden the notion of money so as to make it indistinguishable from general liquidity (M3). But then we find ourselves wandering off into a boundless bog in which the liquid can no longer be distinguished from the solid.

Monetary analysis will continue to get bogged down in such confusions as long as no clear methodical distinction is made between those units of money that can directly effect a payment and those that cannot. Only those units that are directly exchangeable for a supply of goods or services have the payment function and can consequently be said to have an effect on economic activity and prices. A cheque, which is of course a claim on a bank, can only be said to effect a payment when it is handed to someone in return for a supply of goods and services, as long as it is not converted into cash. If it is, then it is the bank-notes which the bank hands over that effect the ultimate payment. It is by looking for the *ultimate* direct exchange of this sort that the real mechanics of money can be discovered.

3. It is a conviction widely shared by monetary technicians that all bank deposits should be included in the money supply, time deposits and savings deposits being called 'near'- or 'quasi'-money.

But the population of a country is not counted by adding the 'quasi-living' to the living. It is an error of reasoning to assimilate units of money that have the payment function to those that do not, merely because the latter can be transformed into payment units or at least give rise to such units. An *event* is one thing; the *eventuality* of an event is quite another. The event should be registered, counted and assessed according to its effects. The eventuality, on the other hand, should be assessed according to its degree of probability. Confusion between the two leads to confusion in the monetary regulators.

4. It is a frequently repeated conviction that credit is the same thing as money, and those who believe this justify their beliefs by referring to the well-known adage 'loans make deposits'.

This book retorts that credit is *not* money, and that the formula does not explain, as people pretend it does, the creation of money in a national banking system. A ten-pound note is deposited at a savings bank, lent by it, spent and then redeposited at another bank or at the same bank, once, twice, three times. There are thus, in all, three 'deposits denominated in money', but there is no new money. In order to effect a payment at the request of a customer, the savings bank will have to provide a bank-note or a cheque drawn on another bank. The velocity of circulation increases but not the quantity of payment money.

But the hypnotic power of these glib formulae, handed down from generation to generation should not be underestimated. Jacques Rueff always insisted on explaining the power of monetary creation of a bank by saying that all it needed to do was to 'enter amongst its assets its claim on the borrower and balance this with a credit for the same amount to the customer's current account: in this way the credit has created a deposit and thus money'. Anyone can do that, but that doesn't mean that anyone can create money. What matters is what happens when the customer makes uses of his asset by transferring it or drawing a cheque. The institution, if it is a monetary intermediary, such as a bank, can pay its debt by means of a claim on itself. But if it is not, it is obliged to remit or transfer a claim on a third party without itself creating any money. By trusting blindly to this adage, Jacques Rueff spent his time expecting the birth of new units of money in cases where the pregnancies were false.

5. It is a conviction common to both bankers and university teachers that the clearing process is only a convenient tool for the sorting out of paper claims and that there is no difference between that and what the

treasurer of a company does when he balances his outgoings by his incomings (which explains why clearing is scarcely mentioned in books on money).

This book tries to show that the clearing process is the fundamental mechanism by which banks create claims on themselves that have a full payment function and are added to the supply of central bank money.

6. The system on which credit was based in the past was conditioned by the belief that the essence of a bank's role was short-term credit founded on the discount of a piece of paper (up to three months at the most). It was an equally firm conviction, and a cause of much anguish for certain members of the National Plan, who were looking for resources with which to 'finance the expansion' of the economy, that a long-term bank credit was 'inflationary' and should be provided exclusively by the financial markets.

In fact, money created by discount is no different in essence from money created for a medium- or long-term credit, with the difference, however, that a credit for the purpose of an investment is more profitable to the economy than the discounting of a thirty-day bill drawn by a supplier of barley-sugar on his customer. This belief in the virtues of a discount resting on a commodity has delayed the rational organisation of financing and 'transformation', or investment on the basis of monetary creation, for a long time. The only thing that is supposed to matter is the statistics regarding the volume, velocity and degree of conversion of the means of payment.

It is only by bringing together within the same money-supply definition those elements of money that have direct payment power (M1), without distinction as to origin, that one can hope to have a reliable guide, the need of which is all the greater as economic policy becomes more hazardous. It is a dangerous balancing exercise to try to overcome inflation and stimulate the economy using purely monetary instruments. In order to achieve the first aim, we must slow down the growth of the money supply, whilst the second implies the need to accelerate it. The only way to reconcile such totally contradictory policies is to practise a *selective*, well organised distribution of new money. This in turn implies that first of all the varieties of creation of money should be properly isolated and grouped in a clearly defined aggregate.

7. It is a matter of overwhelming conviction for some that the quantity theory of money is an abomination, whilst for others it is no less certainly the explanation of everything.

It is the reassuring opinion of this book that both sets of antagonists should forget their differences and admit that all new units of money, whether created for a commercial discount, a long-term credit, an overdraft, or a purchase of gold or foreign currencies by the central bank, give their first holders the benefit of goods and services which are 'unearned' and consequently exercise a kind of tax on the holders of money, which is levied gradually as the units of money change hands.

This is the only possible reply to the question: who supplied the goods or services which the first user of the new unit of money consumed without having 'earned' them? How are they supplied and by what vehicle? Conversely, the holder of a unit of money just before it is destroyed does make a contribution in the form of goods or services that *have* been earned and receives nothing in return. Who is the beneficiary?

Nothing comes from nothing. Goods and services consumed by the first holder of a new unit of money are withdrawn from, or cause a 'reduction' in, the total stock of goods and services available to the holders of money. They are restored when the unit of money is destroyed. The difference between the money that has been created with the payment function and those units of money that have been destroyed (M1) gives a measure of the phenomenon of reduction. The relationships between money, prices and economic activity can be deduced from this, without implying any particular causality, which ought to be sufficient grounds for a truce between the warring factions of monetarists and anti-monetarists.

There is something else we can add to this: the growth of the M1 money supply means that a corresponding quantity of additional 'unearned' rights to goods and services has been created. These rights, which are exercised by the first holders of the new money but which have not been earned by them, are based on a corresponding reduction of the assets of the holders of M1.

Making due allowances for the velocity of transactions, there is an exact correspondence, franc for franc in France, dollar for dollar in America, and mark for mark in Germany, between the addition of new money to M1 and the resulting reduction in the value of the money assets of the population, which is effected through the circulation of payment money as it passes from hand to hand. This reduction is comparable to a tax; though it is not immediately apparent and is hidden among many other factors having a similar effect on the purchasing power of money, it is nonetheless real.

From the earliest times, the right and the obligation to decide the level of taxes, to distribute the tax burden and then collect taxes, has always been regarded as the apanage of the state. For this reason, and for others relating to the generally accepted responsibilities of the state in the guidance of the economy, it is clear that as the notion of money supply gains acceptability, its 'management' will come to be recognised as one of the fundamental functions of government, which in turn means that it will also come under the scrutiny of Parliament. Such a development is inevitable in view of the immense vacuum left behind by the now defunct disciplines of the gold standard (and the dollar standard), fixed exchange rates and budgetary equilibrium. But management of the money supply presupposes reliable monetary indicators, trustworthy means of intervention and, above all, a solid body of doctrine.

To write in these terms of the likely development of public policy on these matters is not to express a preference either for or against the quantity theory of money, but simply to recognise facts. Rather than indulging in sterile skirmishes about purely abstract matters, it would be better to admit the changed reality of the monetary scene and give to the management of the money supply the role, the means and the prominence it deserves.

8. It is a widespread conviction that a bank operating in the Euromarket has the same power of monetary creation in foreign currencies as it has in the currency of the country in which it is domiciled.

This book attempts to explain why this cannot be the case. In the Euromarket, when it is dealing in a currency which is not the currency of the country it is operating in, a bank functions to a considerable extent as a non-monetary intermediary. The Eurodollar money supply is a mass of deposits denominated in dollars and held outside the United States, only a fraction of which are payment dollars deposited in American banks and included in the American M1. The fact that the Eurobanks function as non-monetary intermediaries is the consequence of the absence of a clearing system between them, which would be rendered difficult by the fact that the banks in question are scattered around the world in different time zones and in different banking systems.

9. It is a source of reassurance for some (and concern for others) that the use of cheque books may be extended to depositors in savings banks, without any inflationary consequences, 'on condition', as the official text puts it, 'that any possibility of overdrawing is forbidden'.

This book sees in this condition another example of the many misunderstandings which a better comprehension of the mechanics of money would help to eliminate. There is nothing to stop a savings bank lending to its customers, which is, moreover, what they are doing all the time. It is only by excluding cheques drawn on the savings bank from inter-bank clearing that the payments over and above the payments in central bank money will be limited to internal clearing between the payments carried out by the bank's own customers.

Credit cards provide another example of the sort of misunderstandings to which a too hasty association of credit with money can give rise. People often argue that credit cards are inflationary because they constitute a source of *ex nihilo* monetary creation. This book argues, however, that one should not pass judgments on the inflationary character of such and such a monetary mechanism without having first analysed it rationally. There are no inflationary consequences when the means of payment in question, so far from being created *ex nihilo* are pre-existent and are simply transferred by their holder — who thereby becomes a lender — to a borrower who uses them in the place of the lender. In so doing, he avails himself of a title to goods and services which the lender has temporarily abandoned.

This is what happens with credit cards. The lender is the retailer, whom the customer, thereby becoming a borrower, pays with his card. The customer is subsequently debited and the lender is reimbursed by the credit card company. There has been no creation of new payment money. Various side-effects, however, may thereby be induced. The very ease of use of the credit card may encourage people to make purchases they might not otherwise have made and may thereby concentrate resources on consumption that could have been used for investment. One can also argue that the retailer may cover the money he has lent to his client by asking for a loan from his bank, which may lead to an *ex nihilo* creation of money by the bank. This may indeed be so, but the client would probably have asked for a loan from *his* bank, if he had not had the advantage of a loan from his retailer.

There are many arguments that one can put forward, pro and con, but the important thing is not to confuse the main phenomenon with its secondary or even tertiary effects. To ignore or to overlook the fact that a loan operation involves a contribution or transfer of *pre-existing*, unused rights to goods and services and not a creation *ex nihilo* of new rights, is just one of those errors in monetary thinking that tend to paralyse the whole apparatus of monetary regulation.

10. It is a firm conviction, both in the minds of those who support it as well as in the minds of those who oppose it, that *credit control* is only a makeshift expedient.

In the opinion of the author of this book, however, the other instruments at the disposal of the authorities, such as open-market operations and compulsory reserves, are still more inadvisable because they are used for purposes for which they were not intended. It is natural that the government should wish to control and limit the privilege of monetary creation which it delegates to the banking system. Credit control can be improved and its defects can be largely eliminated.

11. It is a recent belief that the velocity of money should be measured just as much as should the quantity.

This book argues that account should also be taken of the nature of the transactions money is used for. The effect of a transaction is in fact different according as it involves a transfer or exchange, whether it involves an addition of value or whether it effects a conversion of final production into consumption or investment.

In order to achieve this end, this book proposes a new indicator which tries to reflect the extent to which transit through a monetary or non-monetary intermediary affects the conversion that the unit of money precipitates.

12. It is the conviction of traditional teaching, as it derives from the classical authors, that one can explain economic motivation in terms of particular formulae, e.g. 'liquidity preference', 'the propensity to consume', 'choice of uses as a function of interest rates', etc.

This book argues that if human nature is the same as it always was, man's environment, his living conditions and his reactions are not what they were even forty years ago. For a businessman, for example, uncertainty and fiscal, administrative, political and above all *social* problems have a significant effect on his expectations, more significant than interest rates, which are negated by inflation and thus unpredictable in real terms. As for consumers, they have long since ceased to invest in equities and capital goods — nowadays they put their money into consumer durables.

Many facts have changed, but theory has not always changed with them.

13. It is a passionate conviction of the anti-monetarists (or rather the anti-monetarians) that monetarists (or monetarians) are bad economic advisers.

This book suggests that there ought to be a cease-fire between the two opposing parties. The causes of inflation are many and various. They are not confined to the decision to create new money. Nevertheless, inflation is always accompanied by an increase in the means of payment. For this reason, one cannot avoid concentrating on payment money if one wishes to control inflation, because it is one of the ultimate determinants of inflation, the inevitable instrument through which all the supposed causes of inflation produce their effects. For example, a price rise in a floating exchange rate system caused by a rise in exchange rates is accompanied by an increase in the quantity of money. The responsibility of floating exchange rates in this does not diminish; the increase in the quantity of money is only the vehicle of the process, but it may provide a welcome argument for the proponents of fixed exchange rates to use against their opponents who favour floating rates.

The multiplicity of causes of inflation justifies singling out money, both as indicator and as intervention instrument, which does not thereby imply that one should ignore the other factors. Their actions and interreactions remain, and they offer an immense area of study from which monetarians and anti-monetarians alike could profit.

14. It is the conviction of many disillusioned people that monetary regulation is condemned for ever to impotence since the indicators are imprecise and inaccurate, badly defined and crude and, in addition, erroneously applied.

This book rejects such a conclusion. The main obstacle to progress is the uncertainty of present knowledge on these matters. An attempt should be made to devise reliable indicators, efficient and appropriate instruments and methods of approach. One of the great areas of progress of the present day, which the young are hardly aware of but which the older generation appreciates, is the progress of the science of statistics. To attempt to steer the economy fifty years ago was to attempt to steer 'blind', with neither compass nor rudder. Nowadays, we know more or less what goes on; what we don't know is how to *interpret* what we see with any accuracy.

15. Faith in an eventual return to the gold standard system persisted for a long time and still lingers on even today.

This book argues that we should respect the memory of a system that was of immense benefit and which, in the space of a century and a half, prepared the world for the industrial age — though it was the product, as we ought to remember, of exceptional circumstances. The admiration which the gold standard elicits is understandable; what is less understandable, is the reluctance which people seem to have to admit that the reintroduction of the gold standard, however desirable it may be, is impossible because it is based on a parallel circulation of gold and paper. The reciprocal convertibility of these two elements of the system was based on a form of confidence which it is in no one's power to recreate because no one can eliminate from the minds of men sixty years of their history. The persistence of the belief in the virtues of a return to the gold standard is responsible for the total absence of imagination and innovation in monetary affairs.

16. With regard to the international monetary system, opinions are many and contradictory. The 'liquidity' of the system is provided by the deficit of the American balance of payments; this deficit disrupts international affairs; the preponderance of the dollar causes international

monetary matters to be dependent on the internal policies of the United States and left at the mercy of a crisis of confidence which could destabilise the thousands of millions of dollars accumulated on the scales of the American balance of payments deficit. When this threatens, the exchange markets go mad and the American government urges the population to consume less oil.

The truth is that the dollar is no longer capable of fulfilling its role of international currency, but no one knows how it may be replaced. This is the fundamental cause of present monetary disorders: what we ought to be doing is looking for a substitute for the dollar.

The conclusion which this book comes to is that the dollar must be supplemented in its international role by a new monetary unit, which will be extra-national and which will circulate in parallel with the other Euro-currencies outside the borders of nation states, but which will have a remarkable characteristic that other currencies do not have, which will make it possible for the new currency to rival the well-established national currencies. The 'Eurostable' is an example of just such a unit.

17. Many people are prejudiced against the international monetary organisations and believe that the IMF is a 'threat to national independence' and that the SDR is a 'source of inflation'.

This book considers the IMF to be an important institution, which, far from threatening national independence, protects states by imposing a salutary discipline on them. As for the SDR, it is merely a guarantee mechanism, designed to ensure the smooth working of exchanges of credit between states. It does not create any new money.

18. It is the optimistic conviction of many people that a basket of currencies in fixed quantities is capable of replacing both gold and the dollar as an international money.

This book approves of any initiative intended to promote the creation of a genuinely neutral international currency, but it is well aware that such an initiative is only a first step. An artificial currency unit with fixed composition is subject to all the drawbacks of the national currencies that make it up, and one or two others as well. In particular, it is not suited to act as a standard of reference in terms of which the value of other national currencies could be measured.

This book adds to the three traditional functions of money two new ones that are peculiar to our times: that of standard of reference by which a currency may be defined and that of intervention and arbitrage instrument. It also shows that a composite currency based on a fixed basket of currencies is incapable of carrying out any of these functions.

On the other hand, neither are national currencies equipped for this

task and here we have one of the grave deficiencies of the present
international monetary system, namely that its main currencies are all
national currencies, exposed to all the vicissitudes of national politics. But
since we are at last starting to take seriously the task of creating a common
neutral unit of payment, would it not be a good idea to equip it with a
quality that no national currency has or can have, instead of leaving it
exposed to all the weaknesses inherent in national currencies?

19. A conviction that is politically popular is the belief that monetary
agreements between states are all that is needed to set right the disorders
of the exchange markets and the problems they cause in international
relations. Evidence of this conviction is to be found in the European
'snake', the EUA, and the other artificial currencies that have proliferated
in recent years.

There is no doubt that this sort of thing constitutes a step in the right
direction, but it is only the first step. A specifically European monetary
intervention fund will help the struggle against speculation and will help
the authorities to cope with short-term economic crises but it will be no
more capable than the IMF of overcoming structural disequilibria between
states in social, industrial, financial and fiscal matters. A necessary
precondition, without which such agreements cannot be expected to
function either harmoniously or for very long, is that governments should
be willing and able to impose, internally, those measures necessary to
ensure that their external obligations are respected. In the past they have
lacked both the will and the power to do this.

20. It is an oft-repeated conviction, especially by politicians, that
'creative imagination' is the only source of hope for the future. At the same
time, many people (often the very same people) secretly consider that
innovation in monetary and financial matters is wrong and should be
discouraged.

This book rejects such a craven refusal to meet the challenges of the
modern world with appropriate initiatives. Innovation is the very condition
without which there can be no progress, and monetary systems are more
in need of innovation than any other human institutions. But it must be
admitted that public officials cannot be expected to create and *experiment*,
since this implies the right to make mistakes, a right which they are wary
of arrogating to themselves. This is why a new monetary unit with constant
purchasing power, like the Eurostable, should first be tried out in the
private sector, in the Euromarket, in fact.

21. It is the firm conviction of all the faint-hearts and other supporters
of the *status quo* that the Eurostable will not be able to overcome the

obstacles in its path, which derive largely from force of habit, vested interests and sheer incomprehension.

(a) 'Such a unit', people say, 'needs to have borrowers if it is to be introduced into circulation, but no borrower will agree to take on debts in constant terms'. The gyrations of the foreign exchanges and the fluctuating purchasing power of money constitute a source of uncertainty for any businessman who has to borrow. A loan in constant terms, at low interest rates, will be a source of security.

In any case, what counts is less the volume of business than the fact that there would then exist a stable standard of value. Gold had ceased to be used as a medium of exchange long before being officially 'demonetised' but this did not mean that it thereby lost its role of store of value, which is still very much alive and is, indeed, growing. Similarly, it served as a common denominator in terms of which other currencies could be defined, and thus prevented them from drifting apart. Just as it is necessary from the monetary and economic points of view, a stable, extranational monetary unit is also necessary from the political and psychological points of view and it would constitute an incomparable source of prestige, a banner behind which the nations could rally.

(b) 'It is against the nature of things that a currency should maintain its purchasing power'. This would be true of a currency circulating within the borders of a state, but not of a parallel unit circulating in the monetary 'no government's land' of the Euromarket. Such a specifically extranational currency would not be used for initial payments to producers or for final payments by consumers. Circulating between monetary locks, i.e. exchange offices, it would be protected against the laws of the market by the conversion rates.

Of course, the validity of this assertion may be denied, but no one can deny the dangers facing the world economy so long as its monetary system is paralysed.

No fixed exchange rate system will be of any use, and no floating rate system will be able to restore equilibrium, so long as thousands of millions of dollars can flow from one centre to another in a matter of seconds. The traditional weapons, such as central bank reserves and interest rate manipulations, will be quite unable to control huge masses of capital which are bent on deserting a weak currency or besieging a strong one. Even if they could, they would create intolerable disorder in the internal economies of states.

It appears, therefore, to be an act of extreme imprudence not to attempt to stabilise these vast capital flows by attracting them to a stable *numéraire* into which they could be converted. This is all the more so, as there exists an exceptional opportunity to give monetary systems what they most need — namely a stable standard of reference, which can be achieved in the case of a neutral extranational currency reserved exclusively for international transactions.

22. It is a conviction shared by many distinguished economists that 'the real problem is not a lack of willpower; it is a lack of knowledge. . . This impotence in the field of economic theory is largely due to ignorance of economic and monetary reality. . . In international matters, I am convinced, like M. Denizet, that only a system founded on the issue of an additional currency over and above gold has a reasonable chance of success. The creation of such a currency will test the ability of politicians to innovate, and thus protect the world economy and mankind in general from the dangers of ignorance and impotence.' (Valéry Giscard d'Estaing: preface to *Monnaie et Inflation* by Jean Denizet (Dunot).

Here at last are two convictions — in addition to the twenty-first — with which this book is in complete agreement and which it will take as its conclusion.

Glossary

Amortise   To extinguish a debt over a fixed period. Thus, a loan may be *amortised* over eighteen months.

Arbitrage   In financial usage, *arbitrage* is the word used to describe the simultaneous buying of one currency and selling of another in order to profit from the small discrepancies in exchange rates from one financial centre to another that from time to time occur.

Bank/non-bank   In the language of monetary theory a 'bank' is any banking institution that has the power to create new money. This is contrasted with the 'non-bank'. Thus, the National Westminster Bank is a 'bank' whilst the National Savings Bank is a 'non-bank'. The majority of banks operating in the Eurodollar market are also 'non-banks'.

Base-money   The money stock issued by the central bank, so called because it acts as the *base* on which commercial banks erect their pyramid of *bank money*. See also *central bank money*.

Basket of currencies   Since the collapse of the Bretton Woods monetary system, various attempts have been made to define international units of account in terms of something other than gold or a national currency. The most popular method has been the so-called 'basket formula', which consists in defining the unit in question in terms of a quantity of currency *A* plus a quantity of currency *B* plus a quantity of currency *C* etc., the various quantities being imagined to be contained in a 'basket'. The idea was derived from the 'baskets' of goods which economists use to calculate price index numbers.

Binomial   In mathematics, an algebraic expression consisting of two terms joined by + or −. In this book, the term is used to describe a purely bilateral relationship between two banks in the clearing house. Hence also *trinomial* and *quadrinomial*.

Buy spot   To buy foreign currency for immediate delivery; cf. *buy forward*, which is to buy for delivery at some future date.

Central bank money   The money stock issued by the central bank. The general public is familiar with it chiefly in the form of coins and notes. See also *base money, primary money, high-powered money*.

Clearing bank   Any member bank of a *clearing house* (see Chapter 5 in

Part 1). To the extent that they conduct current account business, central banks may also be clearing banks. Also called *commercial banks*.

Commercial bank   See *clearing bank*.

Debt money   Money conceived of as an abstract claim having no backing, whether in the form of a commodity or a quantity of precious metal.

Discount   In financial usage, the selling before maturity of any kind of negotiable paper for less than face value.

Eurobank   See *Eurodollar bank*.

Eurocurrency   See *Eurodollar*.

Eurodollar   A dollar owned by a person or an institution not resident in the United States. Thus, a dollar owned, for example, by a German and lent to a Frenchman is a Eurodollar, as also is a dollar owned by an Arab and lent to a Canadian. Any currency owned by a non-resident of the country of issue may be called a *Eurocurrency*.

Eurodollar bank   A bank specialising in making loans and taking deposits in Eurodollars. A bank operating in a variety of Eurocurrencies is called a *Eurocurrency bank*, often abbreviated to *Eurobank*.

Fiat money   Money devoid of any commodity or metallic backing into which it could be converted. Most modern money is fiat money.

Fungible   If a customer of a bank deposits bank-notes or securities in a bank account and does not insist on having exactly the same notes or securities handed back to him when he makes a withdrawal, the account is called *fungible*.

Gold standard   The monetary system pioneered by Great Britain which lasted from roughly the end of the Napoleonic Wars till 1914 and in which gold coins and paper circulated in parallel as legal-tender money, the paper being convertible on demand into gold at a fixed rate. Gold, in the form of coins or bullion, was also the chief instrument of international payments.

Gold exchange standard   This was a modification of the gold standard for purposes of international trade, according to which the currencies of countries which were themselves on a full gold standard could be used by countries that were not to constitute reserves and effect international payments. In practice, these currencies were first the dollar and sterling and then the dollar alone.

High-powered money   A term coined by Professor Milton Friedman to describe *central bank money*.

Legal-tender money   That form of money which creditors are legally obliged to accept in payment of debts. In practice, this usually means the coins and notes issued by the central bank. In spite of their wide currency, cheques are not legal tender.

M1, M2, M3   See *money supply*.

Monetary intermediary   Any financial intermediary with the power to create money. Those that lack this power are called non-monetary intermediaries, cf. *bank/non-bank*.

Money supply   The quantity of means of payment, whether circulating in the form of coins and notes or held in bank deposits. The varying degrees to which different kinds of financial asset may be considered 'money' has given rise to differing definitions, some very narrow and others very broad. These different definitions are conventionally referred to as M1, M2, M3 etc., in ascending order of broadness.

Near-money   Those financial assets which may not be used directly in payment of goods, e.g. a sum held in a bank deposit account. See also *quasi-money*.

Payment function   The property of being directly exchangeable for a supply of goods or services. A bank-note has this payment function but a bank time deposit has not.

Payment money   Money having the *payment function*.

Primary money   The stock of money issued by the *central bank*.

Quantity theory of money   A theory which states that there is a correlation between the price level in a given economic system and the quantity of money in circulation. In its most extreme form it asserts that the price level is directly affected by a change in the quantity of money and that this effect is in the same direction as the change, so that an increase causes a rise in prices and a decrease a fall. In the eighteenth century, the theory was given prominence in the writings of David Hume and Adam Smith. In our day, it has come to be associated particularly with Professor Milton Friedman and the so-called 'Monetarist' School.

Quasi-money   Another term for *near-money* (q.v.).

Rediscount   To discount a second time. Usually by banks and other specialised institutions, who go to the *central bank* to obtain immediate cash for paper they have themselves bought at a discount.

Reduction   See Translator's Note, page 2.

SDR   The commonly accepted abbreviation for Special Drawing Right. See Chapter 2 in Part 3, entitled 'The International Monetary Fund and its SDR'.

Seigniorage   Historically, the difference between the cost of production of a coin or bank-note and its face value. Assuming that this difference is positive, which it almost always is, it constitutes a source of profit for the 'seigneur', who alone has the right to mint money. In this book, a parallel is drawn between true seigniorage and the benefit enjoyed by the first user of a unit of money created *ex nihilo*, for which he has made no compensating contribution to total production.

Specie   Money in the form of coin or bullion, as contrasted with paper money.

Velocity of money   The rate at which a given money supply aggregate changes hands over a given period, usually a year. For further information see Supplementary Notes on pages 197–205.

S.H.

Index